P9-BXZ-382

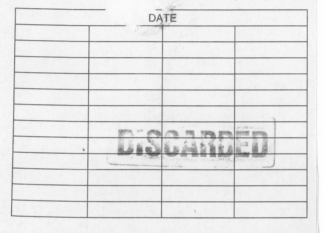

DATE

DISCARDED

BAKER & TAYLOR

HASTENED TO THE GRAVE

Other Books by Jack Olsen

Salt of the Earth: One Family's Journey through the Violent American
    Landscape
The Misbegotten Son
Predator: Rape, Madness, and Injustice in Seattle
Doc: The Rape of the Town of Lovell
Son: A Psychopath and His Victims

HASTENED TO THE GRAVE

The Gypsy Murder Investigation

JACK OLSEN

ST. MARTIN'S PRESS
NEW YORK

Design by Nancy Resnick

Library of Congress Cataloging-in-Publication Data

Olsen, Jack.
    Hastened to the grave : the gyspy murder investigation / by Jack
Olsen.—1st ed.
        p.   cm.
    ISBN 0-312-18362-3
    1. Homicide investigation—California—San Francisco Bay Area.
    2. Aged—Crimes against—California—San Francisco Bay Area.
    3. Gypsies—California—San Francisco Bay Area.   I. Title.
HV8079.H6057   1998
364.15'23'0979461—dc21   98-10239
                                                              CIP

First Edition: May 1998

10 9 8 7 6 5 4 3 2 1

For Su

The Gypsies are here. Eyes the color of stars. Dressed in history. Dressed in rainbows. . . . The men look like pirates. The woman look like whores. Tall women, heads back, bold stare, easy hips. What right have they to walk as if they had never known pain?

—Jeanette Winterson, *The Green Man*

It seems that the Gypsies, men and women, are on earth only to be thieves. They are born of robber fathers, brought up for thieving, educate themselves for it, and end up nicely as full-blown thieves.

—Juan Miguel Cervantes de Saavedra, *La Gitanilla*

HASTENED TO THE GRAVE

An Easy Touch

FAY FARON ALWAYS answered her phone with a cheery "Rat Dog Dick!" even though she was well aware that some of her callers would gladly garrote her and feed her to the crabs off Pier 45. When she'd first established her one-woman detective agency, she tried answering in a businesslike contralto to create the impression that she employed a receptionist, but a friend complained that she sounded like a table dancer.

This morning's caller was Ken Chan, her lawyer and favorite client, asking if she could drop into his office on busy Union Street to discuss an assignment. "No big deal," he added.

"I'm halfway there," Fay said. You could never tell what Chan meant by "no big deal." On one of his cases she'd ended up chasing rustlers in the Arizona desert, earning a year's supply of flank steak for herself and Beans, her Rastafarian dog and confidant.

ONE GOOD THING about Ken Chan, she reminded herself as she climbed into the rattly old car she called the Frog Prince, he's quick pay, unlike some other lawyers. She was $68 delinquent on her veterinary bill and a week or two behind on less important accounts like electricity and telephone. Some of her clients hadn't paid up in years, but she would rather skate naked across the Union Square ice rink than dun a customer. She considered herself a relaxed and forgiving soul, lighthearted, playful, famous among her friends as an easy touch for men, women, dogs, cats, gerbils, lizards and goldfish. It was one of the reasons she was usually broke.

THE SESSION IN Chan's small third-floor office wasn't five minutes old before she realized that this would be a simple research job—no tricks, false closets or mirrors. The client was an Anglo-Russian expatriate named Hope Victoria Beesley who believed she was being hustled out of several hundred thousand dollars by an odd-jobs worker whose name abruptly appeared on her property deed as co-owner. Chan said that the elderly widow's house was worth $500,000 and stood out from its Sunset District neighbors by virtue of the sheen on its lustrous green roof. The inside was so lavishly decorated that the place had been featured in *Better Homes and Gardens* alongside rococo old mansions from Nob Hill and Pacific Heights.

"What's the guy's name?" Fay asked, pencil poised above the legal-size yellow paper that she customarily used to take notes. She was acutely aware that other investigators utilized minicassette tape recorders resembling Fig Newtons; she planned to buy one when she caught up on her bills or at the turn of the millennium, whichever came first.

"Teeny," she heard Chan answer. "Danny Teeny. A big guy. The client says he looks like a beached sea elephant. See what you can find on him, will you, Fay?"

She asked how to spell the name. Despite a high IQ and prodigious verbal acuity, as shown in her weekly newspaper column "Ask Rat Dog" and other published and unpublished writings, Fay had never heard a name she couldn't misspell or mispronounce. "God gave you so much, dear," a teacher had told her in childhood. "He just didn't give you spelling."

Chan said, "T-E-N-E."

"Odd name," said the PI. "That'll make things easier. How many T-E-E-N-Es can there be?"

"*Two* E's," he reminded her. "T-E-N-E. How much time do you need?"

Fay asked herself, Why are lawyers always in a hurry? She collected her notes, zipped her down vest from Eddie Bauer over her flowered print dress from Laura Ashley, smiled sweetly and said, "Will yesterday be soon enough?"

2

Skip Tracer

DRIVING HOME FROM the lawyer's office, Fay felt invigorated. Her carrot-cake-and-baked-oatmeal diet was producing a steady flow of energy, just as she'd hoped. She shook her head as she thought of the money she'd wasted on other people's idea of miracle foods—sprouts, wheat grass, lecithin, ginseng, various picolinates and chelates, beta-carotene, dried nettles, everything but unicorn horn. She hadn't ingested a shred of "health food" for a month and felt twenty years old again, or about half her age. This very morning she'd biked two miles to the Golden Gate and two miles back, and when she got home she felt like making the trip again, and did. She planned to cycle to Alaska someday. It was only—what? Three or four thousand miles? She hoped Beans could keep up. He was just the right size to feed a family of grizzlies.

FOR TWO YEARS Fay and her dog had lived in the Marina, a sunstruck part of San Francisco that belied Mark Twain's well-worn quote about the coldest winter he ever spent. Her office-apartment was a five-minute walk from the beach and a bracing stroll from dozens of restaurants where she could replace some of the calories that she burned off on her new rope-jumping regimen, which consisted of nine hundred acrobatic jumps in varying positions, or as many as she could manage before fellow residents started banging on the walls. When the north wind blew off Fisherman's Wharf, a faint iodine scent made her imagine a tourist at Alioto's slurping an oyster or cracking a Dungeness crab. She found this another useful dieting aid.

INSIDE HER THREE-ROOM office-apartment, Fay offered Beans some leftover chicken curry soup, enough to lick but not enough to cause the same unfortunate reaction that a full bowl had caused the last time. He was a two-year-old golden retriever–German shepherd mix that she described as "the world's first canine Rastafarian" for the dreadlocks behind his floppy ears. The dog was clumsy and undisciplined and a profuse shedder of zigzag hairs of the same gauge as speaker wire, but there was no question that he meant well.

With her best friend at her feet, the private investigator installed herself at her Star Wars control center. This was the part of her work that she enjoyed the most. Admirers were convinced that she could produce the vital statistics, credit records, shoe sizes, blood types and personal histories of anyone from Governor Wilson to Vlad the Impaler, although Vlad might take a while. Of course skip tracers weren't supposed to have access to credit reports and other confidential information, but what were friends for? Fay called her personal network the Friends of the Rat Dog Dick Detective Agency and tried to give as good as she got.

HER DINING ROOM was draped in swags of spaghetti wire and patch cords that climbed like May Day ribbons to a multiple socket in the four-bulb chandelier. Her desk consisted of a heavy oaken door laid across two filing cabinets and spray-painted to resemble the finest Carrara marble. To the left of her workstation was a microfiche reader that she'd bought at a county salvage sale for $25. It served her well as long as she remembered to pull the plug at the first sign of smoke. On utility shelving to her right were a battered black-and-white printer that oozed copies according to its mood and a vintage fax machine that spat tightly curled messages with charred edges. At her fingertips was a crotchety old Everex 286 computer that she called Evie, or sometimes Evil Evie, attached to a Hayes modem that ran at 2400 baud, the slowest rate available from her favorite electronics shop, where her account was too seriously in arrears for an upgrade.

A RED LIGHT winked on the answering machine that she'd picked up at the Goodwill, but she decided to ignore it for the moment. Like the pilot of a transoceanic jet, she sat among her humming machines and blinking lights to launch her journey into the private world of—what was that name again? She consulted her notes and found "Danny Teeny." She hoped Ken Chan hadn't misspelled it. Then she remembered that it was pronounced "Teeny" but spelled T-E-N-E. Or was it the other way around?

For a start, she punched "Tene" into a data bank that claimed to hold every listed phone number in the United States. She expected a bare minimum of hits, if any, for such an unusual name, but Tenes turned up in New York, Boston and its suburbs, Los Angeles, Chicago, Philadelphia, San Diego and several smaller cities, plus a few in the San Francisco Bay Area.

She switched tactics and dialed the online number for the Social Security Master Death Index, a listing of names and Social Security numbers of citizens who'd forfeited their privacy rights by dying. More Tenes appeared: John, Mary, Angelo, Tina, Larry, Tom, Frank, Steve. The name Pete Bimbo Tene popped up and sounded remotely familiar, as did Pete Tene Bimbo, but Fay couldn't remember where she'd heard them. Several Ephrem and/or Ephraim Tenes turned up; one of the Ephrems also seemed to be named Brian or Bryan. A few listings were so baffling that Fay decided they were simply errors, typographical or otherwise.

In other handy data banks she discovered that some living members of the clan seemed to have two or three Social Security numbers, some had none, and some were using numbers that belonged to the dead. A few SSNs checked back to the wrong names, and vice versa. In court records, the names of several Tenes and Bimbos and Tene Bimbos appeared on restraining orders. An infant Tene, twenty-three days old, had died under peculiar circumstances. Another Tene had been killed in a parking lot. One had been arrested for picking pockets, and other members of the clan had misdemeanor records. There were also evictions and charges of welfare fraud.

Fay cruised the information superhighway every day but she'd seldom encountered such mystifying files. How could these Tenes expect old-age benefits if they didn't pay into their own Social Security accounts? What was the point of building up a retirement equity for someone else, or for the dead? She wondered if the Tenes were a Mafia family, running some kind of scam. She called a network friend, a detective who worked organized crime; he told her that the name Tene meant nothing to him.

IN THE EVENING, she took her sidekick on his regular evening frisk to Marina Green, then decided to file the Tene mystery in a far corner of her mind and go to bed. She'd studied creative writing at Arizona

State, authored *A Private Eye's Guide to Collecting a Bad Debt*, and regularly critiqued detective novels in a column called "The Gumshoe Letters" in the *San Francisco Review of Books*. On this cool winter night she decided to lull herself to sleep by plotting out still another project: a novel about a skip tracer. She got as far as the title—*Lily Kills Her Client*—when her concentration began to slip.

Then Beans licked her face, a pigeon cooed on her balcony, and the steam heat system hissed and knocked, a triad of events announcing the arrival of dawn. Her clock said five-fifty. Darn, she said to herself, I gotta stop sleeping so late.

3

Tracking a Tene

SHE STARTED HER new day by rearranging her document files so they wouldn't come crashing down while she showered. She kept most of her papers in crates along the wall of her art deco bathroom, where they rose six sinuous feet like Oriental acrobats. The W to Z folders stayed damp from bathtub runoff, but A to V were dry. A shorter stack of wanted posters, legal documents and back copies of dog-lover magazines perched atop the water closet at a slight angle.

At 9:00 a.m., after a bracing ride to Seal Rocks with Beans gallomping behind her bike, Fay called the Department of Motor Vehicles to request the driving history of Hope Victoria Beesley's friend Danny Tene. She learned that a Dan Tene had been involved in minor traffic matters but otherwise seemed clean. He was the registered owner of a metallic-gold Corvette. Fay reversed the license number through the system and this time the owner came back as Sal Lamance. Same address, same car. She wondered why Danny Tene needed two names. It was perfectly legal under California law, but . . . odd. Maybe this job wouldn't be as simple as she'd thought.

*　*　*

SHE DROVE HER 1982 Tercel to the San Francisco Medical Examiner's Office and learned that a photocopy of the police report involving the dead Tene infant would cost $25, an offer she was obliged to decline. She perused City Hall records and found that a Dan Tene resided in a nondescript neighborhood, stood six-three, weighed two-eighty, and had been born in New Jersey in 1957 or 1962—the printing was faint— which made him thirty or thirty-five.

After a hasty carrot cake brunch with iced damiana cappuccino, she dropped by Ken Chan's office. "I've been trying to connect Tene with Mrs. Beesley," she said after reporting her preliminary findings. "So far—no connection. What do we know about her?"

The lawyer described his client as an irascible eighty-two-year-old eccentric who alternated between spinning fascinating tales about her past and cussing him out. "Most of the time I really enjoy her, but she can be hard to take. Hates lawyers, doctors, politicians, bureaucrats, Americans. She calls Russians "Bolsheviks." Has an opinion on every-thing, usually negative. You name it, she hates it. Except the English. She was born Russian, but she's proud of holding U.S. and English passports. She looks down on Asians and lends them money at eighteen, nineteen percent. She's got about a half million dollars on the street. Sometimes a debtor skips to China and she gets stiffed. That's where I come in. It's tough work, and she's never satisfied."

Chan said the old woman had offered several explanations of how the opportunistic Danny Tene came to be listed as co-owner of her luxurious home with its stained glass windows and objets d'art in jade and ivory and precious metals. The bare home, minus contents, had been appraised by the city at $373,000, but it was worth more on the open market.

"She doesn't remember how she met Danny," the lawyer continued, "but it might have been when she was taking a walk. He offered to help her out—housework, gardening, handyman. Told her he enjoyed help-ing old people and did the same things for his mother. After a while he asked if he could rent her empty garage—"

"For his gold Corvette," Fay interrupted. "California license 1PLL244."

Chan ignored her display of expertise. "One night Danny men-tioned that he needed a place to stay and since Mrs. Beesley had five empty bedrooms, why couldn't he just move in? Next thing she knew he was a permanent guest."

"Was there any—uh . . . you know?"

"Not likely. She's under five feet, weighs ninety pounds. He's huge. And he's fifty years younger. But . . ." He shrugged. "Who knows? Maybe you can find out."

Fay said that sexual profiling wasn't one of her specialities.

Chan smiled. "After a few months Tene got her to sign a joint tenancy deed. Said it would legalize their living arrangement. She didn't suspect anything. She'd taught English, and he was her tenant, wasn't he? Simple enough. She also speaks Russian, French and German, and she can get by in Mandarin and Cantonese and some Chinese dialects I've never heard. Learned 'em in Hong Kong."

"Hong Kong?" Fay was a busy traveler herself, a compulsion that had begun when she'd said to herself "I'd rather be anyplace but here" while enduring 120-degree heat in the playground of Royal Palm Elementary School in Phoenix. Since then she'd been to fifty states and four continents and had enjoyed every trip except the midwinter freight train ride from Mount Shasta to Seattle.

"Mrs. Beesley was in Hong Kong in World War Two," the lawyer explained. "She spent three years in a Japanese concentration camp."

Chan said that Danny Tene had promised the old woman $75,000 in return for her signature on the joint tenancy agreement. Chronically worried about money, she'd accompanied her roomer to City Hall and signed in front of a notary. After the document was recorded, the handyman dropped out of her life. "That was two or three years ago, and she hasn't seen him since. She's hurt, but what can she do? She had no idea what he was up to, and she had other things on her mind—opera, philanthropies, costume parties, entertaining. She likes to dress in her Russian costumes and play piano in charity wards with a group called the Half-Notes. Shakes her tambourine and does dances she learned in Russia. A *very* busy old lady."

Fay said, "Hope Victoria Beesley doesn't sound like a Russian name."

"She was born Nadia Malysheff. Married an Englishman named Beesley and renamed herself after the Hope diamond and the queen. She says she came from a family of aristocrats—doctors, teachers."

"What makes her think she's being scammed?"

"A year after she signed the joint tenancy agreement, the Assessor's Office raised her taxes. She sent a note to Danny saying something like, This thing that you recorded, whatever it is, you gotta unrecord it because it's costing me money. Danny ignored her. He had what he wanted. The joint tenancy agreement makes him co-owner of her house. When she dies, he'll own it outright."

Fay nodded. She'd heard of a few similar cases. Big-money scams had been based on the fact that the phrase "joint tenancy" actually meant "joint ownership" under the law. She wondered when California politicians would learn basic English.

"After another year or two," Chan continued, "the midnight calls started. Someone would ask if she was still alive. She got six or eight hang-ups a night. She was sure it was Danny or his relatives. Then she broke her hip and was bedridden and scared to death in that big empty house. As soon as she could walk, she took a cab straight to my office, told me she wanted Danny off her deed. I filed a recision action. He's fighting it. That's why I called you."

"I was surprised to find so many Tenes in the data banks," Fay said. "And so many interchangeable names and Social Security numbers."

The lawyer frowned. "Oh, that's not unusual for Gypsies," he said.

"Gypsies?"

"Yeah. Didn't I tell you?"

4

Life and Hard Times

BY THANKSGIVING WEEK 1992, the lady known as Rat Dog Dick found herself wondering what real Gypsies looked like and where they hung out and why one of them seemed to be relieving a ditsy old woman of her house and possessions. Didn't Gypsies go around shaking tambourines, playing violins and dancing the—fandango? The *flamingo*? Didn't they read palms and stare into crystal balls? As a child, she'd glimpsed a Gypsy encampment in the saguaros outside the Phoenix city limits, but the brightly colored skirts and chattering dark-haired kids disappeared down the blacktop and she never saw them again. In her busy life, she'd given Gypsies little thought. She vaguely remembered that they'd originally come from Egypt—thus "Gypsy"—and that the word "gyp" had something to do with their earliest activities in England—or was it Rumania?

EN ROUTE TO northern Marin County to interview a client, she drove a few blocks off-course to check on Danny Tene's current address on Fifteenth Avenue. It turned out to be an ordinary-looking building, and not a tambourine in sight. She considered a short stakeout, but the Frog Prince was too conspicuous. With the odometer at 150,000 miles, she'd made the mistake of ordering a repaint job in a distinguished-looking "hunter's green," but the car had emerged the color of a St. Patrick's Day hat. Until she could raise the cash for a re-repaint, the old Tercel was useless for surveillance.

She returned to the freeway, crossed the Golden Gate Bridge, and soon was passing through Sausalito, an artsy-craftsy town of painful memory. Ten years earlier, a local mugger had clubbed her in the face and stolen her wallet. Thirty-six hours after the mugging, a freak storm sank her houseboat. Penniless and homeless, she faced a $26,000 loss unless she could prove that the leaky old boat had been unseaworthy when she bought it. A harbormate informed her that a previous tenant had changed his name to a mantra that sounded like "om hadji all in free" and joined a Breatharian cult in Texas. It took Fay two days to find the ex-hippie's cave and talk him into signing an affidavit verifying that the ancient hull had shipped water for years. Lawyer Ken Chan was so impressed by her investigative feat that he handed her a list of uncollected judgments and offered her a fifty percent commission. Working out of a telephone booth, she located three deadbeats in her first week. An admirer commented, "Fay, you chase down people like a rat dog chases rats."

After a few more successful searches, she was advised by the authorities to get an investigator's license or "cease and desist." Using savvy acquired from *Rockford File* reruns, she aced the examination on her first try and immediately took an ad in a bar association newsletter: "Misplaced your witness . . . estate heir . . . client? Don't be embarrassed!

Call Rat Dog Dick, the skip tracer who finds people like a rat dog finds rats."

On the whole, her offbeat professional name had worked out well, except for the occasional call for advice on getting rid of household vermin, or chauvinists asking for "Rat Dog Dyke." From the beginning, the flashy sobriquet proved irresistible to the media. In her role as the beautiful skip tracer from San Francisco, she'd appeared on national TV shows, including *Good Morning America, Oprah, Joan Rivers, Larry King* and *Jenny Jones.* A typical newspaper article was headlined "Rat Dog Dick: Not Your Average Investigator." Another read "Rat Dog: Hound on the Trail of Rascals." The *San Francisco Examiner* advised its readers that "Rat Dog's the Name, PI Work Is the Game." Columnist Bill Mandel referred to Fay as "the Maltese Faron" and described a memorable colloquy:

> "Where'd you get a name like that?" I asked.
>
> "Where'd you get a name like Bill Mandel?" she asked . . .
>
> She rolled up her pants a few turns and crossed one sinewy leg over the other (or maybe she crossed the other leg over one; in the excitement, I forgot to take careful notes). Then she hooked a long, elegant finger under my chin and pulled upward.
>
> "Look me in the eye when you look at my legs, Mandel," she snapped. . . . "There are six jillion stories in the Naked City . . . I'm one of them."
>
> "Well," I said, shifting my gaze back into the forbidden zone.
>
> "Just give me the publicity, buddy," she said. "I'll watch my legs for you."

A profile in an investigators' newsletter called Fay "the best-looking skip tracer in the U.S." She had flawless skin, a springy woof of lemon-colored curly hair, razor-straight features, and eyes that flickered from gray to blue behind her mirrored CHiPs sunglasses. Although her figure had attracted stares since junior high school, she wasn't pleased by a journalist's suggestion that she "must have been designed in a wind tunnel" and another reporter's reference to her "giant gazungas." Friends reminded her that a voluptuous figure wasn't necessarily a liability in a city where the hypermammiferous Carol Doda had become famous by displaying her enhanced assets atop a piano in North Beach. Fay preserved her own natural shape by adding and subtracting weight with such regularity that her cells were too busy to get tired and sag—or so she figured. So far, into her early forties, her system seemed to work. Her business card showed a woman in slouch hat and trench coat arching long legs over the logo "Rat Dog Dick Detective Agency." Women took it in the lighthearted way she'd intended, and so did most men.

BACK FROM HER half-day trip to Marin County, Fay fired up Evie the Everex and to her surprise found another address for a Dan Tene in a data bank she hadn't consulted. Beans was skilled at reading her intentions and was already rubbing his backside against the door to the hallway. He enjoyed reconnoitering new neighborhoods, always looking over his shoulder to keep her in sight.

On the drive to the new Tene address she passed a Russian Orthodox church on California Street, another on Geary, and a smaller one a few blocks beyond. She recognized a demographic irony: hardly a Russian lived on the tony Russian Hill—the rents were too high for immigrants and their offspring—but parts of this western section of San Francisco seemed as Russian as Sevastopol.

The blocky apartment building at 486 Funston Avenue was four stories high and shaded by old established trees that were even taller. A sign next door bespoke the influx of Asian-Americans into the solid old neighborhood: "San Francisco Bible Church—Sunday Worship. Cantonese Service 9:30 A.M." The original color scheme of the apartment house appeared to be cream and white, with a brick facing and stucco walls that looked as though they hadn't encountered a paintbrush in decades. Naked wood was visible, and shields of oyster-colored plaster showed where earthquake damage had been patched. Broken windows exposed some of the lower apartments to wind and fog. Fay asked herself, Hasn't the owner ever heard of routine maintenance?

She circled the block, hoping for a chance sighting of Danny Tene or his Gypsy relatives, and thought briefly about letting Beans use the rest facilities in the isthmus of trees and shrubs that separated quiet Funston from the four busy lanes of Park Presidio. She decided not to stop after she spotted tents and sleeping bags under the thick canopy of trees. When she first moved to San Francisco in 1976, the homeless had tended to hang out south of Market Street and in relaxed areas like the Haight and North Beach. Now they were found wherever there was cover, even on the dark sands below the Cliff House and in the well-scrubbed lanes and flowered doorways on Nob and Telegraph hills. She wasn't surprised to see them camped along this sylvan stretch.

On her third circumnavigation of the block she noticed that a pickup truck had stopped in front of the apartment building and disgorged two dark-looking men, one of average size and one built like an out-of-shape 49ers lineman. The big man walked with the rolling gait usually associated with chafed thighs. He wore a white shirt, jeans and dainty loafers that would have been suitable for an evening of ballet. His blue-black mustache and thinning black hair looked newly wet.

Fay drove to a pay phone to report that she'd just seen Danny Tene in the flesh.

"Fay," Ken Chan said excitedly, "I've been trying to reach you." He lowered his voice. "We've lost Mrs. Beesley."

5

Death in the A.M.

THE USUALLY STOIC lawyer appeared rattled as he beckoned the PI into his cramped office with its leaning stacks of books, briefs and legal filings stuffed with whereases and wherefores. He informed her that his client's body had been found in her home a few hours earlier.

"I drove out to see for myself," Chan said. "Her eyes were open. Mrs. Beesley owned twenty wigs, but her head was bare. Just a few wisps of white hair. Helpless . . . pathetic." He rubbed his eyes. "She'd've been *so* embarrassed to be seen like that."

"Was it a natural?" Fay asked.

"I don't know. She was eighty-three, weak, ailing. We'll know for sure when the medical examiner gets finished."

"You don't think Danny Tene—?"

"If everything she told me was true, she hadn't seen him in two or three years."

The lawyer looked down and shook his head slowly. Describing his client earlier, he'd seemed distantly tolerant, almost bemused, as though discussing a crotchety old character in an Anne Tyler novel. But he was clearly touched by the death.

"You won't see many like Mrs. Beesley," he said. "She'd sit right over there and tell me off, like I was one of her eighth-grade students in Hong Kong." He touched his fingertips together. "She lived from the steam age to the space age and never missed a thing."

"Any survivors?" asked the practical PI.

"Her son Montagu lives in Australia. He's a psychiatrist. They haven't spoken for years."

Fay began to feel a sense of loss for this lonely woman she'd never met. It was her old chickenheartedness kicking in again. She always tried to discipline herself to think of her clients as names (sometimes misspelled) on legal-size yellow paper. But how could anyone not feel a twinge of sorrow for Hope Victoria Beesley, naked and dead without her wig, her only living relative an estranged son halfway around the world?

She asked Chan how his client's death affected his prospects in the civil case against Danny Tene. "It'll be a hell of a lot tougher now," he replied. "Mrs. Beesley was our main witness."

"I'll keep digging," Fay said.

Chan said he wasn't sure her estate could afford her fee.

Fay said, "Fee? *Fee?* What the heck's a fee?"

6

The Executor

THE NEXT MORNING Fay and her furry companion returned to Chan's office to meet the dead woman's sole heir and executor, Barry Hughes. As usual, Beans' head and shoulders protruded from the passenger window like a big-game trophy; a traffic cop had warned her that the combination of dog and Frog Prince could be construed as reckless driving and advised her to get rid of one or both or risk the consequences. Fay risked the consequences. When it rained, Beans rode in front with one paw on her thigh.

BARRY HUGHES TURNED out to be a fortyish Englishman with fluffy silver-gray hair curling over his collar. Chan performed the introductions. "I say," the man said, "did you say . . . *Rat Dog Dick?*"

"Call me Fay," she said.

The executor's easy manner suggested that he would be more comfortable behind a Whitney's ale and a Woodbine cigarette. Fay liked him at once, her standard reaction to strangers. She tended to admire everyone until they proved undeserving, and sometimes longer.

In a charming British accent, Hughes described himself as the dead woman's best friend, "completely and utterly." He said he and his wife had stopped off at the Beesley home to pick her up for Thanksgiving dinner the day before she died, but "Mrs. B was feeling poorly and didn't want to go. I told her I'd drop around in the morning and take her over to Sausalito for breakfast. She always loved the view from the Golden Gate Bridge." But when he arrived the next day, he said, he found her dead in bed, her body locked in rigor mortis. A fist was clenched and her arm pointed straight at the ceiling in what appeared to be a final irascible gesture.

Fay drew the Englishman out while Chan leaned back in his chair and listened. Hughes explained that he worked as a service representative for Pacific Bell and had met "Mrs. B" over the phone. "She rang up to complain about annoying calls from a chap named Danny Tene, and I was the only rep who could understand her accent. She spoke upper-class English with European overtones and a hint of Russia, the Far East, kind of polyglot. She was like a lot of old people who call the phone company. They just want a point of human contact. When she mentioned that she'd lived in Hong Kong, I told her I was there many times as an officer in the Royal Navy and it was one of my favorite places. Well, that did it. She rang me up day after day. Wouldn't talk to anyone else. Pretty soon I learned that she was looking for someone to help her get back to Hong Kong for some kind of intestinal surgery. She'd had the procedure before—she called it a nip and tuck—and she didn't trust American doctors."

"Or lawyers," Chan put in.

"She gave the impression that she was down on her luck. I arranged to put her on our Universal Lifeline Service to save her a few dollars as a senior citizen. That was really all I could do. She insisted that she wanted to meet me—couldn't I please drop by her house so she could thank me for my kindness? When I put her off she sent a packet of pictures. Most of them were falling apart—they'd been taken from Moscow to Manchuria to Hong Kong and who the hell knew where. The older pictures showed a petite, pretty woman in jewels and Russian dance costumes and fancy settings. You could see she'd been a knock-out."

"Was she married?" Fay asked.

"Five or six times. And she'd had hordes of admirers. But right now I could see she needed a friend. Well, she was persistence personified. One day she called and said she was yearning to sit down with someone and talk about Hong Kong. She laid the guilt trip on me—Oh, Mr. Hughes, I'm a poor old lady, I'm all alone. She sent me a packet of testimonials from former students. She'd taught English, typing, and Pittman shorthand to the Chinese. They all said what a good teacher she was. When I got off work I dropped by her house on Balboa Street to return her pictures. I was surprised at the size of the place, but plenty of penniless old folks live in homes too big for them. That's one reason they're penniless. She greeted me like royalty and showed me into a drawing room with a ceiling twelve feet high and carved antique furniture that must've cost a bundle. The drawing room had the same atmosphere as Sotheby's. She set out tea and cookies on a silver tray and she couldn't wait to show me her British and American passports."

"She lived alone in that big place?" Fay asked.

"She had one lodger left, in an apartment on the top floor. He was a chap of about sixty, tall, overweight and with very sloppy habits, at least by Mrs. B's standards. She treated him like a bloody peasant. Didn't allow him in the kitchen. Used to leave him notes. She'd berate him for coming in late or trying to smuggle a girlfriend up the stairs. She told me she frowned on visitors—no sex please, we're English, that old story. She'd thrown out a female tenant for boinking the roomers, and she threw out her last lodger, too. Well, we ended up talking all afternoon. She was completely and utterly fascinating! Feisty, vain, imperious. Vulnerable, too, though she tried to hide it."

Fay asked, "Why'd she use the name Beesley?"

"Because it sounded British. Came from her second husband. He abandoned her in Hong Kong just after the war. Before Beesley she'd been married to a Russian nobleman, and after Beesley she was married to a Frenchman who took over the Beesley persona to get into the States, and then she married an Italian baron but divorced him after she caught him sleeping with his mother, and finally she married a dentist who died. I wouldn't have put it past her to marry again, even at eighty-two. When she wasn't calling you six kinds of sod, she could be charming. Under all that bombast there was something soft and feminine, you know?"

Chan was nodding slowly behind his desk. "She tried to believe that people were good," the lawyer said. "She was frugal but she was trusting, too. I hate to think how many people took advantage of her."

"How'd she get so naive?" Fay asked. "You'd think after all that travel—"

"Old age," Hughes interrupted. "She lived a little too long and a little too hard. Life stopped for her in the sixties. After that she lived in her memories. And, I say, what memories! I've always been a war buff, but she was an encyclopedia of military history. She had firsthand knowledge of the Sino-Japanese War, the Chinese civil war, the Russian Revolution, both world wars. She survived torture, hunger, disease, strafings, bombings, everything but poison gas. She made a couple of great escapes, met Churchill, Eden, Mao, warlords, admirals, generals. She was a guest of Chiang Kai-shek and Madame Chiang. When she first came to San Francisco, socialites tore each other's hair out to get into her parties."

He shook his head. "But she was such a mark," he said. "She lent one of her tenants ten thousand dollars and the bloody bostid screwed himself rigid in Vegas and never came back."

"She kept me busy," Chan put in. "She grew up in China. She felt comfortable with Asians."

Hughes said, "I used to take her shopping and she would bargain in Cantonese."

After more reminiscing, the threesome got down to the business of the Tene connection. Hughes confirmed that the old woman despised the corpulent Danny and referred to him as "the mugger." But she used similar pejoratives to describe doctors, lawyers and most other Americans.

Fay asked, "Why on earth did she sign a joint tenancy agreement?"

"I don't know," Hughes said. "Maybe he caught her in a weak moment. I got the impression they might have been intimate at one time. A business arrangement, you might say."

"I got a look at him yesterday," Fay said. *"Ugh!"*

"He's one repulsive fucking creature," Hughes went on. "Pardon my language." Fay didn't mind, but she avoided such words herself. Her standard expletives were "rats," "criminy" and, in extreme situations, "jiminy Christmas." A well-meaning friend had suggested that she update her vocabulary by repeating "fuckety fuck" in front of her mirror until the words flowed naturally. It didn't work.

". . . And he was so much younger than Mrs. B," Hughes was saying. "But don't forget—she'd always enjoyed the company of men. Sometimes old women have to buy their companions. She told me that Tene slouched around her house as though he owned it. Then he began pestering her to make him her sole heir. When she wouldn't change her will in his favor, he pulled the joint tenancy trick and took off."

Chan asked the Englishman how often he'd seen Mrs. Beesley in her final months. "Over the last year's time," Hughes responded, "I went from someone who chatted her up on the phone to being her main caregiver. After she hurt her hip she was almost bedridden, and she'd ring me for help. She had no one else. I started out bringing her little gifts of food and ended up making her breakfast every morning before I went to work. She'd have starved otherwise. I even used to bawth her.

She was very proper about such things, and it embarrassed both of us, but she became incontinent. What choice was there? Old people all alone in the world—well, *someone* has to care for them."

Fay winced. She was unmarried, and someday she might be old and alone. Would there be a Barry Hughes to help her? She would rather be dead than dependent on strangers. But Mrs. Beesley had seemed independent, too, till old age dragged her down. Then she'd given away half her house and died.

"I cleaned the place," the sole heir and executor was saying. "I did her washing and laundry. Sometimes I thought, Dear God, how did I get myself into this? She could be an awful bitch, bawling me out for not doing enough, but I kept reminding myself that she was old and tired and frightened. And . . . a fascinating human being. I don't regret a bit of it."

Fay scribbled notes as the insiders eulogized the strange woman who'd touched both their lives. But after a while a disturbing thought bedeviled her concentration. Was it a coincidence that the body had been found just seven days after she'd been brought into the case? Was foul play out of the question? She didn't pretend to any special medical knowledge, but who ever heard of a corpse pointing its hand at the ceiling? Not even the dear departed were exempt from the law of gravity. It didn't take a forensic scientist to conclude that the woman's body must have been turned face upward after rigor mortis set in. But . . . by whom? And why? She scribbled "MURDER??" and underlined it twice.

To Fay, a longtime fan of James Bond and Hercule Poirot, the possibilities were endless. Mrs. Beesley had a knack for raising hackles, and a number of suspects came to mind. Among these was Danny Tene, of course. He had a valuable home to gain, and he'd been lurking in the background for years. Where did it say that he couldn't return and kill the old lady in the middle of the night, or hire a hitman to do the job? But . . . with what? A blow-dart fired from a rooftop? A ray gun?

As Hughes and Chan began to discuss wills and statutes and inheritance laws, a silly scenario crossed Fay's mind. She'd made a career out of sexual harassment cases, incest, reuniting lost parents and children, finding hidden assets and missing witnesses and lost loves and bail skips and deadbeat dads. She'd tracked down the daughter of a European countess, the missing son of a self-made millionaire, a playboy who fled to the Virgin Islands with his cook, a befuddled man who exiled himself to the Catalina Islands under the impression that he was Paul Gauguin, and dozens of others. But she'd never solved a murder. What a break this could be! She would find Mrs. Beesley's killer and . . . write another book!

"He's already got it," Hughes was saying to the lawyer.

"Got what?" Fay asked.

"The house," the Englishman said. "It's Danny's now, you know. His lawyer changed the bloody locks. I found seventeen thousand five hundred dollars in a drawer the day she died—that was her petty cash— but I haven't been able to get back inside. She kept her money in a safe and other hiding places. I know of three hundred thousand dollars that she transferred from a Shanghai bank on her own signature. And that's just one transaction. She was as tight as a duck's ass and always paid cash, said she didn't want to depend on banks. She's got money tucked away, all right. But where?"

"Let me do some checking," Fay proposed. "I'd hate to see Tene get it all."

Hughes nodded and said, "It'd be nice to inherit something besides her bills."

LEAVING THE LAWYER'S office, the PI marveled at how quickly Hope Victoria Beesley had changed from a euphonious name into a fully fleshed human being whose death mattered and who deserved much better than she'd received from the citizens of her adopted city. Fay was still touched by the sentimental reactions of Chan and Hughes, but then she'd always been exquisitely touchable. She'd once annoyed a movie companion by breaking into sobs during the opening credits. "You're good-hearted, Rat Dog," the TV interviewer Larry King characterized her on the air. "They all were. Philip Marlowe was and so are you!"

She wondered if the Beesley case would pay off and realized just as quickly that it didn't matter. An interviewer for USA Today had asked why she'd failed to crack down on a particular millionaire deadbeat, and she'd answered, "Oh, I had fun on the job!" And anyway, Mrs. Beesley was no ordinary woman or she wouldn't have evoked such emotion. And . . . what if she'd been murdered?

Fay stopped for some Moroccan takeout and headed home to the Marina, still deep in thought about the case. Suddenly she became aware of a dull orange headlight approaching the Frog Prince from dead ahead, the driver madly clanging his bell. She'd turned the wrong way into Powell Street. After a quick U-turn, she muttered, "He won't try *that* again."

The cable car receded in her mirror.

7

Graziana

BACK ON THE paper trail in the morning, she drove downtown and punched "Tene" into the assessor's data bank. Out popped a Mary Tene who'd married a Philip Steiner and thus become Mary Steiner in the records. It looked as though she was heavily involved in rental property. Fay cross-checked court records and found several eviction actions filed against the tenants of an apartment house that the Steiner woman had inherited from a man with the unpronounceable name Liotweizen.

She also found "Tene Danny" on the deed of the Beesley home at 1045 Balboa, together with entries showing that the original owner was in the process of trying to get him off the paper. Too late, Fay said to herself. Mrs. Beesley is in no shape to fight.

OVER A SOLITARY lunch of dim sum and green tea, she ruminated about her findings. Could Mary Tene Steiner be related to Danny? Surely they were both Gypsies—Ken Chan had said that Tene was a common Gypsy name, like Yonko, Bimbo, Marks, Emil. She wondered where Mrs. Beesley fit into the Gypsy world. Had she met them in her travels? Did she associate with them as she associated with Asians? And what about Liotwhatever? Was that a Gypsy name too? "Steiner" sounded German. Steiner Street was a major thoroughfare that ran the length of the northern part of the city. Maybe the woman had borrowed the name from a sign. The only commonality in all the Tene legal filings seemed to be the advanced age of most of the people with whom the family dealt and the frequent notarizations of their legal papers by a woman named Nicole Nicholson.

Fay drove to the Sunset District to search out the notary. She'd always enjoyed the untouristy old neighborhood with its rows of ticky-tacky houses in flamboyant pastels: turquoise, flamingo, canary, burgundy, plum, fuchsia, mauve. Early paint salesmen must have made fortunes here. She liked the homeyness of the local watering holes, even though she seldom had time to visit. She laughed as she passed a sign in a barroom window: "We steal from drunks." She knew who was inside: fun-loving souls like her. They would be wearing pins proclaiming "Up the 49ers" and "Irish whisky makes me frisky." She licked her lips to remove salt from an imaginary margarita and thought about dropping in on the way home.

The notary wasn't hard to find but not very communicative. "Tene?" the woman said, frowning hard. "Tene? I don't remember."

"Gypsies?" Fay offered. "Long dresses? Dark hair? Gold earrings?"

The notary shook her head.

AT HOME THAT night Fay perused a list of names she'd taken from the eviction filings at the courthouse. There'd been many entries for Graziana Gandolfi, who apparently had been the subject of a lengthy eviction proceeding, and almost as many for Dimitri Egoroff, whose personal beef with Mary Tene Steiner was still in court.

Fay opened her phone book and found no listings for Egoroff, but there was a G. Gandolfi at an address in the Sunset. A plummy female voice answered the phone, and Fay identified herself as a private detective working on a case involving a woman named Mary Steiner.

The empty air was intimidating. "Hello?" Fay said. "*Hello?*"

The woman asked, "Who did you say you were?"

Fay's quick repeat of her name was followed by another silence. "You can find me in the phone book?" she offered. "Under . . . Rat Dog Dick Detective Agency?"

"Under *what?*" the woman asked.

"Rat Dog Dick. Would it, uh, make you more comfortable to check my listing and call me back?" She was used to dealing with the shocked and the dubious, especially via phone. As soon as they heard the word "detective," they were convinced they were en route to San Quentin for unpaid parking tickets. And why on earth were they being called by a "Rat Dog Dick"? She'd learned to work around the problem.

At last the woman said, "Yes. I knew Mary Steiner. But . . . I really can't talk about her."

THEY TALKED FOR an hour. Graziana Gandolfi said she was under court order not to discuss her legal entanglements, which seemed to involve eviction proceedings and some kind of harassment action, but she had no problem discussing Hope Victoria Beesley. In her rich, mellow voice, she said she'd come across the old woman's name and address while making the same document searches as Fay. "I took the Balboa bus and knocked on her door, but nobody answered. I went back later and an old lady invited me in. Maybe five feet tall. Good-looking for her age, spoke with a British accent. I thought, She must've been a hot number when she was young."

Fay asked, "What did the house look like?"

"Decadent. Run-down. Lots of antique furniture. Floors scarred and scuffed. Original plumbing, and only one bathroom. She had a beautiful piano. I was thinking, This place may need work, but it'd be a dream come true for me!"

"How big?" Fay asked.

"Five bedrooms. Three floors. Maybe five thousand square feet. A nice little pied-à-terre."

Fay was trying to remember if she'd ever heard the name Graziani Gandolfo in connection with the stage or opera. She didn't want to show her ignorance by asking.

"As soon as I mentioned the Tenes," the woman went on, "Mrs. Beesley just glowered. She said, Oh, Danny! For a second I thought she was gonna spit. She said, Imagine a grown man still calling himself Danny! It should be *Daniel*, followed by a middle initial and a last name. She said, He calls himself a single man but he's not. He's got two brothers and a mother and a sister."

"Did she mention any first names?"

"His brothers, Teddy and Kelly. A sister, Theresa. His mother, Mary."

"Mary . . . Tene?"

"Mary Tene Steiner. She married Philip Steiner when he was eighty-three and she was in her thirties. He stayed alive for ten more years and she finally inherited."

Fay was becoming confused by all the names, never her long suit, and tried to steer the phone conversation back to her late client, Mrs. Beesley. "Tell me, Graziani—"

"Graziana."

"Sorry. Did Mrs. Beesley talk about a document she signed for Danny?"

"Talk about it? I couldn't shut her up! She was still angry about the Tenes. How old people dwell on minutiae! She said Danny lived in her house and the joint tenancy papers made it proper and legal."

"Did she have any dealings with his mother?"

"With Mary? I warned her to be real careful about that woman. She cost me forty thousand dollars and a year of my life. I asked Mrs. Beesley if she had a family to look after her, and she said she had a son but they didn't speak. I said, Well, maybe you should mend your fences with him. She didn't seem to care. You could see she was losing it a little."

"She's lost it a lot," Fay said. "She died the day after Thanksgiving."

"Oh, my God," the woman exclaimed. "That explains something."

"What?"

"I saw Danny and his mother at the Beesley house the other day. Do you suppose they scared the living daylights out of her? They were good at that, you know."

"At what?" Fay asked.

"Frightening people. Especially the elderly. But nobody wants to hear about it. Not even my lawyer."

Fay suppressed a gasp and said, "I know somebody who wants to hear about it." The two women made a date to meet.

8

Burial at Sea

A FEW DAYS later, Ken Chan reported that postmortem examinations had revealed that Mrs. Beesley died of "atherosclerotic heart disease" and "cardiopulmonary arrest." Fay drove to the City Department of Health to check the death certificate. It confirmed that Hope Victoria Beesley, eighty-three, a Russian-born teacher, had died of natural causes. Darn! Fay said to herself. There goes my murder case.

On New Year's Day 1993, the eccentric old woman's body was cremated and her ashes scattered off the Marin Coast, north of San Francisco, following her last wishes. Danny Tene filed an "affidavit of death of joint tenant" with the City Assessor's Office and became sole owner of the house.

WITH THE SEA burial, everyone except Fay seemed to feel that the case was closed. "Look," she told Ken Chan, "I haven't found a smoking gun, but this whole deal looks bad."

Barry Hughes said that most of Mrs. B's assets had proved to be in her house and its contents, and he'd inherited precious little cash. "I'm sorry, Fay," he said, "but I don't know where I'd get the money for any more investigating."

"Don't mention money," Fay said. She was thinking of her upcoming session with the plummy-voiced Graziani—or was it Graziana? "I'll just write my report and take it to the police," she said. "That'll wrap things up."

DRIVING TOWARD THE meeting place in a Chestnut Street cappuccino bakery, Fay realized that this case was shaping up like so many others: long hours, low pay and lost sleep. As usual she couldn't back out. She was nosy and often wasted time probing for irrelevant tidbits and lore, another reason she was usually broke. She *had* to get to the bottom of things. She'd worked a case involving an Amtrak ticket clerk and ended up learning the story of American railroading back to the golden spike at Promontory, Utah. Customers of the Rat Dog Dick Detective Agency realized that she would handle their cases gratis if they could excite her curiosity. She frequently reunited adoptees with their birth parents and wrote it off as "reunion work." She tried to track down a call girl whom a soldier had loved in 1954; after one week, the client's money ran out, but the fruitless search continued for months, in and out of every flophouse and whorehouse in town. After five years she was still working the case of a missing alcoholic beauty whose son had burned down their mansion and hanged himself. The original client was long dead, but Fay refused to give up, even after a friend told her she should change her business name to the Pro Bono Detective Agency.

She considered how she'd been throwing herself into these frustrations for a dozen years and didn't care because she was having so much fun. Before becoming a PI, she'd moved about the world finding jobs, boyfriends and apartments, only to depart three or four months for other jobs, boyfriends and apartments. In her early twenties she'd composed her epitaph: "Here lies Fay Faron. She didn't have to work very hard." She served sherry to poets in New Orleans and sherry trifle to bankers in London. She clerked at I. Magnin, led bike tours on Cape Cod, and drove an ice cream truck (she still heard the bell in her dreams and jumped from bed to unwrap a Frostee-Cone for an imaginary customer who always turned out to be Beans). She hostessed at a Mafia bar in Boston, monogrammed shirts, covered the resort beat for the *Santo Domingo News* in the Dominican Republic, filmed a travelogue on the River Kwai, and sold vacuum cleaners in a part of Appalachia without power ("But just think, missus," she told the housewives who answered her knock, "when electricity gets here, you'll be *ready!*"). She'd finished up her vagabond years as an associate producer for KGO-TV, the ABC affiliate in San Francisco, fine-tuning an innate talent for drama and intrigue.

Sometimes she interrupted her work as Rat Dog Dick long enough to reread her old files for sheer pleasure. She considered them her private soap operas, stories of hate, misery, cruelty, altruism, every extreme of good and bad, with F*A*Y F*A*R*O*N getting top billing, at least on her unpaid invoices. She doubted that her agency would ever net more profit than the average espresso stand, but she didn't mind as long as she could afford kibble and curry. She'd long since diagnosed her central neurosis as a childlike abhorrence of injustice, which she considered a genetic disorder and therefore untreatable. Growing up in Kansas City, Minneapolis and Phoenix, she was always yelping "That's unfair!" on behalf of herself or other children. She didn't regard her oversensitivity as a credit or discredit; it was just something she had to live with. So did the people she tracked.

The Landlord

GRAZIANA GANDOLFI PROVED to be a robust woman with a glowing complexion and a thatch of dark reddish hair that perched on her head like a puff. She described herself as an administrative assistant, "a glorified secretary." Fay admired her modesty but was surprised that she didn't hold a job better suited to her mellifluous voice: news anchor, perhaps, or third mezzo from the right in a Greek chorus at the Opera House.

In person the Gandolfi voice was even richer and the enunciation more precise than on the phone. The handsome woman spoke Spanish, French and Italian and said she'd once planned to become a translator at the UN. Her language skills were intimidating until Fay realized that they were unconnected to any sense of self-importance. The faintest Mediterranean intonation was explained when she said her family had emigrated to the United States when she was four. She appeared to be in her mid-thirties, amply built but pleasantly proportioned. "I'd kill to be a size ten again," she said after they'd talked for a few minutes.

"Me too," Fay said. They discussed taking out a contract on diet guru Richard Simmons.

WHEN THE CONVERSATION turned to Mary Tene Steiner and her brood, the Gandolfi expression changed. Plainly, this was no joking matter. She explained that there'd been a settlement in her court fight with the Steiner woman, but she was legally gagged by the terms of the agreement. She had plenty to say about her lifetime hero, the man she called "the landlord." She said she hoped someday to be able to forgive Mary Steiner and the other Tenes for what they'd done to her personally, but she would never forgive them for their treatment of old Konstantin Liotweizen.

"Mary stole his apartment building and his money and everything he had," the woman said. "I watched it happen. Then she put him in a home to die."

"You lived in the big place on Funston?" Fay asked. She was thinking of the building where she'd caught a glimpse of Danny Tene.

"I moved there in the mid-seventies. I had a lovely second-floor apartment, two-sixty-five a month, a good deal. I had a view of the Park Presidio. You know how rare that is in San Francisco—a bay window filled with trees! The landlord was a White Russian army officer who was exiled to China. He came here with his mother in the twenties. He was almost eighty when I met him, still very strong: broad shoulders, built like a steer. Soft, delicate hands, slender fingers. He had a wide Slavic face like Pope John Paul and a loud military voice and a fringe of white hair and the same strawberry birthmark as Gorbachev. His eyes were the clearest blue. He read the *Examiner* and the *Chronicle* every day without glasses, till Mary Steiner cut off the deliveries."

"Was he a Communist?" Fay could never keep such matters straight. Back in Arizona, there was never much discussion about political parties because even the liberals were Republicans.

"Heavens, no! He was a White Russian to the death. He voted Republican, but he spoke highly of Roosevelt and the WPA. He never complained about taxes. He loved American culture, history, music. He believed in education and had a degree in engineering. He could talk about *anything*. After we got to know each other, we talked for hours. Can you imagine? A man in his eighties and a woman in her twenties!"

"He wasn't a little boring?"

"Not till he started repeating himself. But that was much later."

"What were his tenants like?"

"Old folks. Old *Russians*. I was the only one under seventy, the only one working, and just about the only one who wasn't fluent in Russian. People lived there thirty, forty years. They knew a good thing. I had a full-time job, so I didn't see much of the others. Sonia Ellis lived right above me. She was Russian Jewish, in her eighties, and she'd lived in China, like the landlord. All the exiled Russians passed through Harbin or ended up there. It was in Manchuria, and I think it was one of the last stops on the Trans-Siberian Railway. Mrs. Ellis was very bright, very cool, drove an old Toyota. At night you could hear the mah-jongg tiles clacking in her place. Tulia Hartman was another nice old Russian lady. Very Jewish. You know, Eat now, we'll talk later?"

Fay nodded. The expression also described her Baptist mother in Arizona, now devoting her life to caring for her dying husband.

"Anna Atamasov lived in 304 for twenty years. She was ninety, a retired nurse, deaf, almost blind, spoke no English. Sometimes I'd walk her around the block to put a little sun on her face. It was a sin the way the Tenes forced her out—the worst kind of elder abuse."

"Who else lived there?"

"Tamara Baruksopulo lived on the third floor with her son Dimitri. She was a beautiful woman, in her eighties, an artist, very energetic. Worked at the Bank of America for years. She had dyed brown hair to midback, big brown eyes, very few wrinkles, graceful hands with long artist's fingers. Her son was an inventor. Eccentric, talky, intelligent. He and I fought against Mary. The others were too afraid."

"Were you tight with the tenants?"

"Only the landlord. He was the grandfather I never had. He would phone me to say good night in Russian: *Spokoynoy nochi.* He'd say, Have good dreams! He always wore a brown hat with a feather, and he'd tip it when we passed in the halls. Old-world politesse. I worked downtown, and he'd leave his door open and wait up for me. Sometimes I'd be tired and my feet hurt and I just wanted to go to sleep, but he would beckon from the front window and I would have to sit in his front room for a while because, well—" she shrugged—"anything else was out of the question."

"Didn't he ever go out?"

"Once in a while he took the bus to the Safeway. He could only carry a few items because his knees were stiff from arthritis. I'd shop for him, pick up *pirozhki*, the little Russian pastries, and sweets—he *loved* sweets. Years back he'd owned a Russian deli on O'Farrell and then another on Geary, and he still watched his pennies. That was his shopkeeper's mentality. Maybe he should've been a Swiss, like me."

"Swiss?" Fay said. "I thought your people were Italian."

"Italian Swiss," Graziana said. "From the Alps."

"Can you yodel?" Fay joked.

"Yodel? No, but I can speak the dialect."

Fay smiled and waited for a demonstration, but the woman was preoccupied with the eulogy. "I'll tell you how frugal he was," she continued. "One night a young guy put a gun in his back and demanded his money. The landlord said, You should be ashamed of yourself, stealing from an old man. Go out and get a job! The robber took off. The landlord told me he'd had three dollars in his wallet. I said, You risked your life for three bucks? He said, Listen, young lady, I worked hard all my life for my money. I'm not giving it to some bum in the streets."

"Was he pretty well off? I mean . . . at the end?"

"I saw some of his statements from Wells Fargo, and he never kept less than five hundred thousand in savings and seventy thousand in checking. Our building was appraised at just under a million. And he had other investments. You could call him cheap, niggardly, thrifty, but you could never call him greedy. He could have charged us three times as much rent. He wouldn't buy anything for himself. I bought him pants, a jacket, a fifty-five-dollar hat at I. Magnin's. I enjoyed buying things for him; he was such a nice man. He needed teeth and ate baby food to avoid the dentist. I think he had the first dollar he earned as a laborer in the sugar mill."

"Sugar mill?"

"In Benicia, near Martinez, when he first came over in 1927. He loved to talk about those days. He'd call me at my office and tell me how he survived the revolution only because his mother prayed for him, how he'd opened a Russian deli and sold bread for a nickel a loaf and worked from dawn to midnight and grabbed a pickle out of the barrel for his supper—all the sad old tales. *Horatio Algeroff!* I liked to listen to him, but sometimes he drove me nuts. He admired black people—he'd never seen them in the old country and he found them fascinating. But he said, Never trust a Chinaman. He told me how the Harbin peasants would drop a fishing line to steal food from the windows below. I'd say, Well, they were *hungry!* And he'd say, So was I, but I never stole. It was no use telling him there were degrees of hunger."

"Was he religious?"

"Oh, yes! On Saturdays I drove him to this hole-in-the-wall Russian Orthodox church. The only way you could tell it was a church was by the round steeple. The candlelight was dazzling, beautiful. The congregation stood up during services, and it was a hardship for him with his bad knees, but he never complained and never missed. Twice a year he dressed in a starched white shirt and a double-breasted blue suit, very distingué, and I would drive him to the Russian veterans' club in an old Victorian house on Lyon Street. He commanded respect because he'd fought alongside Baron Peter Nikolaevich Wrangel."

Fay looked up from her scribblings and said, "Peter *who*—?"

"A White Russian general. The veterans sat around and toasted Captain Liotweizen and the czar and griped about Stalin and the Communists. The landlord told me that the worst insult at the club was to call someone 'comrade.' "

"Was he ever married?"

"Eugenia died in 'seventy-one. Every Sunday he visited her grave in the Serbian Cemetery up in Colma. He showed me a picture of her lying in her coffin. She had curls and a broad face and wore a little hat. He kept her piano dusted and polished."

"Sounds grim."

"He was *never* grim! He had a young man's fascination with the oddest things. He liked to watch the bison in Golden Gate Park. I took him for treats at Knopp's Bakery, and he said that no human being could ever eat enough *pirozhki*. He taught me to say *kuritsa* for chicken, *spasibo* for thanks, the days of the week, the months. *Odin, dva, tri, chetiri, pyat*—that's one to five. Every week I had to drive him to Ocean Beach to watch the sun go down. There's all these parked cars, people necking, smoking joints, and I'm sitting in the front seat with my landlord. Sometimes I'd say to myself, Is there something wrong with this picture?"

"Every woman knows the feeling," Fay said.

"One night in March 'eighty-six, I came home from work and he wasn't at the front window. His door was shut and locked. Another tenant told me he'd fallen and broken his hip. I took the next day off and went over to University Hospital to see how I could help. I told him not to worry about the building; I'll take care of the mail, the rents, everything. He said he already gave the master keys to a woman. I said, A woman? I asked her name and he wasn't sure. I said, What? I was astonished! I said, How could you give the keys to a stranger? I'm here, I've done all these things for you all these years. What the hell were you thinking?"

"How on earth did he get together with a woman?" Fay asked.

"He said he met her just before he broke his hip, but he wouldn't say where or how. I could see he was being evasive. I said, Listen, I don't want anybody else having keys to the building. I'm the only tenant who's not there in the daytime. I rushed right home and changed my lock. I talked to my mom about what was going on and she said, Well, he's getting senile. He needs somebody to look after him. I said, Maybe I can help him. She said, What? Quit your job? I said, I can hire a Russian woman for the daytime. If I can listen to those same stories a hundred times, so can somebody else. And she can do a little cooking and cleaning. That night I went back to the hospital, and as I was walking into the landlord's room a woman walked out with her head down. She wouldn't engage my eyes and neither would he. She was about forty, dressed in black, wearing a bandanna shaped into a turban. I thought, What an odd bird."

"Mary Steiner, right?"

"He wouldn't tell me her name. Said she was just a friend. I could see he didn't want to discuss her. Well, it wasn't my place to question his choice. A few days later she brought him home in an ambulance. She was wearing a white nurse's outfit. Somebody asked who would attend to the landlord's accounts. The woman said, I have his power of attorney and I'll be writing his checks."

"Scary," Fay commented. "What a quick move."

"A couple of nights later he phoned and sounded terrified. I went down to his apartment and kept him company for a few hours, but he wouldn't say what was bothering him. I sat with him again the next night, but I couldn't always be there, so I bought him a four-hundred-dollar TV, thinking it would occupy his time. He'd never owned one."

"Did he watch TV?"

"I couldn't tell. After a few months his door was locked and nobody answered. I tried to phone him, but he had a new unlisted number. His newspapers were cut off. One day I pounded on his door for a long time and it opened a few inches. I said, I want to see the landlord. The woman opened the door a crack. I said, Who are you? She said, I'm his nurse, Mary Steiner. I said, Well, I'm his friend Graziana. She said, He's tired, he can't see no one right now, and shut the door."

"She'd just moved in?"

"Right under our noses. Within a few months the relatives started showing up. At first we thought the fat one was her boyfriend—they weren't that far apart in age, and they yelled and argued like a married couple. I called him the Neanderthal till I learned that his name was Danny Tene. There were two younger brothers, Teddy and Kelly, and a kid who seemed a little slow. I don't think any of them went to school. I heard one ask, Who owns Mexico anyway? Every night the littlest one would go from door to door and yell, Lemme in, lemme in! Teddy was in his late teens and kind of dapper in a dark way. Kelly was younger and pudgy, had an angelic face, but you could see he would look like Danny before long. I learned later that Gypsies regard fat as a sign of success."

Fay asked, "How'd you get along with Mary's kids?"

"Nobody got along with 'em. When they weren't yelling and screaming, they were screaming and yelling. They roamed in and out of the landlord's apartment. Then the woman across the hall died and Mary and the kids took over her apartment. They kept their door open and barricaded the hall with an old cabinet so they could see who tried to visit the landlord. Old friends were allowed a few minutes and then eased out. Mary would say, Mr. Liotweizen's tired. You've had long enough. She never left him alone with anybody."

"Not even you?"

"Nope. For a while I was puzzled and hurt. I wondered what happened to our friendship. I loved him; we were like family to each other. Now he didn't call, didn't say good night, didn't show his face. There was no use bringing him *pirozhki*. No one would answer. I couldn't figure out this woman's hold on him. She began collecting the rents. What could we do but pay? If we questioned her authority, she reminded us that she had his power of attorney."

"Didn't you *ever* get in to see him?"

"One night I heard him yelling, Kelly! *Kelly!* I decided that the Gypsies must be gone and I let myself in. He was lying in bed next to a big can of ravioli and a milk carton. He said they set out his food every day or two and left it there till it was gone. I was appalled! Food was always so important to the landlord. Now he didn't seem to care. He wasn't getting fruit, he wasn't getting vegetables, he wasn't getting anything fresh. At ninety, who could live like this? I said, Would you mind telling me what the hell's going on? This woman isn't taking proper care of you. She's collecting rents and threatening to throw people out and acting like she owns the place."

"What'd he say?"

"He said, Don't worry, Graziana. His voice was so weak I could hardly hear. He said, Marushka's the manager now. I asked if she was a paid employee, and he said he sometimes helped her out a little. He showed me a canceled check for twenty-five thousand made out to Sal Lamance."

Fay recognized the name but didn't want to interrupt.

"I went into shock!" Graziana continued. "The landlord *never* spent that kind of money. I said, What's this for? He said, Well, Sal Lamance is Danny Tene, Mary's son. It's to repay them for helping me get out of the hospital. They needed a car. I yelled, Look at all the times I drove you! Did you ever buy me a car?"

"Didn't he get angry?"

"Oh, no. We were so close. That's just the way I could talk to him. I saw another canceled check for twenty-five thousand and asked why there were two, and he said there'd been a problem with the first check. I tried to tell him he was being taken, but he didn't want to hear about it. A day or two later a gold Corvette shows up in our parking garage on the first floor. It had fancy gadgets and big bass speakers. A friend ran the license number through the DMV, and it was registered to Sal Lamance at Mary Steiner's address."

"I wondered about the two names when I first ran the records," Fay said.

"A few months later I got an urgent call from a doctor. The landlord had been rushed to the UC Medical Center and they'd found my name in his wallet. I got there just as Mary Steiner was walking in. He was pale and trembling. His ankles looked like grapefruits. The doctor pointed to a smear of excrement on his thigh and asked who'd been taking care of him. Steiner piped up, I'm his nurse! The doctor said, This gentleman needs a higher level of care. Maybe he should go to a convalescent home. No, no, I said. He hates those places. It would kill him."

"Sounds like he was already dying," Fay pointed out. "Of neglect."

"Of course! The doctor warned us that he wouldn't survive without better care and exercise. When we got home, I said to Mary, You've got three strong sons. Can't you put him in the shower once in a while and wash him off? Can't you walk him around? She went inside her apartment and slammed the door. The next day she ordered a hospital bed and parked him in it—exactly what he didn't need. That's where he stayed from then on, immobile. It finally dawned on me that for some reason or other, he'd been sentenced to death. The squatters were gonna cash in. But . . . how?"

Fay said ruefully, "Now we know."

"Yeah, and I could've put myself through Stanford for the price I paid fighting her in court."

Graziana walked to the restaurant counter and returned with a refilled cappuccino and a wafer-thin slice of chocolate decadence. Fay tried to decide: Should I sit here and let her eat in front of me? And . . . lose our rapport? It was too big a risk. Carrot cake wasn't on the menu, so she ordered a raspberry brioche.

"Where was I?" Graziana asked as she dabbed daintily at her lips with the filigreed paper napkin.

"Mr. Liotweizen was in a hospital bed at home," Fay said, retrieving her yellow notepad.

"A few weeks later I sneaked inside to talk to him and Mary Steiner came running into the bedroom. She said, Get out! He's tired. You're disturbing him. I said, I just dropped in to say hi. She threatened to call the cops. That only made me angrier. She disappeared across the hall and came back and said, The cops are on the way. I said, Listen, you're the one who called 'em. I'm not leaving."

"What was the landlord doing?"

"Lying in bed with his mouth half open. I'm not even sure he knew I was there. Danny Tene wandered in, rubbing his crotch. I said, Don't do that in front of me! Later I saw him doing the same thing on the street. I guess it's just something he does. A couple of uniformed cops arrived and Mary grabbed them at the door and claimed she'd caught me touching the landlord's bedclothes. It was a clear sexual innuendo. I couldn't believe she would fight so dirty."

"Did she bring charges?"

"She threatened to, but the cops talked her out of it. I was still upset. I went to the Sixth Avenue police station and talked to a desk officer. I said, Listen, am I in trouble here? This female cop told me the responding officers hadn't even filed a report. She said, You know, Ms. Gandolfi, there's something weird about those people."

Graziana sighed and continued, "Later on I was sorry the police didn't take action right then. So much misery would have been avoided. Months went by without a peep from the landlord. Sometimes I wondered if he was alive. Steiner's dog would bark all night, meaning that nobody was in her apartment. I wondered where she and the kids spent their nights. Who was taking care of him? I would always knock, but I never got an answer. They'd sealed him off—no phone, no newspapers, no contact with old friends or relatives. They didn't even let him go to church. To them he was just an old wreck waiting to die. One day a housing inspector came through the building. He said, You know, Miss Gandolfi, somebody should tell the district attorney what these Gypsies are doing to this man. It gave me an idea. Maybe the authorities *would* give a damn."

"That's their job," Fay said.

"Supposedly," Graziana said, looking annoyed. "I called the mayor's commission on old people. They weren't interested. I called the landlord's nephew in Los Angeles. He was the only heir. I told him his uncle was being mistreated. I sent him documents by FedEx but never heard back. Later I found out he told somebody, This Gandolfi woman, she's just a tenant. What the hell is *her* interest? I wrote him a letter and called him a jackass. I was his uncle's best friend, for God's sake!"

Graziana trembled with intensity, and Fay reached out and touched her arm. "Don't be upset," she said, but she was becoming upset herself. She imagined her mother in Arizona, helpless in the face of the same cruelties in her final years of life. It couldn't happen, she reassured herself. I'd never let it happen. *But what if I wasn't around? What if Mom was alone?*

Graziana lowered her voice. "You have no idea what it's like to know that something evil is being done to a person you love and you can't do a goddamn thing about it. You can yell and scream and make a thousand complaints to the cops and the family, but—nothing happens. And the next time you see this person who means so much to you, this person you love like your own family, he looks a little closer to the grave. At night I would lie in bed and think about my own old age. Would somebody help me if I needed it? Break down my door if they had to? I lost sleep. My work suffered. I talked to a couple of lawyers, and their attitude was, Shit happens. One of my friends said, Hey, Graziana, this is Life 101. Live with it! I said, What about fraud? What about abusing the elderly? What about letting a helpless old man lie in his own filth?"

"Inhuman," Fay said. She looked at her watch. It was 10:45 p.m. They'd been talking for an hour and a half.

"I called the police on them," Graziana went on, "and a cop came out and said it was a matter for Social Services. I drove down to this big monolithic building on Otis Street and told a social worker that an elderly man was being taken for his money. She said, What're you to him? I said, His friend. She said, There's nothing I can do. She looked at me as if I were a little odd."

"Well, you *are!*" Fay couldn't resist saying. "You care about right and wrong, Graziani. These days, that's *odd.*"

"Anyway, I went from there to the Public Guardian's Office, and a very pleasant man said, Well, I *do* believe you, Miss Gandolfi, but we're not an investigative body. Why don't you try to become Mr. Liotweizen's conservator? So I retained a lawyer. She said, I understand your position, but a judge probably wouldn't grant you a conservatorship because you're not related. She gave me no hope and sent me a big bill."

"It's a wonder you didn't give up."

"Well, would you?"

"Heck, no," Fay said.

"I didn't think so. That's why I'm talking to you. Most people wouldn't understand. Next I called the priest at the Russian Orthodox church. I said, One of your oldest parishioners is being taken advantage of. He listened patiently and said, Well, it's very sad. But I can't involve the church."

Fay asked, "What about the other tenants? Didn't anybody care?"

"One day old Mrs. Atamasov's daughter came to visit, a bright woman in her fifties. I grabbed her and tried to tell her what was going on, but she didn't seem interested. The Gypsies were trying to scare her mother into moving out, but we didn't know it at the time. My own mother said, Why are you going to so much trouble? Nobody else cares. I said, That's *precisely* why I'm doing it. But I also thought, Graziana, what a blooming idiot you are!"

"A *good* kind of blooming idiot."

"Word must've got back to Mary Steiner that I was trying to save the landlord, and she raised my rent from two-sixty-five a month to three-sixty, which is illegal under city law. I asked the Rent Board, Who is this Mary Steiner? I said, Konstantin Liotweizen owns the building. How can another person raise our rents? They told me that Steiner must have some kind of financial interest and suggested I look up the property records at the County Recorder's Office. All I could find was a joint tenancy agreement dated Thursday, April third, 1986, with a shaky signature that didn't even look like his. He'd signed that paper less than a month after she met him."

"Did you know what joint tenancy meant?"

"Not at the time. So after a few weeks I snuck in and asked the landlord what the hell was going on. His voice was weak, but he gave me the impression that the paper was only a technicality. I didn't see him for a long time after that. He was incommunicado. In the spring of 1988, two years after Steiner and her Gypsy kids moved in, I heard that he was dying. Jim Egoroff and his mother lived on the third floor, and Jim said he could hear him banging on the pipes in the middle of the night. Strange things were happening to some of the older tenants, and Egoroff said that Steiner was trying to scare us all away."

"Why scare away paying tenants?" Fay asked.

"So she could bring in new tenants and jack up the rents."

"But you said Mr. Liotweizen never cared about rents."

"*He* didn't. But Steiner *did*. And she was running things. I didn't see the landlord again until the middle of November. He was in bed watching TV with the sound off. He seemed glad to see me, but his voice was almost gone. I remembered how vigorous he'd been when I first met him. I told him I was worried about being evicted, and he lifted his head and said, Not while I'm alive. I wanted to ask him what was going on, but there was no time. I knew his heart was in the right place, but I'd also seen the power Steiner had over him. So I got out a pen and paper and helped him draft a statement saying that I couldn't be evicted by anybody except him."

"Did he sign it?"

"Yes. And he signed an addendum to the effect that he still intended to leave everything to his nephew and not to Mary Steiner. Not knowing civil law, I thought it was binding."

Graziana's mellow voice was beginning to fray. "Soon afterward," she pressed on, "we heard that Steiner had dumped him in a convalescent home called Hill Haven. I visited him every few days and brought him *pirozhki* and baby food. By then he was easily agitated. One day he asked if I would wash his socks, because he didn't think the home did a good enough job. I said, Look, I have to come here after work. Why don't you talk to your precious Marushka about your socks? He said, Oh, Graziana, you always treated me better. I trusted the wrong person."

"He knew he was being taken?"

"I don't know *what* he knew. I told him it wasn't too late. I said, Get rid of her! He said, Ah, there's nothing I can do about that. I said, Of *course* there's something you can do. But he was too old and feeble. He told me his affairs were in order and he'd left everything to his nephew. I thought, So be it. Let the poor man enjoy his last days in peace without those Gypsy vultures squabbling over his bones."

Fay asked, "How long did he last?"

"Another year. He was a strong man, he wouldn't go gently. In the second week of December 1989, I got a call from old Sonia Ellis. She said he'd died suddenly on the morning of December ninth. No one had even notified me. Mary Steiner wanted some of the tenants to ride with her in the funeral car. We went on our own."

"What happened at the apartment after that?"

"We expected things to settle down. The nephew would inherit the building and get rid of Steiner, her kids, her dog and her disposition. But weeks went by and she still acted like the boss. Then somebody noticed an ad in the *Examiner* for prime rich huge apartments and called up the listed number. Guess who answered? She described herself as the owner and manager of twelve beautiful apartments overlooking the Park Presidio and she was asking eleven-fifty a month. That was three or four times what the landlord charged! We couldn't understand. What apartments would she be renting? Our building *never* had vacancies, except when somebody died. People stayed forever. I expected to die there myself."

"She owned the place under the joint tenancy laws, right?"

"It was even better than that. Or worse. She produced a revised will that made her executrix, gave her the building, and split the rest of his estate between her and his nephew. After taxes and expenses, the nephew ended up with twenty-eight thousand."

"But Mr. Liotweizen was a millionaire!"

"He was worth between one and a half and two million, if you counted his apartment building."

"What happened?"

"*Poof!* His money went with the wind. He died believing he'd left everything to his blood relative. But the new will left the nephew nickels and dimes. I didn't know where to turn. I'd already yelled my head off to the cops, to the city, to lawyers, friends, everybody. Nobody believed me."

"Maybe they believed you but didn't care," Fay said.

Graziana nodded. "My own lawyer said I was nuts to be so emotionally involved. He told me not to worry as long as I paid my rent on time; the Rent Board wouldn't allow Steiner to evict me without cause. She tried to reject my monthly payments and pretend I was delinquent, but I was persistent. I got so mad I wrote on the bottom of one of my checks, 'Mary Steiner is a thief, liar, and cheat.'"

"How'd she react?"

"She just cashed the check. She'd changed a lot. No more nurse's uniforms, no more Gypsy scarves or long skirts with yards of material. She started dressing like a teenybopper—short skirts, patent-leather heels, thick makeup. She'd waltz down the hall in expensive ballerina shoes and ruffled leotards. She didn't have a clue about how a forty-year-old woman should look. She'd always had dark straight hair to her shoulders and a trim figure for her age, but she started wearing curly wigs and putting on weight. She was *always* in my face, loud, aggressive. One day she shoved me across my threshold and ran down the hall and fell. She jumped up and yelled that I'd knocked her down. Tamara Baruksopulo was right there. She said, Graziana, you never touched her! Her heel got caught! The cops came to arrest me for assault. Tamara's son Jim Egoroff talked them out of it. He said, Please, officer, Graziana is *such* a nice person. She would *never* harm anyone."

"What was Steiner up to?"

"None of us knew that some Gypsies make a good living off stunts like that. It's called the slip-and-fall. They threaten to take you to court if you don't pay up on the spot. But Mary had a different motive. She flat wanted me out of the building. It wasn't just a matter of getting higher rents from fresh new tenants. Jim Egoroff and I knew too much about her. And we weren't being quiet about it. I wasn't surprised when her lawyer gave me notice to move. When I didn't budge, they filed an unlawful detainer ordering me off the premises in three days. The complaint accused me of all kinds of horrible crimes. Listen to this."

Graziana looked around the bakery and lowered her voice as she read a line from a crumpled legal document that she pulled from her purse: "Defecating and urinating on the garage floor."

"*You?*" Fay said, her voice skittering upward.

"Can you imagine? I hired an attorney and went to the Rent Board. I got a restraining order against Steiner and she got one against me. We took depositions and the case dragged on till my life savings were gone. At a hundred and fifty an hour, it doesn't take long. Finally the emotional toll became too great. Steiner got her way. I just gave up and moved."

10

"Old Men Die"

FAY FOUND IT hard to collect her thoughts after hearing Graziana's saga. The Beesley affair had been disturbing enough, but the new information made Danny Tene come across as a petty operator compared to his mother. Were they teacher and student? Had Mary Steiner trained her brood to exploit the elderly? In her mind Fay ticked off the properties that had slipped into the same Gypsy family's hands: old Philip Steiner's house on Thirty-third Avenue, Hope Victoria Beesley's showplace in the Sunset, Konstantin Liotweizen's four-story apartment building on Funston. Had other homes been involved? Probably, Fay said to herself. It's obvious that these people parasitize the elderly. That's their *occupation*. They're skilled, and they're prospering.

She was still preoccupied with her dark thoughts as she parked the Frog Prince in front of the cluster of tourists at the entrance to her building. Her corner was a popular stop on a bus line that served Chinatown, the Marina and Fisherman's Wharf, and visitors were intrigued by the 1930s tone of the area. They unholstered their Nikons and Minoltas to shoot the building's heavy iron gate and art deco turquoise trim and the Rastafarian dog salivating into the chrysanthemum pots on the second-story balcony. Sometimes Fay wished she could snatch one of their expensive cameras to replace her battered Kodak with the scratched lens. California's no-fault divorce law had cut down on most peep-work, but there was still a small demand. Fay tried to avoid such assignments. Staring through a lens at sexual athletes wallowing in their own body fluids wasn't her idea of a respectable occupation. And how would she explain to her Baptist mother?

Some of Fay's ultrasophisticated neighbors resented the tourists, but she enjoyed the busyness of her neighborhood and momentarily joined the outside visitors gawking at her building. The place was full of surprises. Her own apartment was entered via a high arched doorway that looked restored from a Roman palazzo. Ceilings vaulted up and up, supported by thick stone walls. In November 1989 the building had withstood a tremor that measured 7.1 on the Richter scale and took seventeen seconds to turn the surrounding area into flaming piles of Lincoln Logs. A fellow resident had explained proudly, "Most of the houses around here were built on fill, but ours was on the spot where they put the World's Fair. Solid ground. And built solid." The story of my life, Fay had said to herself at the time.

She was exhausted from the marathon session with Graziana. She checked her phone messages and e-mail, walked Beans around the block, kissed him on the nose, and repeated her bedtime mantra, "I love my big old dog and my big old dog loves me," a message which she also wore on a sweatshirt. As usual, the Rastafarian dog dozed atop her covers till she turned off the light, then slid to the floor with a thump. In his earlier life as a puppy, before she singled him out at the pound, he'd never learned how to lie down gracefully. He snuffled and sniffed all night long and kept waking her up. She decided she wasn't the only one dreaming about Gypsies.

IN THE MORNING she skipped breakfast and steered the Frog Prince toward Colma, a hilltop part of town where cemetery plots were still available for less than the price of Italian white truffles. She'd always enjoyed driving the back streets of San Francisco, never considered returning to Kansas City or Phoenix or even Santo Domingo or Paris. She embraced every kindly description of her adopted town: "the cool gray city of love," "Baghdad by the Bay," "the last great metropolitan village." Unlike many of her friends, she didn't roll her eyes whenever she heard Tony Bennett singing "I Left My Heart in San Francisco."

Bright sunlight flashed off the polished faces of the tombstones in the little Serbian Cemetery. Most of the inscriptions were in the Cyrillic alphabet, and Fay asked the friendly custodian to point out the grave of Konstantin Liotweizen. The middle-aged woman smiled and said, "Oh, yes. Konstantin Konstantinovich. He came here every Sunday for years. Brought me candy from his deli. Or sardines. Such a good man. He lit candles and sat by his mother's grave and his wife's. Here, let me show you where they're resting together."

The woman led Fay to a small plot near the entrance and translated the inscription on the flowered marble slab:

LIOTWEIZEN

EUGENIA
1–5–1971

KONSTANTIN
KONSTANTINOVICH
9–8–1897 12–9–1989

At the bottom of the tombstone, "Liotweizen" appeared in small Roman letters.

Fay couldn't decide between anger and rage and settled for incomprehension. "It's a real shame that nobody did anything for him," the custodian was saying. "He ends up in a cheap casket. Strangers end up with his money."

"How d'you know that?" Fay asked.

"We hear things, see things. I watched Mary Steiner and her fat son pour liquor on the grave. Then they did a little dance."

"On the *grave*?" Fay asked.

"That's a Gypsy way of saying thanks."

AT CITY HALL, Fay examined the old Russian's death certificate. In a medical scrawl that looked more like Farsi than English, the attending physician had listed the causes of death: "right cerebrovascular accident, acute; arteriosclerotic vascular disease, generalized arteriosclerosis." No autopsy had been performed.

Once again Fay sought out an interpreter and found a clerk from the pages of Trollope. "It means he had a stroke," the man said, barely looking up from his desk, "and hardening of the arteries. With old people, that's pretty much generic."

"Nothing unusual?" Fay asked hopefully. "Nothing . . . suspicious?"

Uriah Heep raised gelid eyes in a cryogenic stare. "He was ninety-two, lady. Old men die."

11

Dom, Lom and Rom

FAY PHONED TO cancel an afternoon bike-and-quiche date with a new friend who gave promise of adapting to her antic manner and style, unlike some of his predecessors. She'd videotaped their first date from arrival to departure, thinking it might work in a TV documentary. To her surprise, he hadn't complained. "Besides, I might never see him again," she explained to a girlfriend. Ever since college, her relationships had come and gone in four-year increments—she could pinpoint historical events by remembering which man she was seeing at the time—but ever since she'd become involved in the Beesley case, most of her dates had been with Beans.

She waded into the stack of papers atop her faux-marble desk to make sure she wasn't overlooking any urgent business. She owed her newspaper syndicate an "Ask Rat Dog" column, but that could wait another day or two. She scanned a letter from a reader who claimed to be Lyndon Johnson's illegitimate daughter and wanted to know how to find a publisher for her tell-all memoir. Another correspondent asked if Fay had seen her ex-husband; he once waited tables in a food court in downtown Rochester, New York. No, I haven't seen old Harold lately, Fay said to herself as she turned to some unfinished business. She was still on the trail of a Thai woman missing in Chinatown with several million Hong Kong dollars, and a friend's bookmaker who'd skipped owing a hundred large on a sixty-to-one shot, and a key witness in a Mexican custody case.

She pushed the papers aside and thought of old Konstantin Liotweizen, moaning for help in his empty apartment. She wished she could ignore the case in favor of more lucrative ventures, but her personality made it out of the question. Who knew what Mary Tene Steiner and her brood were up to at this very moment? How many other old people were they abusing? It didn't take a Rhodes scholar to discern their basic MO: trick the elderly into signing away their homes and savings, then wait for them to die. It was a geriatric variation on the old sweetheart scam that had been separating the lovesick from their fortunes for eons. Fay was shocked at the blunt inhumanity. Mrs. Beesley and Mr. Liotweizen had lived rich, worthwhile, active lives, with friends, families, marriages, *histories*. How could anyone treat them with such cruelty?

She remembered seeing a TV documentary in which European Gypsies flogged dancing bears and jerked them around by chains attached to nose rings. She'd never viewed evil as an absolute—*malum in se,* as lawyer friends like Ken Chan called it—nor did she believe that evildoing was racial or hereditary in nature. She wondered if some of the harsh Gypsy ways might have been passed down from generation to generation, not by genes but by some kind of warped tradition, or as a reaction to their own mistreatment, harshness begetting harshness. She wondered how they'd managed to endure as an identifiable race without a flag, a homeland or even a written language. Gypsies *were* different; they *had* to be. If she understood them, she might be able to save some lives. Who were they? Where did they come from? And why did some of them seem to be living off the elderly?

SHE DROVE TO the downtown library and emerged with an armload of books. Back home, she shared a Hungry Man chicken pie with Beans, switched off her phone, stacked the books alongside her bed, and dug in. Within a few minutes she'd discovered that many of the oldest clichés about Gypsy history, including some believed by their own historians, were fanciful. This short, swart race hadn't originated in Atlantis or Babel, as some Gypsies claimed with a straight face, or even in Egypt, as Fay and many others believed. Nor were they directly descended from Cain or any Biblical figure. Originally they were a Caucasoid caste of nomadic musicians, drumbeaters, dancers and craftsmen whose exodus from the Punjab region of their native India started around 1000 A.D. or maybe a half-millennium earlier. No scholar seemed sure. As she turned the pages, Fay soon realized that there were no certainties about Gypsies, not in their history, their culture, their sociology, or even in their names. Gypsiology was one of the least scientific of the anthropological disciplines.

In ancient Persia, she learned, Gypsies had been called "Dom." Later, in Armenia, they were known as "Lom," and as their travels broadened, they became "Rom," "Roma," and "Romani" as well as the misnomer "Gypsies." The latest demographic guesswork put their population at eight to twelve million, spread across forty countries. Proud Gypsy spokesmen claimed that their number included politicians in Spain, a nuclear scientist in Rumania, poets and writers in Yugoslavia, academics and at least one commercial airline pilot in the United States, but some leaders were dubious. "We don't even have a Gypsy baker," John Tene of Boston was quoted in Fay's reading matter. "Not even a Gypsy janitor. We look at the plane in the sky and we say, How does it stay up there? We look at buildings and we say, How does the cement hold it together?"

Fay was surprised to learn that there were upward of two million American Gypsies, most of them barely literate both by choice and tradition. No one knew the exact count, least of all the census-takers. The U.S. Rom were divided into sixty tribes and four *vitsas* or nations: Kalderasha, Machwaya, Lowara and Churara. They spoke Romany, the unwritten language of wanderers, an Indo-Aryan dialect of Sanskrit that had been salted through the centuries with words from Arabic, Slavic, Greek, Farsi, Germanic and Latin, picked up on their travels.

THE MORE FAY read, the more it became clear that if segments of the Gypsy population were antisocial and opportunistic, there was plenty of reason. As a race, they'd been shunned and abused by non-Gypsies for centuries and all but forced into illicit means of making a living. The predations of Mary Tene Steiner and her brood appeared to be simple escalations of a history of mutual contempt and misunderstanding that dated at least to 1100 A.D. when a Georgian monk described the Roma as "wizards, famous rogues, adept in animal poisoning," neglecting to mention that they were also expert at animal healing. In the Balkans in the 1300s, Gypsies were enslaved for minor offenses or for no offense at all. In Greece, footloose Romani families had to pass themselves off as pilgrims while dodging the authorities and eking out a living as fortune-tellers, ventriloquists, magicians and snake charmers. To keep from being put to death for heresy and witchcraft, Gypsies of the late Middle Ages declared themselves Muslims, Catholics, Zoroastrians, Russian Orthodox, Greek Orthodox, Protestants. They were pleased to be mistaken for Moors, Tartars, Egyptians, Saracens or just about any race as long as it ensured their survival. At the time of Columbus, Rom leaders convinced gullible Italians that they were on a secret mission for the Pope, then left town.

The anti-Gypsy prejudice was pan-European and unrelenting. Around 1530 A.D., Henry VI referred to "outlandysshe People callynge themselfes Egyptians" and banished them from his kingdom. A French politician complained that Gypsy visitors "emptied the purses of all into their own," leading the Bishop of Paris to order the excommunication of anyone doing business with palm readers. At the time of the Inquisition, the Roma were falsely accused of spreading the bubonic plague, thus placing them one order below the true carriers, which were rats.

By the seventeenth century, bands of English Gypsies were scratching out marginal livings as tinkers, pot menders, horse traders, clothespin peddlers and musicians, but they were still considered subhuman. Shakespeare assigned the name Caliban (from the Romany for blackness) to a sinister character in *The Tempest*. Such creatures made easy targets. In the eighteenth century, two dozen Gypsies were tortured to death for cannibalizing a group of Hungarians who were later found alive and healthy. European countries deported thousands of Rom to America, and colonial newspapers soon began referring to "the Gypsy problem." Between 1801 and 1803, Napoleon exiled whole shiploads of Gitanes to death by fever in the Louisiana swamps. Fin-de-siècle racists spread word that Gypsies stole babies from cradles and drank their blood, a convenient racial libel that was still circulating among the ignorant a century later.

FAY LET A book slip from her fingers and thought, What a long, sad, pathetic history. Of course they distrust us; how could it be otherwise? She wondered how much of the prejudice was the Gypsies' own fault, or how fault could even be determined in such a sordid historical tableau. Did centuries of oppression justify the exploitation of doddering old San Franciscans who didn't even know the meaning of the word "Romani?" Maybe so, in Gypsy eyes. And maybe not. Assigning original blame was an impossible job.

She resumed her reading and learned that most Gypsies, unlike most Jews and other oppressed peoples, stubbornly resisted acculturation or even interracial friendship, refusing to send their children to school lest their *romanipe* or Gypsiness be contaminated by outside ways or their children bullied and mugged. Such clannish ways, justified or not, had often fueled distrust. In the late 1930s, the mad geneticist Adolf Hitler classified the Rom as *rassenverfolgte*, racially undesirable, and ordered "Z" (for *Zigeuner*) tattooed on their arms. In the Gypsy Holocaust or *porajmos* that followed, Nazi assassins killed as many as a half million Romani with gas, bullets and medical torture. The able-bodied were worked to death. Angry survivors discarded their animosity toward the non-Gypsy world long enough to guide Allied spies and POWs along their old smuggling routes and to pass secret messages in a tongue that other Gypsies translated.

Despite their wartime service and sacrifices, the benumbed Rom entered the second half of the twentieth century as the same old pariah population. In the standard encyclopedias, they were described as "having the mental image of a child of ten," "quarrelsome, quick to anger or laughter, unthinkingly cruel," "deceitful," "fickle," and "superstitious." The English publication *The Independent* quoted a typical attitude: "A bullet in the head is what they need. . . . If I were dying of cancer I'd buy a shotgun and take out six of them."

Even in modern times, Fay learned, the worldwide repression continued. France required Gitanes to carry *carnets de circulation* that were regularly checked by officials to keep *familias* from lingering too long in an area. The Swiss and Italian governments sanctioned forcible adoption of Rom children. By the late 1990s, Gypsy caravans were still being sacked on the back roads of Europe, encampments bulldozed in France, Romani women sterilized in Czechoslovakia, clans restricted to government reservations in England, and thousands deported from Germany. (*Everyone hates the Gypsies*, blared a recent headline in the influential newsmagazine *Der Spiegel*.)

Now Fay began to see why almost all of the Rom continued to revile outsiders, refused to drink from the same containers, put deadly curses on non-Gypsies, and rationalized stealing from their oppressors. They even had a derogatory name for non-Gypsies: *gaje*, literally translated as "peasants" or "serfs" but closer in tone to the Yiddish *goy* and the Hispanic *gringo*. Sometimes the word was written as *gadze*, but in any form it was no compliment. The American public seemed to reciprocate the resentment. A *New York Times* survey rated Gypsies the least trustworthy of all ethnic groups, even below the "Whisians," a nonexistent group inserted in the poll as a test.

THE MORE FAY read, the more she realized that the racial animosities seemed to be self-perpetuating. An old saying of African-Americans came to mind: "They break our legs and blame us for being lame." Gypsies told tales about Auschwitz and Mauthausen and rehearsed their children in dolorous anthems of hurt: "Some evenings, like some other evenings, I find myself envying the respect you give your dog . . ." "The whole world hates us. We're chased, we're cursed, condemned to wandering throughout life. . . . We survive as hounded thieves, but barely a nail have we stolen."

But that single nail, according to a hardy Romani legend, was the gold spike intended for the sacred heart of Jesus. Before dying, a grateful Christ on the Cross had given Gypsies a heavenly license to steal from the *gaje*. Cynics argued that the Gypsies told the story backward; Romani blacksmiths had forged the three spikes impaling Christ, and in his last gasp, Jesus had banished them to wander the earth forever.

Legends and counterlegends were fueled, as always, by the toxic combination of ignorance and prejudice. "When God came down to earth," said a villager in the movie *Time of the Gypsies*, "he took one look at the Gypsies and took the next flight back." Another myth held that the once-powerful Rom nation had lost its standing when God parted the Red Sea for the Jews but chose to drown their pursuers. Gypsy children were taught that these stories could be verified in the Bible. Few of them double-checked because few of them learned to read.

FAY FOUND HERSELF agreeing with the balanced reasoning in the French author Jean Clebert's study *The Gypsies*, and realized that it went a long way toward explaining the anti-*gaje* bitterness of clans like the Tene Bimbos:

Above all else, Gypsies are feared: if the truth were known, they are not liked. When they are not held openly in contempt, the Gypsies, men and women, receive the benefit of that recurring little dose of racism which one day puts the blame for something on flashy South American adventurers, and the next on North African coloured people. So it is that the Gypsies, and they alone, are held to be vagabonds, beggars, thieves and weavers of spells.

Fay put aside her homework and stared at the curtain that glowed and darkened with the traffic below her apartment. She fell asleep wishing she'd studied ethics and morals instead of English and journalism.

12

Gypsy Cop

THE MORNING AFTER her midnight cram course, one of Fay's police pals phoned with the name of the local Rom expert: Inspector Gregory L. Ovanessian, Star Number 1444, of the SFPD Fraud Unit. She called him and had hardly mentioned her interest in the subject when he said, "Hey, come on down! Let's talk."

"Now?" she asked.

"Now!"

She'd always admired enthusiasm and spontaneity, qualities that she seldom saw in others. She drove straight to the Hall of Justice and squeezed the Frog Prince into a tight space on Bryant, coming within a few inches of violating her all-purpose parking rule, "Close is enough," meaning within a yard of the curb. A bearded man in a pith helmet and Bermuda shorts held out a cardboard sign: "WILL WORK FOR DEWARS." As she slipped him a dollar, Fay thought, Only in San Francisco. What a great place! Even our panhandlers are cool.

* * *

INSPECTOR GREGORY OVANESSIAN was in his mid or late thirties, dark, bespectacled, and as welcoming and personable as he'd sounded on the phone. She felt an extra rapport because he had a handsome scimitar nose like her favorite comedian Danny Thomas, and also because he appeared to be fighting a battle with weight while still managing to look lovable.

"Are you a Gypsy?" she asked as he guided her to a stiff-backed municipal chair in his small office.

Ovanessian explained that he was of Armenian descent, spoke Russian, and could make himself understood in a few of the seventeen Romany dialects. "I deal with Gypsies in their own language," he said, smiling. "They're not used to that. It gives me an edge."

A sign that had been confiscated from a palm reader's *ofisa* gave the impression that he might tell fortunes when he was off shift, and his walls were lined with photos of "wanted" Gypsies. Ovanessian followed her stare and said, "They'll come in here and point and say, How come you got my Uncle Frank up there? I'll say, Thanks, I didn't know who he was till now. A con man called the other day and said, What do I have to do to get you to take down my picture? I said, Turn yourself in, dude!"

Fay briefed him on the Liotweizen case in detail, and the detective appeared to listen closely. As a uniformed patrolman, he told her, he'd been summoned to the apartment building on Funston in response to complaints that an elderly gentleman was being abused. As he recalled, the reports had proved unfounded. In a polite tone, he asked if she was working a specific case.

She told him about her Beesley assignment from Ken Chan and how she'd done some investigating on behalf of executor Barry Hughes.

"I see," Ovanessian said. "But . . . who's your client?"

She hadn't thought about it lately. "I guess, uh—nobody," she admitted.

"Then why're you still on the case?" He didn't seem nosy, just curious.

Fay said, "I guess because no one else seems to care." She didn't want to sound like a cardboard heroine, so she added, "I'm just finishing up. Any investigator would do the same."

He asked if he could take a look at her files.

"Anything I can do to help," she said. "I'd be honored."

* * *

THE SFPD'S GYPSY expert showed up the next morning accompanied by an assistant district attorney. Fay saw it as a good sign. They weren't just ready to investigate, they were ready to prosecute. She turned over a stack of documents, including birth and death certificates, real estate records, wills, hospital reports and Tene Bimbo genealogy, and the two men pored over every item, chatting to themselves with the same sense of indignation as Fay's. After three hours, they asked a few questions, thanked her and left.

Fay sighed and thought, At last. The pros are on the job.

13

The Name Game

FOR A FEW days she tried forgetting about Gypsies and bringing some sorely needed income into the agency, but as usual she found that once she'd dipped into a subject, she couldn't rest till she'd learned more. She returned the books she'd borrowed and picked up some library files and pamphlets on Gypsy crime. She quickly came across a statement by Roland Anderson, former chief of the Weston Police Department in exurban Boston, an expert on the Rom:

> They don't hold jobs or pay taxes. They pull their kids out of school and sell 'em into marriage. They buy judges and cops. They overwhelm the welfare system and Social Security. You should see some of their rap sheets—forty different names and dates of birth. One of 'em showed me sixteen driver's licenses. I've known honest Gypsies, working every day, but most of them are into their own version of organized crime or benefiting from it.

In reports from an organization called Professionals Against Confidence Crime, Fay learned that criminal Gypsies routinely changed names, Social Security numbers, drivers' licenses, hair colors and home addresses. A Los Angeles Gypsy named Dritchko (born Mihailovitch or Yovonivich or Mitchell or Marks or Spicer or whatever name his parents plucked from their imaginations) would come under suspicion and within a day or two turn up in Kansas City as a Chicagoan named Steve Murphy. If the police closed in, he would disappear into a safe house in Queens as a Slav immigrant named Lubovitch, and then move on to Boston, Miami or New Orleans until the exhausted police ran out of funds or interest. In a year or two, he would resume his activities as a Los Angeleno named Dritchko.

BACK HOME, FAY spent an hour on the phone with fellow PIs and some friends at the Hall of Justice. Everyone told the same story: Rom criminals were as hard to prosecute as the Mafia; in fact, some lawmen referred to "the Gypsy Mafia" as though it was as well organized as the tightly held group that originated in Sicily. She also learned that detectives like Inspector Greg Ovanessian might be the wave of the future in anti-Rom law enforcement. Frustrated police departments were now assigning full-time Gypsy cops (known to the Romani as *jawndare* or *jondade Romano*) to confront the specialized crime. On the Gypsies' behalf, there appeared to be strict limits on how much misbehavior the Roma culture (*romanija*) would countenance before disciplining their own miscreants or even handing them over to the authorities. In one of Professor Ian Hancock's scholarly articles about his own people, Fay read that Gypsy law contained strong prohibitions against violence and murder. Most illegal behavior by Roma criminals seemed to involve white-collar crimes against elderly victims and were committed in daylight to avoid the *tsinivari*, the fearsome nightriding ghosts that still frightened some Gypsies. A gray-haired *gaje* homeowner would be approached and informed that his driveway needed resurfacing and the crew had just enough sealant left over from another job to do this one on the cheap. On completion, the fee would mysteriously treble, and the next rainfall would wash away a thin coating of used motor oil that had looked black and viscous when applied. Similar work was done on courtyards and roofs.

In the time-honored home-invasion scam, a Gypsy criminal would knock on an old person's door and after being admitted would be followed by a half-dozen more, milling around like circus clowns and grabbing cash and valuables. During their getaway, they would slip the loot into preaddressed envelopes and drop them into mailboxes. In a variation, a lone Gypsy woman and her small child, oozing chatter and charm, would ask a householder for a sip of water. While victim and visitor conversed, the child would toddle through the rooms snatching jewelry and cash.

In store diversions, women flooded shops while specialists slipped into back offices to empty safes and cash drawers. In a variation, a child would throw a temper tantrum or pull down a shelf of merchandise or use a corner of the store as a toilet, and in the ensuing chaos his grown-up companions would fill deep inner pockets and speed off in waiting *mobeles*, all in a few minutes. In the unlikely event that one or two were arrested, a Gypsy middleman would show up with the bail money, and the malefactors would resume their activities in another town.

FAY LEARNED THAT bands of criminal Gypsies still swarmed into unsuspecting communities, overwhelming the locals by sheer numbers. They settled into motels, sometimes taking entire wings, and deployed to work their scams in Cadillacs, Lincoln Town Cars, luxury RVs, and 4×4 pickups pulling Airstream travel trailers. In one such expedition, twenty Rom males took the widely scattered elderly of Los Angeles for an estimated $10 million in six months. Organized groups were divided into teams of specialists: body and fender workers, hot-toppers, pickpockets, hocus-pocus and flimflam artists, insurance-fraud experts, sweetheart-scammers, strong-arm panhandlers, slip-and-fall experts, method actors who slapped the sides of cars and claimed they'd been hit, odometer wizards, welfare cheats, and palm readers (known as "agents") with their many variations on fortune-telling, including the burning of "evil" money in *bujo* (dishrag) schemes, a trickery that once netted $850,000 from a single mark in Beverly Hills.

Fay remembered reading about a high-stakes scam by a local fortune-teller named Jackie Peters, wife of Larry Bimbo, the local Rom Baro ("big man"). The Peters woman, also known as Jacqueline Thompson, was envied by her fellow seers for her skilled manipulation of the Chinese, whose superstitious immigrants, flush with smuggled bankrolls, flocked to her Polk Gulch fortune-telling establishment. She got off with three years' probation after pleading guilty to bilking a hysterical woman of $230,000 to remove a curse. A San Francisco court ordered restitution of $100 a month.

What a bargain, Fay said to herself. No wonder Gypsy thieves thrive in our system.

A Missing Safe

FAY RETURNED FROM a biking vacation in New Mexico to find that there was no word from the SFPD Fraud Unit about the Beesley or Liotweizen cases. She was a little disappointed—two months had passed since she'd opened her files to Inspector Greg Ovanessian—but she often dealt with police and knew they were overworked. The delay probably meant that they were trying to do a thorough job. In their visit to her office, the *jawndare Romano* and the assistant DA had discussed charges ranging from fraud, larceny and grand theft to a relatively new offense called elder abuse. Every PI knew that white-collar crimes were hardest to prove and siphoned large segments of time from priority cases of violence. For once she would have to be patient.

BARRY HUGHES PHONED with discouraging news. After three months of being locked out of the Beesley house by Danny Tene, he'd returned under court order to collect Hope Victoria Beesley's antique furniture and other personal possessions as heir and executor of the estate, and all he'd found was "junk, junk and more bloody junk! It took me four trips to take the stuff to the dump."

Fay asked, "Did you look everywhere?"

"Everywhere I could, considering Tene and his lawyer shadowed me every inch of the way. Mrs. B learned to sew jewels in her clothing in the POW camp in Hong Kong and I went through her wardrobe piece by piece. Nothing! There's one last hope. She talked about keeping her money and valuables in a wall safe."

"Didn't you look?"

"With them watching? Not bloody likely. I'll get back in and go over the walls inch by inch. I did find a faded Union Jack with pictures of King George and Queen Mary in the center. Mrs. B had kept it since the war. A nice bit of history."

Hughes said that the estate's financial health was poor and worsening. He'd come across $14,600 in a bank account but it disappeared in the sinkhole of inheritance taxes, probate costs and legal fees.

"To put it plainly," he said in his pleasant accent, "Mrs. B left *no* estate. The Tenes got the house and everything that wasn't riveted down, and I got a little cash that went straight to the lawyers. Still . . . I wouldn't have missed knowing her. I'm out of pocket a few thousand, but Mrs. B was worth it."

"And something might turn up in the safe," Fay reminded him.

"If I can find it."

NOW AND THEN Graziana Gandolfi phoned with new information. The man she called "the landlord" had been dead for three years, and almost all of the old tenants had been squeezed out of the building on Funston, but it appeared that they maintained a Slavic network of the insulted and aggrieved. "Who's still living there?" Fay asked.

"Just Jim Egoroff and his mother Tamara, on the top floor," Graziana said. "She's been there forever."

Fay remembered Dimitri Egoroff as one of the few tenants who hadn't been intimidated by Mary Steiner. Graziana provided his phone number, and Fay called. "I thought you'd be evicted by now," she said.

"Nevuh!" the man replied in a robust voice. "I'll fight those bloody bostids to the end."

Well, well, Fay said to herself, Another Englishman.

15

Murder by Neglect

DIMITRI NICOLAYEVICH "JIM" Egoroff turned out to be a forty-two-year-old Russo-Australian whose dark hair, black mustache, straight black eyebrows and muscular arms put Fay in mind of a Cossack warrior or a Mexican huckstering velvet paintings in a Tijuana bazaar—she couldn't decide which. He bought and rebuilt old cars and described himself as a military engineer who consulted for British Leyland and other auto manufacturers. Among his inventions were a temperature-sensitive serving plate that automatically kept hot foods hot and cold foods cold, a mini jet engine for automobiles, a voice-actuated refrigerator door, and a servo-controlled military tank that spun around so that it always faced the enemy. He was also developing a system for deconstructing Greek amphoras in such a manner that the voices of the potters and their apprentices could be reproduced across the centuries. *A little more clay, please, Ulysses. . . . I'm on my lunch break, Achilles. . . .*

"I pop over to London, the Falklands, Abu Dabai, Moscow," Egoroff told her in his Crocodile Dundee accent. "I started stying in my mum's apartment when I came to San Francisco to visit her." Now, he said, he intended to make it his permanent residence, "especially since the bloody Tenes are trying to throw me out."

Fay met him at the front door of Mary Steiner's apartment building on Funston, and he insisted on the grand tour, guiding her first to a large street-level carpark that appeared to be empty as far as she could tell through the murk. Something furry skittered across the cement floor and her gasp echoed off the unpainted walls. "Not to worry," Egoroff assured her. "They're well-behaved Gypsy rats. They don't bite."

Upstairs, the long interior halls were lit with yellowish bulbs that served more as glow-in-the-dark guideposts than illumination, and several had burned out or were missing from their sockets. Egoroff led her from shadow to shadow to a set of gray-bleached back stairs that looked more like scaffolding, leading to a disused patch of garden in the rear— "My mum raised beautiful flowers before she fell ill." Nothing but weeds protruded from the hard crust. The last survivor of the old garden, a dark brown begonia flower, had dried on its stem under a protective outcrop of wood.

The stairs creaked as Fay shifted her weight, and she was relieved when the tour ended and the guide escorted her to his third-floor apartment. At the moment the place resembled the storage room of an abandoned art museum. Egoroff seemed as impervious as a teenager to the clutter and mess but eager to show the work of his mother, Tamara Baruksopulo, whose name Fay remembered hearing from Graziani—or was it Graziana? Apparently Tamara B, as Fay elected to think of her, had specialized in creating paintings and sculptures too massive to be hefted by anyone except an Olympic weightlifter. One by one the proud son showed a bronze bust of President Kennedy, a five-foot charcoal of author Aleksandr Solzhenitsyn, a life-sized oil of White Russian General Peter Wrangel wearing a caracul hat and a George's Cross, and oversized paintings of the bearded Leo Tolstoy, Peter the Great, Sergei Rachmaninoff and other Slavic notables. There were also forest scenes, ducklings, flowers after the style of Georgia O'Keeffe, a boy in a sailor suit, and a sensitive oil portrait of a black man whose children the artist had served as godmother.

Egoroff treated his mother's artifacts with touching reverence. He picked up a balalaika and strummed one tinny chord. "She brought this all the wye from Harbin, China," he said. He opened a battered old photo album and displayed fading pictures of "my mum" as she'd looked in the old country. With her petite figure, heart-shaped face and glowing skin, Tamara B bore a strong resemblance to Hope Victoria Beesley, née Nadia Malysheff, whose ashes now drifted in slants of plankton off Marin County. Fay imagined cameo likenesses of both Russian women on display in a museum in St. Petersburg.

"Where's your mother now, Mr. Egorhoff?" Fay asked.

"Egoroff," he said. "She's in hospital." It didn't take much prodding to draw out the family bio. With his White Russian parents, he'd spent his first nine years in the Far East and learned a farrago of languages and dialects, including Cantonese, Russian and Ukrainian. He talked rapidly, sometimes almost staccato, but with an engineer's precision of phrase. He was outspoken on the subject of what Mary Steiner and her brood had done to his mother's longtime admirer, Konstantin Konstantinovich Liotweizen. His pronunciation of the last name sounded like "Lit-VAY-zun." That was close enough for Fay; she'd avoided saying the name till now.

"I could quite understand how Steiner fooled a ninety-year-old man," the engineer recalled, "because she fooled *me* as well. I asked him, Konstantin, where did you find this lady? He said, Well, Dima, she came round to visit me in hospital after I broke my hip, and she offered to help me home. He gave her his power of attorney so she could help him handle his accounts. He died with fifty or sixty thousand dollars in the bank. I'd seen his check registers and passbooks. He was worth twenty times that much."

"How did she impress you at first?" Fay asked, and added, "Others seemed to take a dislike."

"Not me. When she first brought Konstantin home, he told me to have a bit of a talk with her and tell him what I thought. From her looks, I had only slight reservations. She didn't look exactly evil, but she looked . . . naughty? Or *capable* of naughtiness? D'ya follow my meaning? I thought she might be of foreign extraction, but that didn't matter to me. As a child, I was taught by my parents to look beyond race. In Harbin there was a big sign over the entrance to the botanical garden: Entry strictly forbidden to Chinese and dogs. In a Chinese city! I was taught to avoid that kind of attitude."

"Did you know any Gypsies as a child?"

"A few came to Harbin and I was warned to keep away from them—the same sort of talk you always hear about Gypsies. I didn't know that Mary Steiner was one. She wore a droshy or whatever they call it on her head, and I asked her, Are you of Spanish or Italian descent? Greek, perhaps? She said, I've a bit of Spanish, a bit of Italian, a bit of Irish, a bit of this and that. I said, Well, I know you're not an American because you've got a slight accent. She said, I *am* an American. But I'm also a Gypsy."

"She didn't try to hide it?" Fay asked.

"She seemed quite proud! She made out to me that she was a widow, alone. Said she had plenty of time to look after Konstantin, and what's more, she enjoyed it. She had a nice smile, seemed personable, clever, diplomatic, eager to please. She said, I hear you've got an elderly mum as well. I'll look after *her* too. I just *love* older people. She said, I've had losses in my own family and I need something to take my mind off my problems. It's so nice of Mr. Liotweizen to give me a roof over my head. She said she wouldn't take any pay."

"You must have been impressed," Fay said.

"I reported to Konstantin that she was a lovely human being. I did add that a Russian-speaking person might have fitted his needs better, but that's his business. You see, Miss Faron, in his old age he spoke more Russian than English."

"It's Fay. Or . . . Rat Dog."

"Rat Dog? I'll use Fay. I'm Australian."

She wondered what his nationality had to do with what he called her, but he resumed his story as though he didn't want to lose the thread. "I met Mary's son and he introduced himself as Danny Tene. A daughter turned up and said her name was Theresa—a pretty little teenager, very pleasant, a captivating figure. She wore a T-shirt and jeans. She didn't look Gypsy, so I chatted her up a bit and asked, Are you Irish? She said, Well, I might have a touch of Irish blood in me. She saw my restored Mercedes and said, What a lovely car! She said, By your accent you must be English. I said, I speak the Queen's English, young lady. *You're* the one with the accent. She told me she'd gone to a Catholic school and the nuns didn't treat her well. My impression was that she was a bit of a flirt, looked deep into your eyes, knew how to talk. Later I learned that she was also called Angela. Confusing, indeed."

"Everything about that family confuses me," Fay admitted. "I think that's the way they want it."

"I quite agree. There's so much beneath the surface. In the first weeks Mary Steiner went out of her way to be pleasant. Whenever I popped in to see my old friend, she'd say, Well, look, Konstantin, you have a visitor! What lovely flowers! Sometimes she'd be giving him a bath and have her blouse undone, ya know? He told me later that he hadn't enjoyed himself so much since his wife died. I called him a dirty old man and he just giggled. He said in Russian, She certainly has lovely breasts. I mentioned that most ninety-year-old men wouldn't be interested in breasts. He said, Dima, my son, may I never grow that old."

Fay couldn't suppress a giggle.

"My mother felt it was a definite mistake that he hadn't found a Russian woman to look after him. She said, A Russian lady would *never* show her body like that. This Steiner must be a street woman. But myself, I condoned the arrangement. Why? Because Konstantin was happy! If he wanted to fool around with a Gypsy woman's breasts, well, God bless him. I have nothing whatever against breasts *or* Gypsies."

Fay asked, "Did you notice anything suspicious about her?"

"Oh, yes. The odd happenstance. Her children disappeared for days at a time; then suddenly they'd pop in. It was as though they came through the walls. Visitors swarmed in and out at all hours. In the beginning we wondered why Mary always parked her old Hyundai around the corner on Anza, as though she didn't want us to see the license number. It seemed a bit strange. I would see her walking toward her car and say, G'day, Mrs. Steiner! Would you like a lift? And she'd say, I do *not* accept lifts, thank you. I thought she was confusing herself with Catherine the Great, so I stopped asking."

"What do you think she was up to?"

"Oh, I winkled out her game soon enough. I was driving to an appointment in the Sunset and saw her car up ahead. She parked at a house on Thirty-third Avenue and an old man gave her a very warm welcome indeed. I thought, Well, *well*, what's this? Why is Konstantin's lady love calling on another man?"

"Did you say anything to Mr.—uh, Liotweizen?"

"I said, Look here, Konstantin, I learned something a bit disturbing about your Mary. Just keep your cool for a while and don't be swayed by her breasts till I make a few discreet inquiries. I checked the address in the reverse directory and found that the place was owned by a Philip Henry Steiner. He was a retired engineer and legally married to a woman named Mary Tene. I thought, Hah *hah!* Our Mary isn't the poor little widow she claims to be."

"How did the landlord react?"

"His face dropped. He asked if I was sure. I said, Here's the address, Konstantin. Here's the phone number. Why don't you ring up her bloody husband? He shook his head. He didn't want the proof."

"I think that's called denial."

"But Konstantin, I said, didn't you wonder where all her kids came from, and the dog? I said, She told you a pack of lies, and now she's going for your money. He said, Maybe she's not living with her husband. I told him I'd seen her enter his house. I could see he was shocked. He'd thought he was onto a sweet little thing to provide a bit of harmless fun in his old age. It hurt his sense of propriety to find out that he was involved with a married woman. Konstantin was an upright person, a churchgoer. He liked a little fun and games, maybe, but nothing that looked like adultery."

"Why didn't he dump her right then and there?"

"Because he didn't *want* to, dear lady, and he didn't *have* to. He worked out his own solution. The next time I popped in he seemed bloody cheerful. He said, Look, Dima, everything's aboveboard now. You needn't have worried. He said, I was brought up in the Russian officers' tradition, you know. I wouldn't do anything against our code. He said, Mary's now my official tenant. We've signed papers to that effect. He told me he'd confronted her about her husband and she said, If you're uneasy about our living arrangement, why don't we sign a joint tenancy agreement? That would make it honorable for us to be under the same roof. He said he'd signed to verify that she was just a tenant and not his wife. He told me, It's all legal, Dima. Mary can stay here whenever she wants. He seemed so pleased, and I thought, Well, fair enough. They've cleaned up their act. What did I know? I'm an engineer. My brain is involved with stress factors and magnetic fields and Ohm's law. In Australia we don't have the term 'joint tenancy.' "

"You don't have to be Australian to be confused," Fay said. "It doesn't mean joint tenant at all. It means joint *owner*."

"Well, yes, and didn't we all learn the hard way?"

Fay nodded.

"The next time I visited Konstantin, I noticed a change. He was dopey, disoriented. And Mary was bloody rude. She whispered something in his ear and then she said, Mr. Egoroff, you got ten minutes. Doctor's orders! I'd hardly sat down before she said, Your time is up. Go away! Konstantin said good-bye in a sleepy voice. A few days later my mum made him a couple of *pirozhki* that she cooked in the lightest olive oil and sprinkled with powdered sugar. He always enjoyed delicacies like that. I tried to deliver them and Mary said he was sleeping. Not to worry, she said. I'll see he gets them. An hour later my mother said, Here, I've baked some *vatrushka* for him as well. Mary opened the door again and I said, I'm terribly sorry, Mrs. Steiner, but I forgot to bring these Danish pastries. She brushed some *pirozhki* sugar from her lips. I thought, Well, Konstantin has been sharing his treat with her. How nice of the old gentleman!"

Fay asked, "Did you wonder why she was eating his food?"

"Not at the time," Egoroff answered, refilling her teacup. "But as the weeks went by it was obvious she wasn't only taking the poor bugger's food, she was taking over his life. She would crack open the door and say, I'm sorry, Mr. Liotweizen can't be seen today. Or she'd say, The landlord's asleep."

"Was she actually living with him?"

"At first, yes. When old man Lovaco died on the first floor, she moved herself and kids and dog into his apartment straightaway. Another woman died rather suddenly across the hall, making more space."

"Convenient," Fay said.

"Most. One day I caught a glimpse of Konstantin and asked Mary why he looked so bad. She said, Painkillers. I said, This broken hip is taking a bloody long time to mend. She said, Is that *your* business? I said, Mary, he's my friend. She said, Well, you ought to be able to see that your friend's sick. I'm the one who's looking after him, not you or anybody else. I asked if I might take him for a walk, exercise him a bit, and she said, He doesn't want to. All he wants to do is rest. I said, Well, then, may I ring him up? It's been weeks since we've talked, and we used to chat every day. She said, No! Don't bother him! Why do you think he changed his phone number? Well, Mrs. Steiner, I said, please let me know if there's anything I can do. And give him a kiss from my mum."

"You're a tolerant man," Fay said warmly.

"A bit less tolerance might have served us better, don't you think?" he replied. "A few weeks later I asked her why Konstantin wasn't going to church or his veterans' club or entertaining any of his old Russian friends, and why he hadn't voted in the last election. Voting meant *so* much to him. And I asked why we never saw his face anymore. She just turned away."

Fay asked, "Why didn't somebody make a complaint? To Social Services, or—the police?"

"Well, it was a bit of human error, wasn't it? Or human miscalculation. I confess I didn't want to rock the boat. I was overseas a lot in those days, and I was afraid Mary might take revenge on my mother whilst I was gone. She was already upsetting the other tenants. She kept those old Russian women confused about who she really was. Now that I look back, I realize it was deliberate psychological warfare to confuse them and force them out of the building. One day she turned up dressed as a nurse, the next in a suit, or a miniskirt, the next with a scarf on her head. She wore different wigs and changed her personality to match. My poor old mum has never been sure exactly who Steiner is or even what she looks like. The other old women are afraid of her. I thought it was just a strangeness on Mary's part. I didn't recognize it as part of a plan."

"Neither did a lot of people."

"Well, what could we do? My mum and I never understood why Konstantin had to be kept so isolated. Sonia Ellis glimpsed him sitting in a wheelchair with his head hanging to one side and his mouth open. Mary caught her watching and moved him into a back room where *nobody* could see him. At night we'd hear him cry out. Help! Water! Then he began banging on the pipes. I wondered if he was handcuffed to the heating system, but I thought, Oh, no, that *couldn't* be. Old-fashioned steam radiators make a lot of noise. Once or twice I saw Teddy Tene or his brother Kelly in the halls and told them, Hurry, the old man's calling for help! They would run inside his apartment and the noise would stop."

"How long did you go without seeing him?"

"*Months*. We weren't even sure he was alive. But then we'd hear him banging on the pipes. No one dared ask Mary what was going on, and she was absent most of the time anyway, visiting her husband Steiner, I suppose, or sleeping with the Gypsy husband we learned about later. We saw more of her kids than we saw of her. Danny came round now and again in his gold Corvette or his big pickup, but whenever I asked if he could let me in to see Konstantin, he would look at me and say, Excuse me, who are you?"

"As if you'd never met?"

"Precisely. I kept waiting for a chance to slip into Konstantin's apartment. One morning I saw Mary step outside in her housecoat to talk to a deliveryman. On impulse, I ran downstairs. I smelled feces as soon as I entered. Konstantin lay in bed in the back. There was hardly enough of him to make a dent in the covers. Flies buzzed around his mouth and nose. His eyes were cloudy, unfocused. It was like looking at a death's-head. He had huge bedsores, and his mouth was opening and closing like a carp's. I leaned over and he whispered, Water, Dima. Water, water . . . I started to pour some milk from a cardboard container, but it was curdled. I could see where he'd tried to bite into a mildewed slice of pizza, but he had no teeth. I ran to the kitchen, found a cup and filled it with water. I glanced out the window and Mary was still talking to the truck driver. I said to myself, Quickly, Dimitri. *Quickly!*"

"Could he drink it?"

"His hands shook when I held the cup to his lips, and most of it spilled. He whispered in Russian, It's too late for me. I leaned over his face to hear him better. He said, She caught me like a little chick. I said, Konstantin, is there anything I can do for you? I thought he might want a priest. I thought, My God, this is murder by neglect!"

"If there's such a crime," Fay said, and added, "There certainly ought to be."

Egoroff nodded. "I didn't know what to do. Konstantin said, No, Dima, nothing you can do. I just feel like dying now. His eyes rolled in his head like bloody marbles. I was speechless. I'd never seen a dead man talk. I rushed upstairs and told my mum, Jesus Christ, Konstantin is almost *gone!*"

Fay said, "Was your mother close to him?"

"*Very* close." He paused. "In their own formal Russian way, of course. She was distraught. She said, We must save him, son. We decided to call the police. Graziana Gandolfi popped in and warned us that it was a waste of time, and she was proved right as usual. The cops didn't bother to come. So we alerted one of the social agencies. They came round the next day for a look."

"Weren't they shocked?"

"Not a bit! Konstantin was all cleaned up."

Fay frowned in surprise.

"It baffled me, too," Egoroff said, "till I thought about it. Bloody fool, I'd left behind the water cup. Mary knew that someone had been in his bedroom! She'd changed the linen and fluffed up the pillows and dressed him in fresh new pajamas. She threw out the moldy pizza and curdled milk and replaced it with juice and a platter of fresh fruit. So the visitors went away. And . . . I left the next day for business in England."

"How long were you gone?"

"Three or four months. When I returned, Konstantin was in a retirement home. I visited him straightaway. He looked terrible. I could see he was beyond coming back."

Fay said, "And Mary was running his building?"

"Like a female Napoleon. She tried to force us out by making the place unlivable. The pipes were ancient. Konstantin used to have the plumber in every few weeks for preventive maintenance, but she let the drains back up till the place was positively unhealthy. We were drinking septic water. Sometimes she turned off the main valve and left us high and dry for a day or two. Then it would come out in globs."

Fay asked, "Didn't you complain?"

"To whom? Every complaint went unanswered. A pane of glass fell from a front window and sliced off a Chinese woman's ear. Tulia Hartmane slipped on debris in the hall and broke her hip. The poor old woman, she was horrified of vermin, but she had battalions of bloody bugs and mice in her apartment. I think the Tenes were tossing in fresh supplies of live specimens. Tulia finally gave up and moved in with her son in San Rafael."

"Graziani told me that the other tenants left, too."

"One by one. But our neighbor Anna Atamasov did *not* intend to budge. The low rent suited her fancy, and she was old and deaf and half blind. The Russian Orthodox church was in the next block, and she'd lived in our building for twenty years. Her biggest fears were fire and burglars, and the Tenes began to play on those."

"How?"

"Her apartment was on the top floor, just under the roof, and she talked incessantly about being incinerated. One morning at two o'clock the poor dear phoned and said, Dimitri, the building's on fire! I said, Do you want me to call the fire brigade? What's burning? She said she saw smoke. I ran over and spotted a wisp of haze at floor level. I said, Anna Alexeiva, this is San Francisco, not Vladivostok. It's just a bit of fog coming through your windows."

"She calmed down—?"

"—And went back to bed. Two weeks later she rings me up at midnight and her apartment smells like ammonia. I said, Did you just do a washing? She said, No no *no*. It didn't tweak to me that something was up. Later the smell turned pungent, like rotten eggs. Then the fog came back, a heavy vapor in her kitchen and tapering off into her bedroom. I said, Somebody must be playing games with you, Anna Alexeiva. But *who*?"

"I can't imagine," Fay said sarcastically.

"We summoned the police and they found nothing. After that, Anna would call and say, Something's floating across my floor. The police came several more times, but it was all false alarms. One night I was awakened by footsteps on the roof. I rang up Bob Sanders in 301, and I said, Bob, did you go up on the roof whilst you were having a cigarette? He said, No, and I said, Well, there's people walking round up there. A bit later, I heard someone jumping up and down. After a few days I learned that Anna was packing her things to leave. I asked her daughter, a very nice lady, Excuse me, madam, but why is your dear mother leaving us? We all love her so much. The daughter said, Well, Mama is having a few mental problems. She thinks she sees smoke in her apartment. I said, Madam, your mum's not inventing that! It's recorded with the police. She said, Well, Mama phoned me at midnight and said, You must come right now, darling. I've got devils dancing on my ceiling."

"Don't tell me," Fay ventured. "It was the Tene kids? Up on the roof?"

"Exactly. But I didn't tumble. I thought, My God, the poor dear's really gone round the bend. She's seeing devils! The truth didn't hit me till she'd been moved away."

Fay said, "So that gave Steiner another apartment to rent for twelve hundred a month."

"I'm sure that's what she intended. Away they went, one by one, Konstantin's oldest tenants, till my mum and I were the last holdouts. Steiner's lawyer wrote us a letter saying that we would be evicted if we didn't move because my mum's health had deteriorated and she represented a danger to herself and others. I'd already had her examined by a doctor, and I had her examined again when we got the eviction letter. Look here. This is the doctor's report."

Fay read, "I found Mrs. Baruksopulo's health to be stable and find no evidence that she is unable to stay at home safely."

Egoroff continued, "On December fourth, 1992, when everybody was getting ready for Christmas, Mary's lawyer served us with a three-day eviction notice. My mum went into shock. She was convinced they would throw her paintings and sculptures on the street. It was late on a Friday afternoon and I couldn't find a lawyer for love of God or money.

Steiner thought she had us by the short and curlies, but I finally found somebody at a Tenderloin help clinic who helped us file the right papers."

Fay said, "Didn't they have to make specific complaints against you? To justify the eviction?"

"Oh, they did, they did! Here, take a look."

Fay read a letter addressed to Tamara Baruksopulo of 486 Funston: "Your actions have caused aggravation and upset to the landlord and the other tenants of the building. You have been indecent and offensive to the senses of the landlord and the other tenants. You have been an obstruction to the free use of their property, you have interfered with the comfortable enjoyment of their living space, you have interfered and disrupted their lives and their right to peacefully live without interference."

"Can you imagine the bloody nerve?" Egoroff said as Fay handed back the lawyer's letter. "For thirty years my mum was Konstantin's favorite tenant. Everyone in the building admired her. She's a dignified little lady who stays in her apartment and creates lovely works of art. And she's being accused of forcing her way into people's apartments, babbling, refusing to leave when asked, pounding on doors, screaming, kicking, shouting. Listen to this."

He read aloud from the lawyer's second letter: "Other tenants were terrorized. She follows tenants around the building, tried to force her way into their apartments, and stood in front of a car door to prevent one from leaving . . . regularly calls the police department for irrelevant and inane complaints, terrorized and bothered the young girls, insanely accused one girlfriend of stealing your purse . . . try to act like a member of the family of which you are not . . . cursed Mary Steiner in presence of other tenants . . . touched other tenants when they have not consented to be touched by you. You lock yourself out on a regular basis and annoy people to get back in . . . interfere with workmen, talk gibberish to them . . . shout and scream at the workmen, slam doors, chase the contractor out of the building, leaves the front door open, presenting a danger . . . utilized slanderous, rude and crude language, all to the annoyance of the tenants who are not interested in your insane ravings. These are but a few examples of your conduct."

"Was any of it true?" Fay asked.

"Not a bloody syllable, and we could prove it," Egoroff answered.

"How did you respond?"

"We hired a lawyer and made it plain we would fight. Everyone else had sort of knuckled under, but my mum and I weren't gonna be run out of our apartment. It was a pretty gloomy holiday season. A few days after New Year's Day 1993, Danny and one of his brothers knocked on our door and told my mum they wanted to check for a gas leak in the stove because they'd smelled gas downstairs."

"Were you home?"

"I was gone for the day. The Tene boys always made my mum nervous and she stayed in the bedroom till they left. That evening we had a little snack after the ten-o'clock news—cottage cheese with a bit of sour cream and some wild cherries. We call them *vishni*. An hour later I felt dizzy and started vomiting. I thought I'd had a bad burrito for lunch. Then I heard my mum vomiting. I went to help her and almost fell over with stomach cramps. All night long my mum and I kept running to the bathroom with bloody vomiting and diarrhea. I forced down some milk and ate the center out of a loaf of bread, to absorb the poison, but my mum was vomiting pure green bile and couldn't hold anything down."

"Surely you didn't think you'd been poisoned?"

"We were too sick to think. I drove my mum to the Pacific Medical Center emergency room and they diagnosed acute gastroenteritis. What is that but poisoning, natural or otherwise?"

"She's okay now?"

"She's never recovered. Whilst dressing to come home, she had a stroke. Her right side is totally paralyzed. She's lingering on, but that stroke will be her end. I'll always believe that's exactly what the Tenes intended. I brought scrapings from our meal to the police, but a detective said it was useless as evidence because I might've contaminated it myself. I ended up throwing it away."

FAY WENT HOME and dreamed all night of Gypsies: roguish minstrels making violins cry, smiling women reading palms, barefooted children begging coins, old bent men leading old bent horses. She saw tents, encampments, sheep wagons, storefront *ofisas* with drawn curtains. She saw showbiz Gypsies: Django Reinhardt, Yul Brynner, "The Gypsy Kings," flamenco dancers, Bizet's Carmen, Gypsy circus performers and bear handlers, dancers, magicians, puppeteers. Toward dawn her dreams turned darker. She saw a thousand years of persecution: Gypsies being torched from their homes, driven from their encampments, flogged, impaled, hanged, drawn and quartered, branded, mutilated, broken on the wheel, guillotined, burned at the stake, stoned and drowned: *hated*. She saw panicked Zigeuner, Manouches, Tziganes, Gitanos, Zingari, Tigani, Bohèmes, traveling in rackety old wagons, mending pots and pans, picking rags, sharpening knives, telling fortunes, lifting curses, suffering.

But when she awoke, all she could think of was Dimitri Egoroff and his mother, vomiting blood and bile.

16

Romancing the Aged

AFTER HER REGULAR morning bike ride to the Golden Gate, Fay couldn't wait to call Greg Ovanessian and fill him in on the Egoroff revelations, but first she ran Philip Steiner in her data banks to complete a gap in her files. Nothing significant popped up except the date of the ninety-one-year-old man's death, April 23, 1987, four years after his late-life marriage to Mary Tene. By that time, Fay realized, his Gypsy wife had been dallying with the fading Konstantin Liotweizen for a year.

She thought, Where on earth did this strange woman get the energy to convince two old men that she was their sole companion? She wondered if Philip Steiner was first turned into a helpless vegetable, like Liotweizen. That would have made her nightly performances easier.

FAY CRANKED UP the Frog Prince for the short run to City Hall to double-check the Steiner marriage records. She learned that Philip had been eighty-seven at the time of the wedding on April Fool's Day 1983, the bride a month short of forty-three. It was listed as his second marriage, her first. Her birthplace was given as New York, her mother as Liza Tene, and her father as "unknown." The papers showed that Mary had attended school through the eighth grade.

A will was dated January 1, 1985, and Fay noted that the witnesses had come from a run-down area where citizens sold signatures and blood for a few gulps of Thunderbird wine. The Steiner estate, including his $300,000 house, his bank accounts at Wells Fargo and Eureka Savings and Loan, and his hundreds of shares of stock, had gone to his wife Mary Tene. Death was attributed to cardiopulmonary arrest compounded by pneumonia.

AT THE COURTHOUSE, Fay copied a revealing quote from Steiner's deposition in her 1991 eviction action against Graziana Gandolfi:

> Q: When did Mr. Steiner pass away?
> A: In, I believe, 'eighty-six.
> Q: How did he die, ma'am?
> A: I don't remember.
> Q: Do you have any idea how your husband died?
> A: He had a heart attack or something like that.

Ah, Fay said to herself. True love.

17

The Tene Bimbos

OVER THE PHONE, she got the impression that Fraud Inspector Greg Ovanessian was pleased but not surprised by the information she'd gleaned from Egoroff. She decided that he probably had plenty of evidence of his own. She reminded herself that lawmen were secretive types, sometimes even with each other. Most of them were convinced that PIs were getting rich at the expense of the underpaid police.

She realized that she would never learn anything unless she kept up the pressure, and she phoned again a week later. The *jawndare Romano* swore her to secrecy and said that he'd spoken to an anonymous female informant. "She said her brother and his Gypsy girlfriend have been running errands for a couple of old men, taking 'em food, driving 'em around. Whatever they're up to, they act like it's funny as hell. The sister hears 'em giggling. She thinks the old guys are being poisoned."

"Who's the Gypsy?" Fay asked.

"A young widow. She's Danny Tene's sister Theresa. Now she goes by Angela Bufford."

Fay remembered her talk with Jim Egoroff and said, *"Mary Steiner's daughter?"*

"Yep."

Ovanessian promised to tell her more later. Fay sat with the dead phone pressed to her ear and thought, What are we dealing with here? The Munsters? The *Borgias*?

SHE SUSPECTED THAT Ovanessian had some answers, and she set about building her relationship with the Gypsy specialist till she began to think of him as a friend. As his trust grew, he became more open. He admitted that he'd knocked heads with the so-called Tene Bimbo *familia* for years; cops from coast to coast considered them one of the most active clans in the so-called Gypsy Mafia. In San Francisco they seemed to have developed a subspecialty, zeroing in on elderly Russian-Americans.

Ovanessian told her that the Tene Bimbos had made themselves experts on old age—"They have the subject nailed." He said they knew when the elderly began to fail, when their memories slipped, when their physical abilities dropped off, where to find them, how to spot their homes. And they knew when families were likely to write off their old folks and lose contact.

He told Fay that Mary Steiner's real name was Bessie Tene, although it was silly to use the phrase "real name" in connection with underworld Gypsies, since they were as creative about birth certificates, driver's licenses and Social Security cards as they were about local laws and customs. Folklore held that every Rom baby was given at least three names: a secret one whispered once by the mother, a Gypsy name (*nav romano*), and a street name (*nav gajikano*) to be used in dealing with outsiders. Ovanessian told Fay that Mary Tene Steiner's daughter Angela Bufford had been born Theresa Tene but also used other names. Within Mary's close-knit Tene Bimbo *familia*, members were better known by diminutives like Botchie, Snooky, Dee-eye, Potsy, Guy-guy, Wovie and Baby. Stanley Tene Bimbo, AKA Richard Bimbo, Ephrem

Bimbo and Stanley Yonvanovich, was the youngest of the brothers, a former boxer who'd quit the sport after punching out a relative's eye. His nickname, Chuchi ("breast," or, more closely, "tit," in the Rom tongue), was said to derive from an infantile preoccupation.

The local branch of the Tene Bimbo family tree came into clear view when Ovanessian explained that Chuchi was the husband of Mary Tene Steiner. It was a typical Romani marriage, never legalized but fully accepted in the Gypsy community. The undocumented arrangement left Mary free to batten off old men like Konstantin Liotweizen and to marry them in *gaje* ceremonies, if necessary, as she'd married Philip Steiner. Chuchi and Mary had been together for some thirty years after a teenage wedding arranged by his family.

Criminy, Fay exclaimed to herself after she absorbed all the information, I couldn't understand how she juggled two men at a time. But she was juggling *three* . . .

Ovanessian suggested that she study Peter Maas' book *The King of the Gypsies* for an overview of the Tene Bimbo clan. The patriarch, he said, was Chuchi's grandfather, an alpha figure named George Tene Bimbo, who was arrested dozens of times in the course of conning, robbing, torturing and murdering his way to leadership of his own nomadic tribe. Fay remembered the movie and its peculiar casting: the pale blond Sterling Hayden as the Gypsy king, and the even blonder Shelley Winters as his wife. The only cast member who looked even faintly Roma was Susan Sarandon. Fay thought, Some Gypsies. . . .

18

King of the Gypsies

OVER THE NEXT months, Fay cultivated tenuous friendships with local Romani experts and carefully read the book by Peter Maas. She was impressed by the author's fairness in allowing the embattled Tene Bimbos to speak for themselves. "So I took two-twenty-odd dollars from the man," Maas quoted a Bimbo known as Aunt Hazel. "My mother was very sick, and there were a lot of mouths, you know, that were starving, and things were bad, those were hard times, no coal to put in the stove, no groceries, no rent, and I went and stole. But I didn't hit nobody over the head."

As depicted in the book, the fearsome King George Tene Bimbo was remembered with fondness and awe by one of his descendants. "... He used to bring hungry Gypsies food, the way he used to take them to the hospitals to get them cured, the way he used to try to rent them houses to live in or rent them fields where they could camp and bring them wood and water and feed their horses. ... All the Gypsy tribes recognized him, the Stevensons and the Thompsons, the Adamses, the Williams tribe and the Evans tribe and the Greens and the Uwanowiches, the Demetros, all them people. When they heard the name King Tene Bimbo, they are just like numb, they feared from that name. ... They shivered and lost their tongues."

As an author herself, Fay found *The King of the Gypsies* a balanced report, but a Hollywood friend informed her that the irate Tene Bimbos had been so angry that they'd filed a lawsuit, later dropped, against Peter Maas. They also claimed that a *ramya* or curse had caused the sudden death of the writer's wife, Audrey. One of King George's grandchildren, a self-proclaimed born-again Christian, didn't deny the assertion. "When I curse somebody," she said, "God listens to me 'cause he knows my heart. Not that I wish people dead, ya know what I'm saying? But when you hurt my family, yes, I will curse you, and I will leave the rest to the Lord. And that's what happened to Peter Maas and his wife."

Fay learned that some of the Romani often used such personal tragedies as proof of their dark powers. Fiorello La Guardia, former mayor of New York City, was said to have blamed a fortune-teller's prediction for the deaths of his wife and daughter. In England, the manager of a soccer team painted crosses on his players' feet to ward off a curse after a Rom *familia* was evicted to make room for a new stadium. When the *ramya* was lifted, the club began to win.

AFTER A WHILE Fay realized that her expanding files now held the answers to a few questions that had troubled her sleep:

Where was Mary Tene Steiner when old Liotweizen was crying out for help? Home with her husband Chuchi, of course, perhaps after dropping in on her legal husband, the senile *gajo* Philip Steiner, who was probably unaware of whether he was alone in his marital bed or not.

Where were the Tene children on their long absences from the Funston apartment? At home with their Gypsy father and other Tene Bimbos.

Who were the dark-haired people who sometimes visited? They were Gypsies, mostly Tene Bimbos. Sometimes there seemed to be dozens. One of Fay's informants told her that King George Tene Bimbo, who died at eighty-five in 1969, had three hundred descendants at the most recent count, plus uncounted others who'd drifted away from the clan and its ways. Gypsies, like Mormons and Roman Catholics, believed in big families.

19

Doctored Food

ON A PRETTY spring day in early May, Fay's phone rang. It was her new friend Inspector Greg Ovanessian, passing along the latest revelations by his mystery informant. This time the woman had given her name as Hami and claimed that her brother George and his Gypsy girlfriend Angela Bufford were busily delivering poisoned food to a pair of elderly males. Hami said that she and her sister Nicole had watched the conspirators grind up yellow pills and sprinkle them into takeout dishes at the family's deli. At least one other relative had witnessed the toxic spicing. Fay asked the detective if he knew the names of the target victims.

Ovanessian explained that he hadn't had time; every cop in San Francisco was overworked; important investigations were being postponed, even shelved. To make matters worse, the Fraud Unit's budget had been cut. He told her not to worry—"We've got it under control."

Fay couldn't decide whether he was leveling or putting her off. Maybe he was afraid she would interfere in the case, a constant tension between cops and private eyes. She asked if he couldn't give her something more to go on. "Greg," she said, "I can help you. I *know* I can."

"I appreciate it, Fay," he said, "but cops can't ask private citizens to do police work."

"Are you saying if I developed some info, you wouldn't want it? C'mon, Greg, let me see what I can turn up."

He grudgingly gave her the address of the suspects, a house on Fourteenth Avenue, and warned her to be extremely careful. "This isn't some silly adultery deal, you know."

"I don't do windows and I don't do adultery deals," she snapped. "Gimme a break."

After more wheedling, she extracted the information that the food was being doctored at the French Village Deli in an old neighborhood called West Portal. She decided to find out the victims' identities and turn the names over to Ovanessian. It would be a simple job for an old pro—she wasn't a skip tracer for nothing. If the cops already knew who the old men were, as she halfway suspected, no harm done. But if the San Francisco Police Department was too busy to protect respectable citizens in grave danger, she would be glad to help out.

20

On the Trail

JUST AFTER DAWN the next day she steered the Frog Prince toward the district known familiarly as the Sunset. Locals complained that the sun never rose in this area of Monopoly houses; it appeared as a bilious glow at sunset, and only when it was in the mood. The Sunset was the heart of the Fog Belt, clammy and chilly even in summer. The suicide rate was higher than in the rest of the city. Clouds of salty fog floated the wide streets in spirals and swirls, climbed the houses in ziggurats, and twisted Fay's hair into tight ringlets that could be combed only with pain and suffering. The boxy homes, usually advertised as "one story over garage," leaned together like tired old men. Most were spaced an inch apart to meet the minimum requirements of the city's fire codes. Stucco-over-wood homes extended to the sidewalk and were painted in gaudy colors as though to create their own brightness. A few trees poked from a carapace of concrete poured by contractors over sand dunes that ran in soft ripples all the way to the ocean. The same shortage of land that forced San Franciscans to bury their dead out of town had driven up the price of the average home to $300,000. Movies were shot all over the colorful city, but not in the Sunset.

AT 6:00 A.M., Fay parked the Frog Prince a half block from the Lama lair on Fourteenth. The house was indistinguishable from its neighbors except by a metal grate at the top of the stairs leading to the second-floor door. The garage doors were closed and a blue-white BMW was parked in the short driveway. The neighborhood was silent, and on this morning when Fay needed heavenly cover, the fog had lifted and a flaming disk of sun lit up the scene.

At seven-ten by her official Girl Scout chronometer, Fay felt a nudge on her thigh: Beans signaling a hydraulic need. As his mission was being accomplished against a rare sapling that protruded from the curb like a broomstraw, a blue-haired woman emerged from the nearest house and glared Fay back into the Frog Prince. A few minutes later a group of schoolchildren walked around the car, pointing and chattering. It's that darned bilious green, she said to herself. Why else would Asian kids stare at a 1982 Tercel? She felt uncomfortable and drove away.

ON THE NEXT morning, a Thursday, the comforting fog was back where God intended and Fay was able to set up a surveillance nearer the house. Just after eight, a young woman emerged to pick up a newspaper. Criminy, Fay said to herself, is *that* Angela Bufford? She looked like a Broadway ingenue.

After the woman went back inside, a man backed a Mercedes roadster out of the garage. He appeared to be somewhere in his thirties, with thinning dark hair and the jerky head movements of a chased fox. His oversized glasses put Fay in mind of the guy who couldn't get a date for the prom. Could this be the boyfriend? Hami's evil brother George? He looked more like Pee-wee Herman.

The man drove fast but seemed oblivious to being tailed, even by a rolling neon blob like the Frog Prince. He double-parked in front of the French Village Deli, tucked between the St. Francis Travel Agency and a karate parlor in the West Portal section, a yuppified neighborhood of restaurants and shops near the western opening of the streetcar tunnel under Twin Peaks. In a few minutes he emerged carrying a white takeout container and drove off. Fay followed him to a nondescript house in the Sunset and watched him carry the food inside. Without taking her eyes off the front door, she inked the address on her palm: 2526 Twenty-third Avenue.

A half hour later Pee-wee Herman emerged empty-handed and sped away. She lost him in traffic and doubled back to sit on his house in case he was headed home. Just as she reached Fourteenth Avenue, she was approached by a blue BMW driven by a dark-haired female with light skin. Fay recognized her as the beauty she'd seen earlier and waited till the car was out of sight to whip the Frog Prince into a rattly U-turn. The sports car got away but Fay found it parked in front of the French Village Deli.

From across the busy street, she watched the woman leave the restaurant with a brown paper bag and drive west to a green-trimmed house at 2266 Forty-sixth Avenue. She was in and out with a dancer's brisk energy and blew a kiss to someone as she left. Then she drove to the Stonestown shopping center. Fay found her as easy to follow as the boyfriend. Some tails were good for a day or two, but she felt she could follow these two with a troupe of acrobats and a brass band. So sure of themselves, so arrogant! She felt like jumping into the woman's expensive Beemer and sharing the ride to save on gas.

At Stonestown, her quarry entered the Nordstrom store. She had a haughty upper-class walk, as though a Force Six gale wouldn't faze her or her hairdo. Fay waited five minutes, then followed. She spotted her subject behind a counter in a department called Point of View that catered to older women. The young Gypsy was exuding a look that Fay thought of as "don't hate me because I'm beautiful." Her long black hair matched pools of kohl around her eyes. Her heart-shaped face looked exotic, almost lupine, and her skin was the palest ivory. She looked like someone who ate whatever she pleased. Fay found her highly annoying.

Noon was approaching, and she felt the opening rush of the fight-or-flight syndrome. I'm a civilian, she reminded herself, not a cop. And Greg warned me not to get burned. She returned to her office and ran the morning's addresses on the crisscross directory. The house on Twenty-third came back to a man named Harry Glover Hughes, the other to a Richard M. Nelson. More research established that both men were ninety-three and well fixed. Hughes' home was appraised at $314,000, and his median annual income at $54,600. Nelson's house was worth $272,400 and his income was $56,300.

Fay dialed Ovanessian to scream out a warning: *It's two old men! They're eating poisoned food right now! They won't last the weekend. . . .*

The Gypsy cop wasn't in his office and didn't respond to his pager. No one else in the Fraud Unit seemed aware of the case or concerned about the danger. A female said Ovanessian was out of town and might be back on Monday.

Fay wondered if she should return to the old men's homes and warn them. But what if the Fraud Unit was already on the case? She couldn't risk interfering. She paged Ovanessian every fifteen minutes for the rest of the day.

21

Long Weekend

WHEN SHE COULDN'T raise the *jawndare Romano* on Friday or Saturday, she called an old voter registration contact and wangled his home address. She drove to the house and knocked, but there was no answer. She doubled past the Nelson and Hughes homes and saw no signs of unusual activity—no aid car, no ambulance or hearse. She went through the same routine on Sunday, with the same results. Maybe, she told herself, the poison works slowly. Maybe there's still time to save their lives.

She burst into the Fraud Unit office at 8:00 A.M. Monday. As always, Ovanessian was the picture of professional cool. He listened to her story, scribbled a few notes, told her she'd done a good job, and ushered her out. She realized that he hadn't offered the slightest hint as to how much he knew. This wasn't the first time that the SFPD had made her feel as though she were being patted on the head like a good little girl who now and then managed to stumble on the same information as her betters. Still, she left the office in a calmer state. Whatever the status of the investigation, Ovanessian's attitude could only mean that the cops were on the case. Mr. Hughes and Mr. Nelson would finish out their years.

MONDAY MORNING FOUND her back at her favorite stand: the musty old records at City Hall and the courthouse. The files on "Angela Bufford" made her blue eyes blink. The store clerk was now thirty years old and had used the names Angela Ciampa, Angela Tene and Theresa Tene before moving from the Boston area to San Francisco. Her mother was listed as Mary Tene and her father as an Italian immigrant whose only name appeared to be Ciampa.

Fay was puzzled. A Gypsy mother and a Roman father with a blue-eyed, light-skinned daughter? Not when *I* studied biology, she said to herself. It was peculiar at best.

So were her next discoveries. At the age of twenty-four, Angela/ Theresa had received a generous gift from a Russian-American San Franciscan named Nicholas Constantine Bufford. On an individual grant deed, the eighty-seven-year-old man had turned over half his property to a person described on the document as "Angela Ciampa, his granddaughter, a single woman." Five months later, in October 1984, the odd couple had returned to City Hall to correct the entry and list the young woman as Bufford's wife. A month later, the old man died of a heart attack, leaving his new bride $125,479 in personal assets and a house appraised at $226,000.

Fay thought, So *that's* her scam! She inveigles old men into signing away their homes and properties, and then they die. A little obvious, isn't it?

She copied the documents and dug back into the files. Within an hour she found a joint tenancy agreement between the lucky Angela Bufford and another elderly person: an eighty-five-year-old widow named Helen M. Mitchell. This time the old person had died two months after filing the papers. Fay checked to see how much Angela had cleared on the deal, but she was surprised to find other names listed as sole heirs: Mrs. Mitchell's son, Dwight, and a daughter, Jocelyn. Fay thought, How the heck did that happen? Did Angela let a victim get away?

For a veteran skip tracer, locating the Mitchell heirs was short work. Dwight Mitchell was out of town, but Jocelyn Mitchell Nash was at home in Point Richmond, on the far northeast side of the bay. She was a motivational speaker and ocean racer, and her accomplishments had been well publicized in the Bay Area.

"Tell me, Miss Faron," she asked on the phone, "what would a private investigator want with my brother and me?" To Fay the voice sounded like old-money San Francisco, straightforward, proper and utterly self-assured.

She decided to be just as direct. "Mrs. Nash," she said, "I think a Gypsy woman tried to steal your mother's house."

"You *think?*" the woman answered, and a throaty Lauren Bacall laugh came over the phone. "My goodness, Miss Faron, I *know!* I'm the one that caught her!"

22

Saved to Die

IN THE STICKY late-afternoon traffic over the Golden Gate and Richmond–San Rafael bridges, the Frog Prince required an hour to reach the sail factory, where the rangy Mrs. Nash explained that she was in town between ocean races and speeches about female empowerment. She looked to be in her fifties but was easily recognizable as the blue-eyed model who'd appeared in magazine ads years before. Her long hair was a sleek blondish gray. She had lean jogger's legs, and her bare arms were smoothly muscled from hauling in jibs and halyards.

"I keep moving," she explained as she ushered Fay into a side office decorated in swaths of sailcloth and other marine accessories. "I have absolutely *no* interest in getting old. I tell my groups, Don't retire. Go sailing! There's no midlife crisis when you're halfway to New Zealand."

Fay smiled. "I believe it," she said. She felt the same way while bicycling across Utah. "Have you crossed the Pacific?"

"Four times."

"Single-handed?"

"Only once."

"Isn't that . . . scary?"

Mrs. Nash smiled and said, "Sure it's scary! I was at sea in the worst storm in a hundred years. We pulled friends out of the water for three days. Seven died." She paused. "So you see, Miss Faron—Angela Bufford was no problem for me." Fay was surprised by the abrupt shift in tone.

"I'm afraid I didn't have the sweetest relationship with my mother," Mrs. Nash began as Fay balanced a legal pad on her knee. She tried not to interrupt the story; every mother-daughter relationship was a source of passion and conflict, and every one was different, including Fay's own.

"Mom was wonderful to me and her grandchildren," the woman began, "and she enriched our lives, but there was always some little discord, some little—oh, I don't know. I just wish I'd tried harder now that she's gone. When she began to fail mentally, things became difficult. For one thing, she insisted on staying in our family home in St. Francis Woods, and that didn't make a bit of sense."

Fay knew St. Francis Woods as a settled old enclave adjacent to West Portal and distinguished by stately pillars at the entrance, steep hillsides, sinuous streets, stands of gray-green eucalyptus, and putting-green lawns. There were cushier parts of town—Russian Hill, Sea Cliff, Pacific Heights—but the gracious old homes in St. Francis Woods started at prices close to a half million, and the patrician residents had enough pride to keep up the streets, set out African violets and orchids in pots facing the passing tour buses, and maintain a lovely community fountain.

"Mother had great inner charm," Jocelyn Nash was saying. "She was a San Francisco belle whose parents went broke. She had delightful social graces, knew exactly how to please people. That was what women of her era *did*. At eighty she still had more red hair than gray, a nice figure, knew how to flirt. She always took *such* good care of herself— vitamin pills, exercise, long walks. Women like my mom were *so* concerned with appearances. I'm glad *that's* changed."

So am I, Fay said to herself, tugging down her sweatshirt with the legend *I love my big old dog and my big old dog loves me*. Her interviewee wore Jamaica shorts, a floppy sweater and deck shoes, and seemed perfectly dressed for the setting.

"Whenever I took my mother to the movies and asked for a senior discount," Mrs. Nash continued, "they demanded her driver's license. She came home so proud one day and told me, They carded me again!

She was the oldest of the old-timers in St. Francis Woods, knew every-body's names, their grandkids' names, their family histories. My father bought our lot in 1923. It was a gray Tudor, earthquake-proof. Dad was a teenager in the 1906 earthquake and as an insurance broker he'd written a lot of earthquake policies, so he anchored our house to bedrock by tie-rods. He said, This is *one* home that won't slide down the hill. Well, it's still there. It's not all that big—three bedrooms and some add-ons—but it has a lot of charm. A beautiful view of Golden Gate Park and the ocean."

Fay asked, "What's it worth on the open market?"

Mrs. Nash said, "It finally brought four-twenty-five. But of course that was counting the charm."

"Why didn't you and your mother get along?" Fay asked, thinking of her close relationship with her own mother.

"She had several nervous breakdowns when I was a child," the woman replied after a hesitation. "I had to take over the household at eleven and fourteen and again when I was in college at Cal. So it was nothing new to me when she began to fail and I had to drive down from Port Richmond every other day to look after her. Of course we had some friction. She'd always been loose about money. When she was upset, she ran up all her credit cards."

Fay thought of the plastic deadbeats she'd traced. One had fled to Brazil rather than pay the twenty thousand dollars he'd charged on a dozen cards. "That can be painful," she commented.

"Oh, it got worse. I could see she was beginning to fail when she gave Ronald Reagan's campaign ten thousand dollars. Out of a yearly income of sixteen! The White House sent back a computer-generated letter: Dear Helen, Nancy and I want to thank you so much. Mom thought Ronnie wrote it himself. After that, she built a fantasy world around their friendship. She papered the house with their pictures, turned it into a Republican shrine. I finally had to sit her down and say, Mother, this Ronnie thing isn't real. You're *imagining* it! She was hurt. It took a lot out of her life."

"How old was she by then?"

"Mid-eighties. Then she began to lose track of whether it was time for breakfast, lunch or dinner. She'd tell me she had a group of people coming over, and no one would show up, and she would be hurt again. We had to take her car away because she didn't realize that she couldn't drive safely anymore. And she wasn't taking care of herself. I mean, hygienically. Very unlike my prim and proper mother. After a while I noticed that she stopped eating. She was never a large woman—petite, five-four, wore girl's sizes—but she was shrinking fast. I peeked at her checkbook and saw that she was still sending money to Ronnie, so I took charge of her finances before she starved herself to death."

"This must've taken a lot of your time," Fay said.

"Toward the end, most of my nonworking hours were spent with Mom, buying her food, sprucing up the place, trying to add some light and pleasure to her life. She wanted me to move back in with her, but I knew it would never work. She broke her hip, and she was never the same after she came out of the anesthesia. She didn't have enough money for a nurse or a paid companion. When her hip healed, she insisted on walking four blocks to West Portal every day, the same routine she'd been doing for fifty years—coffee at the French Village Deli, a light lunch, pick up a few items at the health food store and walk back home. But without someone to accompany her, it was a risk."

"From what I've been finding out," Fay said, "it's a risk for *any* old person to go near West Portal."

"Oh? Well, we didn't know that at the time. I finally decided I had to hire someone to take care of her, regardless of cost. But when I brought it up, she said, Jocelyn, I found a girl to live with me! She's a waitress at the French Village Deli and I won't have to pay her! Mom wouldn't provide any details. Said the woman was young and pretty and just about the sweetest person she'd ever met. Well, I was skeptical from the beginning. My approach was, Why would a cute young lady want to move in with an eighty-six-year-old woman? I thought, She's either a scam artist or she's hiding from the law. She's bound to have a boyfriend; what would Mom say when they slept together? She'd be *so* embarrassed! It was a generation thing with her."

"My mother isn't that old, but she'd react the same," Fay said.

"I kept trying to learn more about the waitress, but Mom wouldn't tell me much. It was odd, because she'd never been devious. Finally she said the woman's name was Angela. And one day Mom called and told me to come over at five to meet her."

"Did Angela show up?"

"No, and Mom went crazy. I'd never ever seen her that upset about her *own* kids. She paced up and down and looked at the clock and said,

Why isn't she here? Do you suppose something's happened to her? It was as though Angela was a three-year-old. I was about to leave when this beautiful brunette showed up and apologized for having to work late. She handed Mom some candy, which made it more conspicuous that I hadn't brought a little gift myself."

"What'd she look like?"

"Very attractive. Five-three, five-four, curvy, good legs. Big hair, dark brown. An innocent smile. The kind of chipmunk cheeks that shape a certain kind of face. She served dinner in the kitchen. So sweet toward my Mom, so diffident! I thought, This woman *must* have an ulterior motive. What's going on? It was my father's cynicism rising up in me. I'd have been less irked if she wasn't so gooey. No one is that sweet! I hated her because she was doing all the things a daughter should be doing. She was acting like I was the outsider. So I went upstairs and sulked and wrote checks for some of Mom's bills and tried to separate my stupid emotions from reality."

"Guilt feelings?"

"Damn right! I'd never thought I was doing a good job of making my mother's last years better. I was doing my best, but this Angela woman could outsweet me anytime. I said to myself, How petty of you, Jocelyn! This nice lady makes Mom feel good. Look at them smiling together! Why, she's a gift horse!"

She stopped for a few seconds, then said, "I have to be honest, Fay. Here was someone willing to solve my problem for me. It was a lazy attitude, but I was spread pretty thin at the time. I went home to Port Richmond and decided to let things ride for a while. One day Mom told me that Angela was moving in, but she was vague about the date. I could never nail anything down about Angela—phone number, address, references. I could never make direct contact. And I'd seen her just once. Seemed like she only visited Mom when I wasn't around."

"Weren't you suspicious?"

"Not in the financial sense, no. But in the middle of November 1986, I got a call from a William Pinney Jr. An honest lawyer! He told me that Mom had signed our family home over to Angela under a joint tenancy agreement, and now she wanted to write a new will leaving everything else to Angela. I went into shock! I was the one who kept Mom's books, and she had holdings in Dow Chemical, Eastman Kodak, Pepsico, Apple Computer, Kroger and other big companies. A million-dollar estate! And she was trying to leave every penny to a waitress she'd just met."

"What was Pinney's involvement?"

"He told me that Angela had driven Mom to his office to draw up a new will. He said he asked my mother for some personal information and she couldn't provide it. Her social graces were such that she could sit there and nod and smile and you'd think she was clear as a bell, but she couldn't even tell him how many children she had. And neither could Angela. So Mr. Pinney called me."

"Good for him."

"Then Angela called—talk about nerve! She said her conscience was bothering her. She said she loved my mother but it wouldn't be fair to cut the other heirs completely out of the estate."

"She couldn't get it all, so she'd settle for part?"

"Exactly! My first thought was that this whole deal was between me and Mom and we would settle it together—*right now*. Who the hell needed Angela? I was flat-ass furious. I floored my 'seventy-three Chevy all the way from Port Richmond to St. Francis Woods. It's a wonder I wasn't killed. The leaves were just turning; it's such a lovely drive, but I didn't even notice. I was livid that I'd permitted this to happen and angrier that this awful Angela person was insulting my intelligence. A stranger was trying to grab my inheritance! What was I gonna do in my own old age? I've worked all my life and been divorced twice and I never asked for a *penny* of anyone else's money. This woman was stealing our birthright, mine and my brother's."

"I hope you went easy on your mother. Some of these Gypsies are experts."

"I'm afraid I wasn't kind. I made my poor mother cry. I said, Do you want to disinherit me? *Is that what's going on?* I said, Don't you want me and Dwight to have the house we grew up in? You want this Angela to have it all? You really want to do this to us, Mom? *Cut us off?* Then Angela walked out of the bedroom. I hadn't even known she was there. I got right in her face. I said, Listen, this isn't gonna happen! I'm gonna find out what you have to sign to take this back, and—by God, *you're gonna sign it!*"

"How'd she react?"

"Little Mary Sunshine said she didn't realize that Mom was leaving her everything. If she'd only known. Et cetera, et cetera. I said, Just shut up! I yelled and slammed things around. Mom wouldn't stop crying. I was so angry, I could've kicked that Angela out the back window. She turned cold—I guess she saw the money slipping away—and started to leave. Mom tried to hug her and she jerked loose. It really hurt Mom. Before Angela left, I told her to meet us in the morning or she'd be sorry she was ever born."

"Did she show?"

"Damn right! My lawyer drew up the recision papers and I drove Angela and my mother to a notary public. On the way that woman sat like a stone. Wouldn't respond to me, wouldn't respond to Mom. I felt like slapping her face, but I still needed her signature on a quit-claim deed. After she signed, she walked out the notary's front door and we never saw her again. It broke Mom's heart. She thought Angela loved her. Poor Mom—first the Reagans, and then Angela."

"Why do you suppose she went to so much trouble and then backed off?"

"She thought she'd found the perfect lonely victim. All she saw was a little old lady sipping latte at the deli and walking back to Santa Paula Avenue alone, day after day. She never realized there was a daughter hovering in the wings, and a son, and grandkids. As soon as she realized she was involved with a whole family, she bailed out."

"How'd your mother take it?"

"Crushed. She died a few months later. The doctors said it was from gastroenteritis. I have my own opinion."

"Did you ever ask for help?" Fay asked. "The police? Social Services?"

"It never occurred to me," said the expert on female empowerment. "You do some things because of what you are, Fay. You don't ask others to do them. You do them yourself."

AS SHE DROVE back across the two bridges, Fay thought, There's still an aristocracy in the United States, and it has nothing to do with debutante balls and afternoon teas. I just met a leading member.

Glancing over the hieroglyphs on her yellow pad, she confirmed that the last act in the Mitchell affair had played in 1987. Criminy, she said to herself, that was *six years* ago. And Mary Tene and her brood are still working the elderly? *Where are the police?*

23

Grape Leaves and Couscous

FAY AWOKE AT her usual 5:00 A.M. and waited two hours to call her new friend Graziana. "You won't believe what I found out about Mary's daughter Angela," she said. "No way the cops can ignore this. This case is gonna be wrapped up in two days."

The mellow voice sounded sleepy. "I'll believe it when I'm subpoenaed to testify."

FAY BRIEFED INSPECTOR Greg Ovanessian and handed over a sheaf of photocopies confirming Angela's malignant involvement with the aged. More weeks of silence followed. She was disappointed but didn't want to disturb the detectives while they were making their case.

She continued her daily checks on the Nelson and Hughes homes. Nothing seemed amiss. She got a peek at Mr. Nelson; he looked lively for a nonagenarian. Plainly, he felt at home with his two young friends. For an instant Fay wondered if she'd been looking at the case through the wrong end of the telescope. Could George and Angela be bringing their clients health food?

SHE DECIDED TO supplement her files with a firsthand report on the French Village Deli. When she arrived at lunchtime, a neatly dressed dark-haired woman was dispensing grillades and other *spécialités de la maison* from behind a long counter while exchanging pleasantries with the customers. Could this be the Hami who'd called the police about her evil brother and his Gypsy girlfriend?

The restaurant gleamed. Light mustard-colored walls and a big trompe-l'oeil mirror seemed to double its size. A pair of long-stemmed pink roses accented each table. The specialties were Middle Eastern dishes like hummus and baba ganouj, couscous, grape leaves, baklava, but Fay also noticed cauldrons of home-style soups and thick sandwiches overstuffed with lettuce and tomatoes. There wasn't a sprout or a mung bean in sight. Her mouth watered as she ordered tea and a wedge of tiramisu, described on the menu as "98% fat-free."

Gee, she said to herself, that's a perfect description of *me*—I wish. Sitting at a corner table trying to look inconspicuous, she had to admit that the French Village Deli resembled anything but the command center of a poisoning operation.

When she returned to her office, she learned that a forty-year-old police inspector named Daniel Yawczak had just been assigned to assist the overworked Ovanessian. It looked as though the SFPD was starting to take the case seriously. When Ovanessian introduced her to Yawczak, the new man seemed more interested in her embonpoint than her professional qualifications, but she was accustomed to such attentions and didn't take them personally.

LATER SHE ASKED a police contact about Yawczak's credentials, and he said, "Jesus, Rat Dog, don't you read the papers?" He informed her that Yawczak had a wife and children in the Los Angeles area, where he'd worked as a police officer before coming north. He was the aggressive type of personality who would stare at strangers in the Hall of Justice elevator and ask, "What're *you* looking at?"

At her friend's suggestion, Fay searched Yawczak's name in her computer, making sure to get the *c* before the *z*, and good old dependable Evie the Everex produced a dozen hits from online local newspapers. He'd won a silver medal for shooting a murder suspect in 1990 but was now a defendant in a civil rights lawsuit growing out of the fatal shooting of a suspected purse-snatcher. The legal ramifications would keep him and the SFPD in court for years.

Fay thought, What kind of approach is this to a complex case? A brilliant detective like Ovanessian works full-time on Gypsy cases and can barely keep up. So they shackle him to a cop who's in trouble up to his scalp? She wondered if police administrators were taking the cases seriously. She remembered being warned that cops would do anything to avoid tangling with the Rom. With their scrambled identities and wandering ways, Gypsy criminals were almost impossible to track and convict. Could that be why so many flat feet were dragging at the Hall of Justice?

She called Ovanessian for a progress report. The *jawndare Romano* said the District Attorney's Office had held a meeting to discuss charges but still found the evidence weak.

"Weak?" Fay shrieked. "Against Danny Tene? Angela? Mary Steiner?"

"This isn't the movies, Fay," he reminded her. "Things don't always work out."

"But we've got proof! Criminy, Greg, they've abused old people for *years*. They're working Mr. Nelson and Mr. Hughes right now. I've got videotapes. What more do you need?"

Ovanessian said the filing of charges wasn't his responsibility. He was warm and friendly, as always, but he left her with the feeling that she'd let him down by not producing enough evidence. She fought an urge to yell, *Whose job is that?* but decided not to argue.

IN DESPERATION SHE dived back into her data banks, but found little more on Harry Glover Hughes than his birthdate, June 6, 1899, and some credit information on his $300,000 home near Ocean Beach. A little more data popped up on the other old man, Richard M. Nelson. His nephew Donald lived in suburban Atherton, thirty miles south of town, and owned a prosperous business that made filing cabinets. As Fay dialed the number, she wondered once again why she was taking the time. What could a nephew tell her that she didn't already know?

24

The Nelsons: Fun with Rich and Angie

RICHARD MARK THORWALD Nelson had always been the family favorite. Donald Nelson and his wife Geraldine thought of their uncle as a typical Scandinavian in the slyly whimsical style of the late ventriloquist Edgar Bergen and the pianist Victor Borge. The man they knew as Uncle Dick was never without a quip or a crack, even at ninety-three. He spun stories that went back to the 1906 earthquake, and, unlike most old men, seldom repeated himself. He'd been a storekeeper and a well-paid accountant for Phillips Petroleum, and he was still a sports fanatic, fisherman, world-class conversationalist, and a careful chronicler of his own history. After retirement, he and his brother had hit the open road to accumulate adventures in a battered old travel trailer. Despite a stroke in his seventies, he still enjoyed jumping into relatives' cars and racketing around the countryside. He logged the events of his life on a hand-drawn calendar precisely constructed with ruler and pen: "Cooked chicken." "Dentist again." "To San Jose with Don and Gerry." "Barium enema, GI series." Before going to bed each night, he would draw a perfect X through the square as though to mark another successful day. He was polite to his contemporaries but preferred younger companions. He wore a little brown cap to cover his baldness and dressed in sports jackets and slacks that he'd bought in the fifties. Women took to him instantly. He would enter a restaurant or a department store spewing compliments in every direction: "This lady is the nicest one . . . This one right here is the smartest in the place. . . . She knows how to do her job, you betcha. . . ." He seemed to trust everyone.

Until his stroke, Richard Nelson had hiked almost every day to the beach below the Cliff House and made his way among seaweed-slickened rocks to cast for perch and cod. He didn't eat fish and left his catch dangling in plastic bags from the doorknobs of neighbors, eliciting thanks except from those on extended trips. Wading into the surf with a seven-foot casting rod was beyond his abilities now, but he still walked several miles a day on his cane. He did his own shopping at Safeway, taking a bus and coming home with packages that the clerks wrapped with string to form a handle for his stiffened fingers. He was on several medications and sometimes took a nitroglycerin capsule to relieve a slight angina. To the younger members of the Nelson family he seemed as jaunty as ever, a rare old specimen whose only real handicap was that he did a lot of nodding and smiling but seldom heard a word anyone said.

DONALD AND GERRY Nelson had been only slightly surprised when their Uncle Dick visited them at Thanksgiving 1992 and announced that he was dating. He'd had girlfriends before, some as young as seventy or even sixty-five, so they presumed he'd met another hot item at the senior center. "How old is this one?" Gerry asked.

"Thirty-one," Uncle Dick quipped.

Gerry and Don laughed. The old man was as good at keeping a straight face as Bill Cosby.

"Does she work?" Don asked.

"Huh?"

"Does she work?"

"At Nordstrom," Uncle Dick answered.

The old joker, Gerry thought. He never knows when to stop.

SIX WEEKS LATER the younger Nelsons were visiting their Uncle Dick when Don glanced at a daybook calendar on the kitchen table. The first notation that caught his eye was "Angela lunch," entered in the retired accountant's careful hand almost a year earlier, followed by such entries as "breakfast with Angela," "Angela phoned," "Angela, 3 o'clock, cake, coffee," "Angela brought a cake," "Angela brought breakfast," ". . . lunch," ". . . dinner." In the late-summer entries, Angela became "Angie" and the tempo of the visits increased. The January 4 entry, made just a few days earlier, was "Angie washes woodwork."

Don showed the notations to Gerry, and she was pleased that the spry old man had made a good friend. "It's a nice break for Uncle Dick," she said.

Since the relationship now appeared to be solid, Don wasn't concerned when his uncle confided that he'd lent Angie a little money. "She has a great job at the department store," he explained, "but her old Japanese car keeps breaking down and making her late for work. So I helped her buy something better." The former accountant added, "She'll save money in the long run." It was the sort of favor that good friends did for each other.

JUST BEFORE EASTER 1993, the Nelsons invited Uncle Dick to their annual family brunch on their pleasantly landscaped grounds in Atherton. Over the phone, the old man asked, "Is it okay if I bring my girlfriend?"

"Well, sure, Uncle Dick," Gerry answered. "We'll pick you two up."

"That's okay. Angie'll drive me down."

* * *

AT 11:00 A.M. on Easter Sunday, two dozen friends and members of the Nelsons' extended family were assembled on the front lawn when a blue-white BMW 733i pulled into the head of the driveway. Don walked out to unlock the gate and spotted a smiling Richard Nelson in his perky brown cap seated next to the driver, a dark-haired young woman who looked a little like Elizabeth Taylor through the windshield. She parked the car and ran around to help Uncle Dick climb out with his cane. He announced, "This is my girlfriend Angela."

The woman's pretty face froze into a fixed grin as she followed the old man around the yard to meet the guests. Everyone at the party sensed that something odd was going on. What earthly logic could account for a romance between a man of ninety-three and a young woman of—what had Uncle Dick said? *Thirty-one?* Gerry Nelson took a close look and decided the woman might be even younger.

The male Nelsons were enchanted and querulous. Don said to his youngest son Jeff, "Do you think that's the car he bought her?"

Jeff said, "I don't know *what* the hell to think."

While the partygoers colored Easter eggs, the Nelsons' older son sneaked a peek inside the BMW and reported that the registration tag was made out to "George Lama or Angela Bufford." Don thought, Uncle Dick should be on that paper, not some guy named Lama. I'm sure Dick put up the money. What's he gotten himself into?

In the yard, Angela clung to her elderly boyfriend's arm and seemed to be trying to distance herself from the younger guests. One of the women tried to draw her out about the romance, and she explained, "I had this difficult relationship with my father, and I've always liked older men. Rich and I get along so well, don't we, honey?" He didn't respond, and she raised her voice: *"We have so much fun together, don't we?"* He nodded and smiled.

At the dinner table the woman discreetly fended off polite attempts to pry out personal information. The talk turned to local sports teams—Warriors, Golden Bears, Angels, Giants—and none of the names seemed to register with her. She put the Nelsons in mind of a beautiful black-and-white moth who'd fluttered out of nowhere and into the life of a man with a foot and a half in the grave. Yes, Don Nelson said to himself, that's what's going on. This is about Uncle Dick's money. He must have close to a million. How to explain to a man in his third or fourth childhood that he's being taken for a ride?

Someone asked Angela where she'd gone to school. She mumbled a name and added, "It's in the East."

Foreheads wrinkled around the table, and Gerry Nelson said, "It must be a small school if no one in *this* crowd ever heard of it."

"Oh, yes," Angela replied with an ingratiating smile. "Teeny."

After a while Gerry Nelson summoned the courage to ask her last name. It sounded like "Bew-ford."

Someone asked if she worked. "Oh, yes," she said. "At Nordstrom. In the Stonestown Mall."

The hostess thought she'd never seen so much plastic charm on one face. She behaved like a date who desperately wanted to be accepted by her boyfriend's family. But couldn't she see that everyone was suspicious of her motives? No one could be that imperceptive. She might as well have worn a sandwich board: I AM AFTER THIS OLD FOOL'S MONEY.

"Bufford's an English name," Angela was saying. "Actually my father was English and my mother was, uh—Greek."

The party wandered into the kitchen, and Gerry said, "Uncle Dick, would you prefer mince pie or pumpkin?"

He didn't respond. Angela nudged his thigh and said, "Rich, honey, would you like some pie?"

Uncle Dick gave her a loving look but didn't reply.

Angela said, "He wants mince."

THE NELSONS RECEIVED a thank-you card showing a happy dog and the message: "Had a doggone good time!" A note was written in the careful penmanship of an elementary school student: "Dear Gerry and Don, I would like to take a moment to express my thanks to you and the wonderful gang! I had a great time and enjoyed a delightful luncheon with you! I must add, you have a very handsome family! Thank you very much. Love, Angela."

Both the Nelsons were bemused by the message and wondered why such a brazen manipulator had risked exposure by visiting their house at all. Gerry had a theory.

"When she first met Uncle Dick, she probably thought he was

alone in the world," she told her husband. "Then he brought us into the act, and we were a potential stumbling block. So she says to herself, I'll go down there and charm the Nelsons to pieces. I'll get them on my side!"

"She must think we're a bunch of morons," Don said.

HE WORRIED ABOUT the situation and finally called the SFPD Vice Squad. After he described the problem, a male officer said, "Well, ya know, it sounds like you got a gold digger."

"Well, yes."

"Unfortunately, sir, there's no law against gold digging. As long as he's mentally competent, your uncle can do whatever he wants with his money."

Gerry and Don wondered if the police kiss-off was a dead end. Could adventurers con folks out of their money and never be held accountable? It didn't make sense. There had to be a law.

On the other hand, the Nelson family had always run on a mutual respect, especially for the elders, and they didn't want to step on their uncle's pride and prerogatives. "He may be ninety-four," Don said, "but hey, if this is what he wants to do with his money—"

"It's so upsetting," Gerry said. "I'd hate to do anything to hurt his feelings."

THEY HIRED A private investigator, Jim Smith of Half Moon Bay, just over the dry brown hills to the west. The PI asked them for the license number of the Bufford woman's BMW, and they kicked themselves for not making a note when the car was parked in their driveway.

They worked up a plan and enlisted the assistance of their son Jeff. He phoned Angela at Nordstrom and told her, "I saw you driving the other day. I honked and waved."

"Are you sure it was me?" she asked.

"It sure looked like you. What's your license number?"

"I, uh—I never remember things like that."

That evening Donald Nelson made the half-hour drive to his uncle's house, spotted the blue BMW outside and jotted down the license number: 2XXN906. He wondered if the girlfriend had finally moved in.

* * *

WHILE THE PRIVATE detective was researching Angela's background, Don tried to squeeze more information from his uncle over the phone.

"Say, where'd you meet this Angela?" he asked.

"At the Safeway," the old man answered. "I was in line at the checkstand and this nice-looking lady says, Could you use a ride? Well, you know me, Don."

"You'll go with *anybody*."

"I made a joke about who was gonna eat all the bread she was buying, and she said it was for the French Market Deli. We were laughing about it. In the parking lot, I says, Lemme tell ya where I live. She says, I *know* where you live."

"Uncle Dick, didn't you think that was a little odd?"

"Didn't I think—*what?*"

Don raised his voice. "Didn't you think it was odd that she knew your address?"

"Well, I wondered a little. But she was so *cute!* I thought, Well, I'm not gonna worry about the details. Folks tell ya to watch out for strangers. Well, if I didn't talk to strangers, I wouldn't have Angela today."

"A real pal, huh?"

"Great gal! Stops in every morning before she goes to work. Fixes my breakfast, makes the bed, drives me to the stores. Little things. I don't know what I'd do without her."

The old man paused and lowered his voice conspiratorially. "Did I tell you what she did after I fell?"

Don recalled that his uncle had slipped while going outside for the newspaper. "I didn't know Angela was involved in your accident," he said. *Had the old man been pushed?*

"She said, Rich, I just can't leave you alone after a hard fall like that. At first I thought she meant she would sleep on the sofa. But she put on a pair of my pajamas and climbed into my bed. She said, Rich, I'm here for you. She rubbed my back till I went to sleep. She still sleeps over now and then."

Don asked if he'd ever visited her own home. "No," his uncle replied. "She pays five hundred a month for a dumpy little cottage behind a house on Fourteenth Avenue. Highway robbery! She's ashamed and she doesn't want me to see it. I keep telling her, I've got all this room in my house. Why don't you just move in? She's thinking it over."

INVESTIGATOR JIM SMITH'S report confirmed the Nelsons' suspicions. The hardworking PI unearthed Angela's fortuitous marriage to old Nicholas Bufford and the odd way she'd changed from granddaughter to wife before inheriting his estate. The timing of the death was so suspicious that the district attorney had ordered an autopsy and toxicological report, and the medical examiner had found trace amounts of mercury and lead. Cause of death was listed as "metabolic acidosis due to uremia," compounded by "arteriosclerotic heart disease." No prosecutions ensued.

The sleuth from Half Moon Bay also established that Angela hadn't been truthful about the "dumpy little cottage" and her burdensome monthly rent. She lived in the comfortable duplex house that she'd inherited from her elderly husband and now shared with a boyfriend named George Lama and his family, owners of the French Village Deli. Angela had also lied about the existence of her English father and Greek mother, as well as her attendance at a private Eastern school. She'd quit school in the eighth grade. The few available documents listed her father as John Ciampa of Italy, and her mother as Ann Lina, Mary Tene and other names.

Investigator Smith told the Nelsons that he had run some of the names past a friend on the San Francisco PD's Vice Squad and learned that two Fraud Unit inspectors were working the case.

AFTER DIGESTING THE private eye's report, Gerry and Don Nelson realized why Angela was taking her time about moving in with their uncle. "It would cramp her style," Don deduced. "She doesn't want to sleep every night with an old guy when she can sleep at home with her boyfriend. She doesn't have to live with Uncle Dick to get her hands on his money. She can achieve her goals by other means."

RICHARD NELSON'S WATERY Swedish eyes opened wide when his nephew sat him down in his living room in San Francisco and insisted on spelling out everything he'd learned. Don kept his voice elevated so his uncle could hear, but the old man made no comment except to say

"Really?" a few times. At the end, he said, "Well, I'm sure there's an explanation. I'll just run this by Angela."

Nelson feared that his uncle was set against the truth. He realized that part of the problem was the comfort his old body must be deriving from his first physical contact with a young female in decades. He was living every lonely old man's dream. Another part of the problem was that no one in the Nelson family had encountered anyone like Angela Bufford or could comprehend such deception.

Before he left, the well-meaning nephew sprang a final surprise: the revelation that Angela's 1988 BMW 733i was co-owned by her boyfriend and not by Uncle Dick.

"That's not true!" the old man said with surprising force. "I have the pink slip."

He rummaged through his desk and came up with a large envelope that he'd sealed and stapled across the flap. "That way I can tell if anybody's gotten into it," he explained. Don thought, How did such a careful person ever get involved with a female con artist?

Uncle Dick removed a slip of pink paper. It was marked "title certificate" and affirmed that the luxury car was registered to "Angela Bufford or Richard M. Nelson." Don took a closer look. The fakery wouldn't have fooled anyone but a lovesick old man. A gray line showed where correcting tape had been placed atop another name and "Richard Nelson" typed in. Then the faked document had been photocopied on pink paper.

Uncle Dick was so convinced of his pink slip's legitimacy that he insisted on keeping it for his files even after Don showed him the telltale signs of fraud. "Don, I'm the legal co-owner of that damned car!" he said angrily. "This paper proves it. Angela would *never* lie about something like that."

The frustrated nephew placed a carefully prepared list of Angela's lies and misrepresentations on the table. "I'll leave this with you, Uncle Dick. Please, I want you to look at it. I want you to understand what's being done to you." He reached in his folder and added Angela's marriage certificate and a copy of the joint tenancy agreement in which she was described as her husband-to-be's granddaughter.

"Please," Don Nelson implored his uncle as he was going out the door, "I want you to stop believing what that woman tells you."

The old man didn't seem to hear.

* * *

LATE THAT NIGHT, Nelson drove by his uncle's house before turning south toward Atherton and home. Angela's blue BMW was parked in front. The house was dark.

25

The Law's Delays

IN MID-MAY 1993, Fay Faron heard from a disconsolate Barry Hughes that he had only one more day to search for Mrs. Beesley's hidden safe. He'd been locked out of the house by Danny Tene but was legally entitled to make a final sweep as executor of the estate.

"It's an exercise in bloody futility," the Englishman said. "That damned Danny, he shadows me. If I find anything I'm sure he'll grab it and run."

Fay called Greg Ovanessian and left a message. Lately he'd been the busiest detective in the Fraud Unit, catching cases that went far outside his responsibilities as a *jawndare Romano*. She wondered if the heavy booking was intended to keep him off the Tene case. She told herself to stop being paranoid. Everything in life wasn't a conspiracy.

Ovanessian returned her call an hour later and told her that the case was on hold because the prosecutor was still demanding more evidence. To Fay, the Gypsy cop sounded defensive.

She described Barry Hughes' dilemma and wondered aloud if there was some way that Danny Tene could be spirited from his house long enough for the executor to make a proper search. "Greg," she said in the helpless voice she sometimes used on recalcitrant males, "could one of you guys just . . . occupy his attention?"

"Funny."

"Just an idea."

He said it was a bad one.

* * *

FIVE MINUTES LATER she had another brainstorm. "What if he's wanted?" she said over the phone. "Maybe . . . an old warrant?"

"He's clean," Ovanessian said.

"Suspicion of elder abuse? Fraud? Murder?"

Her friend hesitated and said wearily, "I'll run him one more time."

A few minutes later he called to inform her that Danny Tene was wanted for driving on a suspended license under his alias Sal Lamance. Bond was $150. Technically, he could be arrested and held at the nearest police station until the bond was paid.

"Oh, Greg," Fay asked. "Could you arrange it?"

She took his sigh for a yes.

AT 10:07 THE next morning, May 21, 1993, Fay watched as Danny Tene alias Sal Lamance was placed under arrest. It's a start, she told herself ecstatically. She'd last seen the hefty young Gypsy a few months earlier in front of the Liotweizen apartment building on Funston. It looked as though he'd spent every penny of Mrs. Beesley's estate at Original Joe's restaurant, a popular Rom hangout. The top buttons of his white shirt were undone, revealing a V-shaped wedge of skin. She wondered if he thought male décolletage was sexy. His back looked broad enough for simultaneous games of backgammon.

The big man was unctuously correct toward the officers and immediately called for a lawyer on his cordless phone. Fay had to admire his unflappability. She knew that members of the criminal Gypsy element were accustomed to being hassled and hardly ever served jail time. When they were arrested, local fixers dropped from the sky and posted bail.

As Tene was being led away, Barry Hughes and an electronics expert arrived with a portable metal detector. "You'll be sorry you did this," Danny grumbled.

"I'm just carrying out my duties as executor," Hughes said. The Englishman was dressed for his treasure hunt in a white T-shirt, sweatpants and tennis shoes.

A plainclothes officer led the handcuffed man to a patrol car. "I can't handle it," Tene said after a few attempts to squeeze inside. "I'm too big. Why don't you call the wagon?"

He was shoehorned into the back of a policeman's private sedan and driven off. At the station he gave his name as Dan Tene but said that he'd also used Dan Steiner and Sal Lamance and other names because schoolmates had made his life miserable by laughing at his legal name: Dan Tene Bimbo. He sat patiently, waiting to be bailed out on the minor traffic charge.

INSIDE THE FORMER home of Hope Victoria Beesley, Barry Hughes and his expert dragged the scintillometer from room to room, but all they heard was meaningless squeaks and squawks. "I knew there'd be nothing before we got here," the Englishman complained as he puffed on a cigarette. "The bloody bostids had four months to clean the place out."

At last the electronics technician said, "If there's a hidden safe, I can't find it. For sure it's not made of metal."

Danny Tene walked in as they walked out.

26

Foot-Dragging

AFTER THREE MORE months without arrests or charges, Fay checked her calendar and saw that she'd been on the case for almost a year. So far her total billings had been under $2,000, promptly paid by the reliable Ken Chan, but most of the time she'd been cliffwalking with neither fee nor client. It didn't matter. She had no desire to live in a city where old men were treated like cockroaches.

Every week or two she and an assistant made spot checks at the Hughes and Nelson homes with a videocamera. Twice they filmed George and Angela delivering takeout food to their clients. Fay wondered why the scam was stretching out over such a long period. If Mr. Nelson and Mr. Hughes are being murdered for their money, she said to herself, these people must be using the slowest-acting poison in history. She suspected that Angela had improved her techniques since the suspicious death of her first husband. Fay's flesh still crawled when she thought about Nicholas Bufford's final days. "Angela didn't call the paramedics till old Nicholas was more dead than alive," one of the investigators had told her. "He was rotting in his bed. She made absolutely sure he was gonna die before she called for help." Two neighbors told Fay that Bufford was so emaciated toward the end that they hardly recognized him. No wonder there'd been official suspicion.

Fay wondered if Angela might have found an undetectable poison that took months to work its subtle way through the body. The Gypsy woman seemed to have great patience, uncharacteristic of sweetheart scammers and other predatory opportunists. She didn't seem to have an ounce of empathy, which made her doubly dangerous.

IN SEPTEMBER, DEEP into the case, Fay came to the realization that it would take a boxcar full of physical evidence to convince the DA's Office to bring charges. She'd amassed a thick file of circumstantial evidence, but apparently the timid prosecutors needed something they could hold in their hands and—eventually—show to a jury. It seemed to her that they were demanding a stratospheric level of evidence from detectives who were already swamped and didn't seem interested in the first place.

She felt a little better about Greg Ovanessian and his partner Dan Yawczak when a mutual friend insisted that they were making progress but keeping it to themselves. Fay understood the need for secrecy. Good investigators tended to be close-mouthed, with the obvious exception of herself. Greg and his partner were probably itching to seek arrest warrants. If there was deliberate foot-dragging, it must be by higher-ups in the system. But who? And . . . why?

SHE TRIED TO think of a way to turn up solid physical evidence and thought of trash raids. She'd conducted a few in the past; it wasn't her favorite technique, lurching out of bed at four A.M. to don rainclothes and Wellingtons and sally forth to paw through trash and garbage. But the results could be astonishing. Folks put *everything* in their trash cans. It was as though they expected the stuff to sink straight to the bottom of a sanitary landfill and never be seen again.

Of course, the collection procedure could be dangerous. To Fay, the secret was in careful planning. The best time for a sortie was an hour before sunrise, after the city's muggers went off-duty but before trashmen began their rounds. The trick was to park quietly, yank the lid off the can, pull out the plastic bag, replace the lid and drive away without disturbing the suspects, the neighbors, their dogs or budgies.

She decided that the primary target would have to be Angela Buford's house on Fourteenth Avenue, a dangerous area for a snoopy private eye. From her research, Fay knew that unscrupulous fortune-tellers sometimes did their own garbage snooping to pick up inside information on potential suckers ("Let me see your palm. Yes! You are behind on your payments to the Bank of America!"). The Tene Bimbos were descended from a long line of fortune-tellers; Angela might be on the alert. Fay had also heard that Angela's paramour, George Lama, despite his nerdish exterior and clerkish job at Budget Rent-a-Car, was known to maintain a small armory in his garage and had threatened to put it to use. She pulled up an old rap sheet and found only one arrest, for solicitation of prostitution in 1985. After twenty hours of community service at the Retired Senior Volunteers, the charge was dropped and expunged. Fay found it an interesting choice of punishment for a man who now seemed to know his way around old people and their bank accounts.

She decided to refresh her trash inspecting techniques with a low-key raid at the home of Harry Glover Hughes on Twenty-third Avenue. If he caught her in the act, she could surely outrun a nonagenarian. She checked with the Sunset District collectors to learn their schedules, and at 4:30 A.M. on a Tuesday in late October she stuffed Beans into the backseat for the twenty-minute drive. Her little hatchback was ill-suited for the operation. We're supposed to blend in with the background, she said to herself, but the only thing the Frog Prince can blend into is a rain forest. Well, it was the Rat Dog Dick Agency's entire motor pool. She couldn't afford a rental car, and she certainly didn't intend to ask any of her police friends for wheels. As squeamish as the cops seemed lately, they might throw her in jail. Not that trash raids were illegal. Under the law, the contents of cans at curbside were no longer private. She'd read court rulings on the subject.

As she approached the Hughes neighborhood, she was disturbed to find a lack of fog in the Fog Belt. She parked three blocks away, pulled on canary-colored rubber gloves, and released the latch on her trunk so she could lift it quietly at the scene. Beans awoke on the backseat and she squeezed his jaws shut, an old technique that sometimes kept him quiet. Then she eased the Frog Prince away from the curb, inched toward the Hughes house, made a squeaky U-turn and stopped in front.

She'd barely stepped out when her car alarm went off. Rats! she said to herself. I meant to get that fixed. She careened around the corner of Twenty-third and Ulloa on her baldy tires. She felt foolish and took a therapeutic break on Geary Boulevard to slow her heartbeat. She looked back at Beans. He was asleep. The excitement had been too much for him.

She waited another fifteen minutes, disconnected the faulty alarm, and returned to the house on Twenty-third. No trash cans were in sight.

27

The Collector

A WEEK LATER, Fay returned to the Hughes house. Once again there wasn't a wisp of fog. Or trash. She was looking around the front of the house for the missing can when Beans let out a howl at another dog. He'd been neutered, but he maintained an interest in the occasional crotch.

Fay decided that the Hughes place was jinxed and headed for Richard Nelson's house on Forty-sixth Avenue. Driving through the Oriental enclave that had grown up in the Sunset, she opened her cracked window for a sniff of instant Asia: dried cuttlefish, bok choy, fried rice, soy. She'd always enjoyed the neighborhood's whirligig of people, cars, shops, action. All the scene needed was a ropy-legged pedicab jockey sucking on a cigarette and she'd have thought she was back on the Chung-Nan North Road in Taipei. Long ago, she'd realized that San Francisco was the perfect habitat for a compulsive traveler, "a golden handcuff with the key thrown away," as John Steinbeck had put it. Every country was present, every climate, every costume, every taste in food and drink. Six or eight times a year, by choice or necessity, she left the place that locals called "the City," but she was always happy to return to the "streets that end in stars," as another writer had described it a long time ago. Of course, he hadn't meant the Sunset.

THE RETIRED SURF fisherman and raconteur Richard Nelson lived in a neat house with green trim, so close to the ocean that Fay imagined she heard the hum of the surf. A gleaming metal can stood at curbside. She double-parked, yanked out the plastic inner bag, and was away in seconds.

She covered her kitchen table with newspapers and spread the contents. A fruit fly flew up her nose and a dark speck ascended her arm before she squashed it into a hairy comma. She thought about spraying with insecticide, but she was afraid of contaminating the evidence.

She used two fingertips to lift a grapefruit rind filled with the soggy gray remnants of a casserole. This creation, she said to herself, did *not* come from Wolfgang Puck. She wondered: Is this goop important? Is it . . . poisonous? She forked out a cube of mystery meat, dropped it into a Ziploc bag, and slid it into her fridge. She was pleased with herself. The guys in the crime lab would award her their Good Citizen medal. Even the phlegmatic DA's Office would be thrilled. You wanted physical evidence? *Hey, guys, how's this for physical?* She couldn't wait to see their expressions.

THE NEXT MORNING she pressed her luck with an impromptu collection at Angela's house on Fourteenth Avenue. With Beans sitting guard on the chewed-up backseat of the Frog Prince, the operation went off like the Brinks' robbery. At home she sifted through eggshells, potato peelings and pizza rinds and at last came to something in writing: a moist note signed "Angie."

> Honey meet me at 6 and we'll go look at the Rolls.
> Eduardo is expecting us.

Fay perused the ads in the *San Francisco Chronicle* to learn who sold Rolls-Royces, an item she'd never shopped for. In the evening she dialed several salesrooms but found no Eduardo. She wondered if "Angie" had been referring to dinner rolls and not the luxury car.

The next day she bumped into Ovanessian's partner Dan Yawczak and described her frustrations. Once again he seemed more impressed by her figure than her enterprise. She took the opportunity to ask what was new in the case. Yawczak said he was keeping busy but offered no specifics.

Criminy, she said to herself after the brief conversation was over, am I being nosy? Why the heck am I going to so much trouble? She discarded her thoughts as unworthy. Police inspectors weren't obliged to account for their activities to a PI or any other private citizen. Of course, they collected steady salaries and she collected watermelon rinds, but did it matter? In her mind she still saw old Konstantin Liotweizen, lying in his own excrement. More than once she'd sat upright in bed and thought: *That could be my dad, my mom!* It was all the motivation she needed.

28

Who's Papa?

BY MID-OCTOBER, she was making regular dawn patrols to the homes of the old men and their predators. Harry Glover Hughes seemed to live without discarding food containers or garbage. Fay decided that he must be one of those composting geniuses who know how to transform beer cans and pop bottles into rich brown loam. But her visits to the other two houses kept her running to police headquarters with treasures like the billet-doux she found scrawled on a shred of notebook paper in Richard Nelson's trash:

> Good morning Honey! I was here from 8:30 to 9:00. You were asleep so I did not want to wake you. They called me to work today. Breakfast is in the oven!! Hope you like it. Love and kisses. Angie.

Fay wasn't surprised to find some of Mr. Nelson's personal mail in the trash can in front of Angela's house, as well as a note on a small square of orange paper bearing the legend BUDGET CAR AND TRUCK RENTAL. George Lama's handwriting proved neater than his girlfriend's:

Love, 9:30 a.m. I'm leaving to Hilda for espresso, then to Papa. He forgot the union meeting. But I'll make sure he goes.

Fay wondered who "Papa" was. She presumed it referred to Mr. Nelson or Mr. Hughes. But a retired accountant like Mr. Nelson wouldn't belong to a union. And Mr. Hughes had worked for the state as a highway engineer and saved his money for fifty years. What "union meeting" would such well-fixed old men attend?

Fay wondered whether the bubble-cheeked Angela and her lover were working Mr. Hughes, Mr. Nelson and *other* old men. Behind their clerkish day jobs, were they widening their net? How many victims had they targeted, and how on earth could she learn their names and protect their money—and maybe their lives?

ON A NOVEMBER trash run to the Fourteenth Avenue lair, she spotted a white Mercedes convertible in the driveway and ran license number 2KKR420 through her data banks. Evie the Everex groaned and hummed and produced the information that "George Antone Lama" and "Harry Glover Hughes" were now joint owners of a 1983 Mercedes roadster valued at $20,000. Other sources revealed that the two friends shared three bank accounts.

Ovanessian and Yawczak seemed impressed by her latest findings and promised to add the information to their evidence files, but once again they emphasized that Fay was on her own if she was caught with her hands in the garbage. She thought, How gracious! I'm making their case and they won't even back me up? She suspected that the chilly attitude might be related to Yawczak's legal problems. He certainly didn't need to borrow more trouble.

THE FRAUD INSPECTORS' interest seemed to perk up when she arrived the next week with more specimens from Angela's trash. On a torn white piece of notebook paper she'd found a financial inventory, including bank accounts, stocks and bonds and contents of safe deposit boxes. A scribbled note was appended:

Get $ in credit union both A&G. Look for S/D box gold coins at Citibank. First Commercial, West Portal: $50,127.84.

Another slip of paper bore a notation in an upper corner: "From old Papa." A message read:

Unit New England Life Ins Co Boston Mass 02116-3900
Policy #0463316
Check on gift taxes. Book says gift taxes are subject to monie taxes if kept within $10,000.

A set of soggy bank documents showed that Angela Bufford and Richard Nelson had opened a joint savings account from which the former could make withdrawals but the latter could not. The authorization form for this peculiar banking procedure was signed and initialed by Angela alone. The bank had been instructed to mail statements to her address on Fourteenth Avenue, and the couple's cash-machine code had been changed so that only Angela could make withdrawals.

Greg Ovanessian shook his head when Fay showed him her latest finds. "They're draining these old men dry," he said. He seemed solicitous and grave. She took it as good sign.

WHEN SHE ARRIVED home, the red light was blinking on her answering machine. A woman who identified herself as Nicole had left her home phone number. Fay remembered the name. A month or so earlier, an anonymous caller had tipped police that a certain Nicole Lama knew the details of a poisoning scheme at the French Village Deli. Nicole was believed to be the sister of the Hami who had provided information earlier. But when Nicole Lama was approached by police, she'd proved reluctant.

Instinct told Fay to return Nicole's call instantly, but she hesitated. She knew that several different Lamas lived with Angela in the old Bufford house on Fourteenth. What if an unfriendly one answered the phone?

She called the Fraud Unit and told Yawczak about the message. "Why do you suppose Nicole wants to talk to *me?*" Fay asked.

Yawczak told her he would handle the matter himself.

29

Pills in the Drawer

THE NEXT TIME Fay saw her favorite *jawndare Romano*, she asked, "Have you guys been talking to Nicole Lama?"

Ovanessian looked surprised and said, "Talking to *her?* Rat Dog, we've been talking to the whole damned Lama family."

Fay asked what he meant by the whole damned family. He said there were two brothers, six sisters and their mother, and he'd interviewed several. She asked what they'd been telling him.

"You don't have time to hear it all," he said.

"I'll make time."

THEY MET AT Liverpool Lil's, a restaurant and bar near the Presidio and a gathering place for the dark-suits-and-handcuffs set from the FBI, CIA, Secret Service and SFPD. Fay was happy to live in a city with 3,300 eating places and selected her favorites carefully. She and her friends enjoyed sipping wine in Lil's and listening to the shoot-'em-up lunchtime chatter. Where else could she pick up such scintillatingly *reliable* information about famous cases: Patty Hearst, the Trailside Killer, the Unabomber, the Hillside Stranglers, Zodiac? The lawmen and ex-lawmen went by nicknames like Mahoot, Big Guy, Magnum, Dan the Man, Scrap Iron, Boombuster. A G-man nicknamed Knucklehead was now being called Knucks for short. "What a cool guy," Fay had commented to her insider group of girlfriends. "His nickname has a nickname!" They dubbed the most fetching member of the group Parade Date because he was the only one they would want next to them on a float. Fay liked nothing more than hanging out at Liverpool Lil's, especially if she was accompanied by a cop.

Over the house salad with its "secret" vinaigrette dressing, Fay listened as Greg Ovanessian dispelled much of her doubt and confusion. He told her that he'd heard from another Lama sibling, this one a New

Yorker named Jerry, and he'd sounded angry enough to tear his brother George into little pieces. It seemed that George's affair with the Gypsy Angela was destroying the tight-knit Arab-American family. "Jerry's an excitable guy," Ovanessian told Fay. "He told me not to be surprised if somebody ended up dead."

The fraud inspector quoted the brother as saying that George and Angela had found out about the Lama sisters' tips to police and installed eavesdropping devices under the duplex house on Fourteenth Avenue. When Jerry flew west from his home on Long Island to rip out the bugs, his equally enraged brother swore blood revenge and bought a rifle and handgun at a gun shop and a silencer from a bar owner in North Beach.

Jerry had told Ovanessian that his sisters knew the details of the poisoning scheme from information they'd gleaned through the walls of the family duplex, augmented by some careless remarks in the open. Apparently the conspirators had discovered a heart stimulant that worked slowly and was difficult to trace, especially in the dead. It appeared that Angela and her mother Mary had fled to San Francisco from Boston after a series of gold-digging operations, and that the mother had developed a fresh roster of elderly "clients" at a Russian Orthodox church on Geary Boulevard. Instead of patiently waiting for their victims to die, George and Angela were trying to speed up the process.

As the lunchtime crowd thinned and Fay tucked into her order of raspberry cheesecake *avec Chantilly*—she would bike twice her usual distance in the morning—she asked Ovanessian, "What's the poison?"

"I wish I knew," he said. He told her that Dr. Boyd Stephens, the city's renowned chief medical examiner, had advised him that certain heart medications might not show up in typical postmortem examinations. The commonly used digitalis, for example, would probably go undetected unless toxicologists performed specific tests.

"What about Nicole Lama?" Fay asked. "Did she ever decide to cooperate?"

Ovanessian said that they'd talked on tape, and she was helpful. It appeared that the Lama sister had watched her brother George change from a law-abiding citizen into a hardened hustler in his half-dozen years as Angela's consort. Nicole told the fraud inspectors that she'd been friendly with Angela herself and knew the details of her relationship with old Nicholas Bufford. Angela had been nineteen when she met the

Russian-speaking man at a McDonald's restaurant and drew a bead on his heart and bankroll. Among other devices, she aged herself by wearing long black dresses and little makeup. Soon they were married, and a few weeks later Angela found $50,000 in a shoe box in her elderly husband's closet. She used the money to buy a black Pontiac Trans Am. After her husband's death, she inherited the house on Fourteenth Avenue and sold it to the Lamas. Honoring the Gypsy tradition that all income must flow through the paterfamilias, Angela had handed $100,000 of her inheritance to her natural father, the former fighter known as Chuchi.

Nicole Lama had also told detectives about an early poisoning attempt that fizzled. She didn't know the name of the drug, but George had acquired it from an Asian-American pharmacist, providing free meals in return. George stashed the toxins in an unlabeled brown bottle in a drawer at the family deli. Nicole said she'd watched both George and Angela grind up the little round pills and sprinkle them on take-out items.

"For Mr. Nelson and Mr. Hughes!" Fay said. It was exciting to see the puzzle pieces locking together.

"No," Ovanessian corrected her. "Hughes and Nelson came later." He said that the couple's first target had been a retired longshoreman named Steven. The old man had lived in an apartment above the French Village Deli.

Fay asked Ovanessian how he intended to use the revelations from Nicole and Jerry Lama, and the Gypsy cop said the subject was under discussion with the DA's Office. There were still problems. The conversations were revealing, but most of the information was hearsay, inadmissible in court. Ovanessian emphasized that gold digging wasn't a crime, an observation that Fay had heard before. If there was no victim, he added, there was no crime—another useful rationalization for dropping cases—and the old men were having too much fun to bring charges. In addition to those problems, the Fraud Unit had *workable* investigations in its files, cases that could be solved and prosecuted and that didn't involve a movable feast of Gypsies on roller skates. He left Fay with the clear impression that the Fraud Unit's attention was elsewhere.

DRIVING HOME IN the Frog Prince, she snarled at her windshield: "If you guys need more evidence, why don't you go out and get it? You're the cops! Are you telling me that if the proof doesn't fall in your laps, you don't want it? If the evidence fairy doesn't provide, you give up?" Beans put a paw over his head.

As far as Fay could tell, Mr. Nelson and Mr. Hughes hadn't even been warned by police that they were being poisoned. After she'd provided voluminous reports on her early discussions with Graziana Gandolfi and Dimitri Egoroff, those two crucial witnesses had finally been interviewed, but when Fay inquired about why the Fraud Unit seemed to be steering clear of the endangered old men, Yawczak had snapped, "We can't just bust in on 'em, Rat Dog. You ever heard of civil rights?"

Yes, she thought as she drove toward her Marina apartment, I've heard of civil rights, but isn't there a civil right to be protected from con artists? From killers? *Human lives are at stake here!* She tried to count the months that had passed since she'd presented the Beesley information to the Fraud Unit. Seven? *Eight?* Now there were two more cases involving the same Gypsy family and the cops were still frozen in place. She had a degree of sympathy for Yawczak; he was preoccupied with personal problems and involved in a federal lawsuit that could cost the city millions. But what was stopping Ovanessian? Wasn't Gypsy crime his specialty? She'd never met a more likable cop. He could schmooze in three or four languages with intelligence and wit. She liked his Danny Thomas nose and charm. The most common remark about Ovanessian was that everybody loved him. Fay wondered if that was the problem. Did this case really need a Mr. Cordiality? How about someone with a rotten temper? An overdeveloped sense of outrage? How about someone who would lose sleep if one helpless old man was in danger? How about . . . Rat Dog Dick?

She sighed at her own brassiness. On the other hand, she said to herself, who else is working the case?

Okay, she decided, I'll go to the old men and tell them what's happening.

Then she thought, What a stupid idea. You're a glorified skip tracer, not a police detective. You could blow the whole case. Angela and George don't even know they're under surveillance. But . . . are they? *By whom?* Certainly not by the Fraud Unit. She couldn't escape a dismal conclusion: I might screw up the case, but *how can it be screwed up any worse than it already is?*

30

Showdown

SHE WAS IN the middle of an intense 3-D dream when the ultimate solution to the problem scrolled across her brain like cerebral e-mail. She'd benefited from these midnight epiphanies before and wished she understood the process. She lay awake for a few minutes, mulling over her idea. It was simple enough and required only a little gall, exactly the amount she possessed.

Fay Faron, "registered social worker," would pay a call on Mr. Nelson and Mr. Hughes with a routine health-status questionnaire, wangle an invitation to step inside, then skillfully open the subject of Angela and George. Sooner or later she would drop discreet warnings of their peril and maybe pick up a little hard evidence at the same time.

Just before dawn she said, "Sleep, Beans! It's not morning yet." She tiptoed into her dining room/office and switched on Evie the Everex. Across the top of her monitor she typed, "Richmond Sunset Senior Services." In less than an hour she was printing out her list of thirty "official" questions. She decided to ask her intrepid friend Debra Russo to join the operation as cinematographer. If anything developed, there would be filmed proof that she'd gone to the correct addresses and talked to the right old men.

AT 10:00 A.M., Fay phoned the Nordstrom store at the Stonestown mall and said, "Is Angela Bufford working?"

"Yes, she is."

Fay hung up. Now that she'd pinned down Angela, she had to locate George Lama. It would never do to arrive at the Nelson home at the same time as a takeout delivery of tainted food. En route toward Ocean Beach she took a short detour to Fourteenth Avenue. George's white Mercedes was parked in the driveway of 2367. The bad guys were accounted for; it was time to make her move.

* * *

WHILE DEBRA RUSSO aimed a videocamera through the windshield of the Frog Prince, Fay pushed the "record" button on the cheap microcassette recorder in her purse and climbed the front steps of Richard Nelson's home on Forty-sixth Avenue. After months of illicit trash-collecting, she was only slightly nervous. If the old man acted hinky, she could always leave. Canvassers were an everyday nuisance in the neighborhood.

She knocked. Three staggered glass rectangles seemed to frown from the front door. She imagined a mean old man peeping through one-way glass and cocking his trusty elephant gun with the three-inch slug. As the door began to open, she called out in her cheeriest voice, "Hi! Is Mr. Nelson here?"

"He is," a female voice replied.

Fay thought, No, no, no, *no*! She's at work! She can't be here! *I don't have a plan for this!*

"He *is?*" she said, talking and gulping at the same time. "Uh, may I speak to him a minute?"

"Sure," Angela said. She opened the door wide and smiled. A ray of sun glinted off perfect teeth. Her eyes were dark blue or blue-green, her skin flawless. With a few splashes of peroxide, she could have passed for Barbie. She wore ankle socks and a loose top over a neat skirt and looked as though she'd just finished a springtime cover shoot for *Seventeen*.

Barbie asked, "May I tell him who's here?"

Fay flashed back twenty years to an incident in Thailand. The image in her camera lens had turned angry as a Hill Tribe warrior charged her with a bamboo spear till the desperate photographer bellowed *"No!"* She wondered if the technique would work in the United States. I'm not this brave, she told herself. This sweet young thing is dangerous.

"My name is Fay," she said in a tremulous voice, and thought, Darn! Why did I give my real name? Stay cool, Rat Dog. Act like a professional. Take a deep breath. *Calm down!*

Angela said, "Fay? From . . . ?" She had a girlish voice and seemed pleased at the interruption. But what was she holding behind her back?

Fay said, "Uh—Fay from . . ." She thought of the introductory speech she'd prepared for Mr. Nelson and began reciting in a monotone as though reading for a kindergarten play: "I'm from the Richmond/

Sunset Senior Services and I'm just here to see if everything's okay with him." She backed down a step to emphasize her harmlessness. "If there's any problem. I guess you're, uh—you're taking care of him?"

"Yes, I am." The voice sounded a little less friendly. Did the woman suspect something?

Fay said, "Oh, uh—okay." She hoped the girlish tremor in her voice was going unnoticed. "He's fine then, I guess, huh?"

"Yes, he's fine," Angela answered. Fay marveled at her coolness. She was acting like the lady of the house. "Have you ever met him before?"

"No, I haven't," Fay said. "We're just, uh, doing a survey in the neighborhood." She held out her clipboard and pencil. "And we're, um, uh, going around to some of the seniors and seeing if they, uh, have everything that they need and, uh—allthatkindastuff."

Angela said, "Could you, or can you, or *would* you have any authority of speaking to the *Examiner* people?"

"*Examiner* people?"

The Gypsy lowered her voice and said, "He used to have a paperboy who would throw the paper right up into—"

Fay swallowed hard and said, "Yeah?"

"And Mr. Nelson is handicapped."

"Yeah?" *I just want to get away from here. I am not Kate Milhone or Kay Scarpello or whatever the heck their names are.*

"And the other day he threw it all the way down there"—Angela pointed to the sidewalk—"and he fell."

"Oh, my goodness!" Fay said aloud. *He wasn't pushed?*

The woman lowered her voice; apparently she didn't want her elderly friend to overhear. "I called them already," she said.

"Oh, you *did?* Okay, great."

Fay backed down another step, but the affable Gypsy didn't seem interested in shutting up. "And I asked them to throw it as close as possible so he doesn't have to go down the stairs. Otherwise . . ."

Fay's loud heartbeat made her miss the rest of the sentence. "All right, g-g-g-great," she stammered. "Well, then, thank you very much. Uh—what's your name?"

"My name's Angela."

"Okay," Fay called out as she hurried away. "Thank you. Nice to meet you."

* * *

SHE WAS STILL shaking as she whipped the Frog Prince around the corner to Rivera Street and sped toward her office as though pursued by King George Tene Bimbo himself. She babbled, "That woman! She looks like a dark Loni Anderson! Those same round cheeks. *Good* bones. Same, uh—*you* know—figure. She's the *last* person you'd suspect—"

Debra said, "Who were you expecting? Cruella DeVil?"

"I was expecting a sick old man," Fay explained. "Did you remember what button to push?"

Her staff cinematographer said she'd filmed every harrowing moment.

31

Drugs to the Holy Land

AFTER FAY BRIEFED Inspector Gregory Ovanessian about her latest adventure, she learned that Nicole Lama had phoned the Fraud Unit to report finding two of Angela's wigs in the Lama family garage. Nicole said that George had been sending flowers to old Harry Glover Hughes and she suspected that a disguised Angela was making the deliveries. Nicole feared that the old man had signed a new will, thinking it was a receipt for the flowers. It would list George as executor and sole heir.

Nicole also tipped Ovanessian that the first name of the Asian pharmacist who'd supplied the drugs was Edwin or something similar. She said that the pharmacist had given George the mystery medication in the belief that it was for their father Antone, who had returned to the Holy Land with heart trouble. Apparently no money had changed hands in the transaction.

Ovanessian told Fay that he was trying to learn the name of Richard Nelson's personal physician so he could see if any drugs had been legally prescribed. Via friends at a drug store chain, Fay reeled in the physician's name, address and phone number in an hour. Another fifteen minutes produced the names of the heart medicines prescribed for his elderly patient: isosorbide to dilate the blood vessels and relieve pain, and Betachoron to regulate blood pressure. Both were regarded as safe. The legal prescriptions had been filled at a pharmacy on Taraval Street.

Fay faxed the information to Ovanessian and drove straight to the pharmacy. The clerks on duty seemed friendly and cooperative, and neither was Asian-American.

"What time does Edwin go on duty?" she asked. A man in a druggist's apron looked at her quizzically and said that no one named Edwin worked there.

32

Jerry Lama: Enter Frowning

WHEN FAY OPENED the door of her apartment, the phone was ringing. "Rat Dog," she answered in her usual melodious tone.

"Holy shit," a male said. "There's a real . . . Rat Dog?" His voice was sharp and lightly accented.

"Speaking," she said.

"How come you never called my sister?" He sounded angry.

"Who?"

"Nicole."

"Who's *this?*"

"Jerry."

"Jerry who?" When he didn't answer, she decided that he must be Jerry Lama. He was the only Jerry involved in the case. But . . . he lived in New York.

She asked, "Are you calling long-distance?"

"No fucking way."

Fay thought, Somebody should wash this guy's mouth out with industrial solvent. He thinks he's talking to some street slut. On the other hand, if he's really Jerry Lama, he's just the person I want to talk to.

She couldn't decide how much to say about the earlier message from Nicole. As far as she was concerned, the man on the phone was a member of a very volatile family. She'd been told that they were Palestinian Catholic immigrants who'd lived in New York City, opened a small restaurant in Woodland, California, and then bought the French Village Deli. Mother Gloria still operated the deli with her daughter Hilda. Two other sisters, Nicole and Hami, were cooperating with police.

"Nicole got her ass chewed for calling you," Jerry said angrily. "You should've returned her call."

"Who chewed her, uh—out?"

"Inspector Dan Yawczak. He told her never to call you again. *Never.*"

Fay thought, Whose side are these darn cops on? The more scut work she did for them, the more they resented her. Were they afraid a penis-deprived investigator would solve their case? Was it sexism? Or just the same juvenile competitiveness that kept so many crimes unsolved? She remembered a favorite saying of her old friend Glennis: "Men are just small boys with attitude." It was especially true of cops. Fay didn't care *who* solved the case. The point was that defenseless citizens were being victimized for the sole offense of growing old. It could be happening to anyone's elderly loved ones, including her own. She decided to level with this stranger on the phone. He couldn't be any less cooperative than the police.

"I'm sorry, Mr. Lama," she said. "Your sister left her number on my machine. By the time I got the message I couldn't be sure who'd answer the phone if I called back. Don't your brother and Angela live in that house, too?"

"They live in the back half. You coulda returned her call, no prob, ya know what I'm saying?"

"Well, I thought—"

"I hear you're on George's ass."

"Not . . . exactly." Criminy, she said to herself, this guy certainly skips around. What do they call that? Flight of ideas? *Schizophrenia?*

He was still talking. "They say you're a pushy broad. Who's your client?"

Fay thought, *Broad?* Is this . . . Frank Sinatra? She said, "That's, uh—confidential." She was convinced that if she ever admitted wasting

Hope Victoria Beesley (*above and right*): crotchety, imperious and dead (Courtesy of Barry Hughes)

The Beesley manse in San Francisco (Photograph by author)

Fay Faron on the job (Courtesy of Fay Faron)

The Rat Dog Dick business
logo (Courtesy of Fay Faron)

Fay Faron skip-tracing with her assistant (Courtesy of Fay Faron)

Beans Faron, Private Investigator (Courtesy of Fay Faron)

Fay plans her next coup (Courtesy of Robert Holmgren)

(Left) Angela Bufford: the Gypsy at twenty-five

(Below) George Lama and Angela Bufford at Lake Tahoe, California (Courtesy of Jerry Lama)

(*Above*) Angela Bufford and "Uncle Dick" Nelson at the lawn party (Courtesy of Donald Nelson)

(*Left*) Fay Faron at the Konstantin Liotweizen grave (Photograph by author)

Mary Tene Steiner, driver's license photo

Dan Reed: star reporter breaks the story (Photograph by author)

John Nazarian: PI with
a Bentley (Photograph
by author)

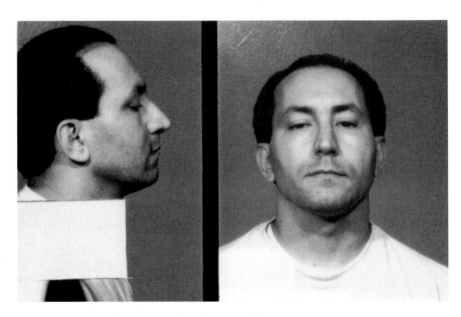

George Lama (John J. Nazarian photograph)

a year of her life out of a childish sense of justice, someone would inject her with benzodiazepine and roll her away on a gurney.

"I hear you know some cops," the man said. His voice seemed a little softer now that she'd halfway apologized for not returning Nicole's call. She thought she heard New York City nuances in his diction but also something vaguely exotic. He said "abawt" for "about" and "suppawse" for "suppose," and he softened his terminal R's.

"I know a few," she said.

"The Fraud Unit, maybe? The guys that can't find their dick in the dark?"

Fay didn't disagree with the characterization. Correctly or not, everyone regarded Fraud as a backwater unit.

"Hey!" he said sharply. "Are you taping this?" My, she thought, what an abrupt person you are!

"No," she said. "Should I be?"

"Look, Rat Dog," he said, "we can help each other, ya know what I mean? But phones make me nervous. Too much fuckin' buggin'."

"Bugging?" she said briskly. "Not by me."

She didn't want this short-fused man scaring the neighbors in her apartment building, so she agreed to meet him in an hour at a nearby place called the Coffee Roastery.

SHE PULLED HER "No Fear" baseball hat over her tight blond curls, threw on her signature trenchcoat from the Nordstrom Rack, and descended her apartment steps two at a time behind Beans. At the restaurant, she parked her sidekick outside and shook her index finger to freeze him in place so she could observe him through the window.

Inside, a man of about forty was dimly visible through a ghostly screen of smoke. He was hatless and coatless and his fingers thrummed lightly on the tabletop. She was a little surprised when she entered and got a better look. She'd pictured Jerry Lama as a cruiserweight with scarred waxy skin and a scowl. Instead he looked like a compact type she'd always found fascinating: lithe, catlike, tightly wound. His bright white teeth were set in light olive skin, his wavy dark hair combed to curled-up wisps in back. His black pullover looked shrink-wrapped and made him resemble a three-quarter-size model of Robert De Niro in *The Deer Hunter*.

As soon as he started talking, she realized that she shouldn't have met him in a restaurant. The last thing this man needed was coffee. He used the F-word as noun, verb, adjective and adverb and seemed oblivious to her unease. She realized that he was too angry to care about social graces, if he'd ever had any. She was thankful that he kept his voice low. And intense. It was like interviewing a Roman candle.

He ignored her comment that winter seemed to be coming a little early. "Fuck winter," he said, and leaned across the table. "The cops have known about George and Angela since last year. That's when my fucking sister first tipped 'em off."

Fay thought, My *fucking sister?* What an interesting usage! I'll have to remember it for my detective novel.

"We've been giving the cops all kinds of information," he continued, "and you know what they do with it?"

Yes, Fay thought, I know what they do with it. "Uh, nothing?" she ventured. She knew she should have replied "*Fucking* nothing," but she didn't want to reinforce his relaxed approach to language arts.

It didn't take long to discover that Jerry Lama's animus was equally divided between the SFPD Fraud Unit and his brother George. The police were "fucking idiots" and George was a "sick fuck," as in "I knew what that sick fuck was doing from day one. He learned the scam from Angela and she learned it from her mother. I knew all about it, but I didn't do a fucking thing."

"Why not?" Fay asked.

He frowned and shook his head. "He's my *brothuh*, for Chrisakes. He was a good guy, too. He changed when he connected with the Gypsy. She walked into the deli and applied for a job as sandwich maker. Told George she lived in a house she'd inherited from her grandfather."

"The place on Fourteenth?"

"Yeah. Later my mom bought it from Angela and let her and George move into the back half."

"Free?" Fay remembered Angela's lament to old Richard Nelson that she couldn't afford the rent on her dumpy cottage.

"Free," Jerry said. "My mom likes to keep an eye on George. He's still her baby boy. George and Angela, they're into all kinds of shit. They cheated the ass off the phone company. I live in New York and he used to call me every fucking day. I said, George, I'd hate to be paying your phone bill. He said, Who's paying? He has a pocket memory dialer that Angela bought from a bellhop. It makes a sound like a coin dropping so he can call free from phone booths. He can call fucking China!"

"What else are they into?"

He stubbed out a cigarette and lit another. "Angela got a job as a bank teller so she could pick out old people and dip into their accounts. She and George drained the fuck out of the ATM machines. George is a master forger—he could sign your name and you'd never recognize the difference. Angela photocopied signature cards and George forged checks and cashed 'em at her window. But the fucking bank caught on. They asked her to describe the customer that passed a bad check for ten grand. She was trying to steer 'em off George, so she says, Hispanic, short, heavy accent. The bank couldn't prove anything, so they fired her."

"Didn't they quit stealing after that?" Fay asked.

"You crazy? George forges another check, puts on overalls, a cap, dark glasses, waltzes back to the same fucking bank. Go figure."

"It's a trade secret, Jerry. Most criminals are idiots."

He looked almost insulted. "George is *not* an idiot. George is *very definitely* not an idiot. What George is is greedy. All he ever says is *I* want this, *I* want that, *I'm* gonna live the good fucking life. Angela is perfect for him."

"What happened when he went back to the bank?" Fay said, trying to keep him on track.

"He told the teller he'd just painted a house and the owner wanted him to cash the check right away. The teller asked for picture ID and George handed her a fake driver's license. She took one look and disappeared into the back. George fucking panicked. He told another teller, Hey, excuse me, I gotta feed the meter, and he split."

"He told you all this?"

"The first pay phone he passed, he calls me in New York, and he's sweating bullets. I said, George, whatta you, crazy? They got your fucking license with your fucking *picture?* He said, They got my picture, but the name's an alias. I said, George, get your ass to Brazil! You're *history!*" Jerry shook his head as though he couldn't believe his own story.

"So what *happened?*" Fay asked.

"What happened? *Nothing* fucking happened. People like that, they lead charmed lives."

"The police didn't go after him?"

"The police didn't get off their fat asses."

Fay asked if he'd passed his inside information to the Fraud Unit. "Every fucking detail," he said. "It checked out, too. Look at this."

He handed her a copy of SFPD report 891151660, confirming that on August 3, 1989, at the Golden Gate Street branch of Security Pacific Bank, a male white suspect had cashed a $10,000 check made out to Mario Mendez on the account of John Coakley. Teller Angela Bufford had dispersed the money in $100 bills. The next day the same man tried to cash a check for $3,000 on the same account. The teller took the check into the back and peeled the new face off the customer's ID. She summoned a security guard, but the man was gone. The case was still unsolved.

"Looks solid to me," Fay commented.

Jerry said, "This isn't the only solid case. I grabbed George's crooked phone ringer and gave it to the cops."

"The one he used for free calls?"

"Yeah. From Radio Shack. Modified. Ovanessian made me return it to George."

"What?"

"He said he was trying to develop a murder case and he didn't want to spook George on chippy stuff."

"Greg never mentioned the bank deal to me," Fay said. "He's always complaining that the DA needs more evidence."

"They got all the evidence they need. Right from the start we knew what George and Angela were up to."

"Who told you?"

"Who else? My brothuh! The fucking motormouth couldn't shut up. He told me the whole scam, said it went back years. He said, Jerry, why should I work my ass off seven days a week for nothing when the Tenes are making a fucking fortune off old men?"

As the session continued, Fay realized that Lama's profanity no longer put her off. There was a lyrical quality to it; she imagined him as the conductor of a symphony orchestra of curses, obscenities and other goat-cries, fading them in and out as Mahler or Bruckner used strings and horns.

"One day when I was here from New York," he continued, "George drove me past an apartment building off Park Presidio and told me

Angela's mother inherited it from some fucking Russian. I said, I thought the mother was married to a Gypsy. George said, She *is*, but the old Russian thought she was single. He said, This is the way her family makes a living. He showed me a corner house on Balboa, said the brother Danny ripped it off from an old lady."

Fay said, "Your brother really trusts you, doesn't he?"

"Not anymore. I told him off good. He crossed the line when he started threatening my mother and my sisters. I could see our whole fucking family going down the tubes. I told my sister Hilda, I do *not* want George and Angela to be bringing these old men to the French Village for coffee. I said, This keeps up, you'll lose the deli."

Fay watched as he walked to the counter with a light step. He set down another cappuccino for her and emptied four packets of sugar into his black coffee.

"Me and my sisters," he went on, "we called the cops thinking the police department was God. That was what—eight, ten months ago?" He looked disgusted. "The dumb fucks."

Fay realized that behind his pulses of of rage Jerry Lama was making sense. His version of the drama paralleled hers, except that he knew the story from the inside and she'd been watching from the cheap seats.

"I found three bugs that George installed in the garage," he was saying. "He wanted to hear what my mother and sisters were saying about him and the girlfriend. He bought 'em at the Spy Factory. That's his favorite store—he likes sneaky shit like that, ya know what I'm saying? Sensitive little transmitters the size of a dime? They're hard-wired from the conduits so they look like part of the electrical system. George installs 'em and sits in the back half of the house monitoring my mom and my sisters. My mom finds out but she doesn't want to turn him in. You know, He's my son, please don't call the cops. That kinda family shit."

"So nobody reported the bugs?" Fay asked.

"Yeah, somebody did," he said impatiently. "*I* did. I had to. What options did I have? At this point Angela has already ruined George and now the two of 'em are ruining my whole family. I could either blow their heads off or turn 'em in. I told the cops those bugs were a violation of my family's civil rights. I found out later that my sister Hilda tipped George off that I was talking to the cops. She said she never saw a human being turn so white. He ran out of the deli and threatened to shoot our whole family and turn the gun on himself. Angela said she was afraid he was gonna shoot her, too. He's crazy enough. He's a fucking hysteric. You never know what he's gonna do next."

"But . . . he's still around."

"Yeah, because my sister sent this off-duty cop to the house to talk him out of killing himself. The cop comes back to the deli but he won't tell me what happened unless we go someplace where we can't be bugged. George has everybody thinking he can bug the French fries. So me and the cop went down the street and shot a coupla games of pool and he got wasted and offered to kill George for me."

"Who is this cop?" Fay asked.

"Just—a friend of Hilda's. Hangs around the deli. Told me he had three disposable guns."

"Disposable?" It sounded like "dispawsable."

"Unregistered, untraceable. I told him, Hey, I don't want George dead. He's my fucking brother. I just want him to clean up his act. The cop says, Don't worry, I'll throw a blanket over his head and shove a gun down his fucking throat. He'll get the message."

Fay put her hand over her mouth. What kind of people were these? *Is this a case for a Baptist skip tracer?*

Jerry said, "I'm thinking, Hey, man, we don't need an asshole like you fucking things up any more than they're already fucked. I'm thinking, Somebody oughta throw a blanket over *your* head, motherfucker." He smiled apologetically and said, "Look, Fay, I know I have a filthy mouth. You were probably warned. I'm, uh—sorry."

"Don't be sorry," she said. She didn't want to risk shutting him down.

"I get upset," he confessed. "George is my brother. Ya know what I mean? We were tight. It's . . . tough."

Fay took a courtesy sip of cappuccino and thought, If my kidneys hold out I might solve this case someday. She decided to stop interviewing in coffee shops. From now on her cluttered office would have to do. Beans would protect her down to his last dreadlock. She looked outside just as her waiting dog sagged to the sidewalk like laundry.

Jerry followed her eyes and said, "Is he . . . okay?"

"He's okay. That's how he lies down."

Jerry rolled his dark eyes and said, "Maybe you should train him better. I mean, a dog that don't even know how to lie down—"

"How does your family get along with Angela?" Fay interrupted. "I mean, all of them under the same roof."

He laughed. "My mother does the see-no-evil number," he said. "She says she doesn't want to take sides. Little does she know, but I think him and Angela caused her heart attack in 1991. She had to go to the hospital for surgery. I think they used my mother as a guinea pig to see how the drug works. Like a dry run."

"What drug?"

"The one they use on the old men. George calls it the magic salt."

"George would poison your mother? As a . . . test?"

"*Angela* would. And Angela runs George. The house is in joint tenancy. That means if my mother dies, George owns it outright. Angela gets her house back and keeps the money my mom paid her for it. She's already told my mom, I want you the fuck outa my house."

"Where do your sisters stand?"

"My sisters fucking *hate* Angela. They got into a free-for-all with her. Nicole ends up in the hospital with a concussion."

He paused to unpeel another pack of cigarettes, lit up, and blew a jet stream past Fay's twitching nose. "That broad's plenty tough," he said. "Fights like a guy."

"Nicole?"

"Angela! After she beats the shit out of Nicole, she has the balls to go to court for a restraining order. She claims my mom went upside her head with a flashlight. But who goes to the hospital with a concussion? *Nicole!* Is this balls or what?"

"I assume Nicole brought charges."

"The cops talked her out of it."

"Which cops?"

"Yawczak and Ovanessian."

"Talked her out of it?" A Biblical passage ran through Fay's mind. "Blessed are the peacemakers." No wonder this case is half dead.

"Ovanessian told me, Whatta you wanna do, slap 'em on the wrist? We don't want 'em for domestic violence. We want 'em for the heavy stuff. He says, Jerry, you have my word. George and Angela are gonna be arrested by Christmas. What he fucking failed to tell me was what Christmas he was talking about, ya know what I'm saying? Right now I'm thinking . . . Christmas 1999?"

* * *

CHRISTMAS 1999, FAY muttered under her breath as she pushed Beans into the back of the Frog Prince and headed for home. It wasn't yet Christmas, 1993. She knew she wouldn't get much sleep.

33

Author's Cramp

SHE AWOKE AT 4:00 A.M., an hour earlier than usual, to work on her novel *Lily Kills Her Client* before cycling to the Golden Gate with Beans. She hadn't thought of her book in weeks, courtesy of the Tene Bimbo Gypsy clan of San Francisco, and she didn't want to lose the thread. Let's see, she asked herself. What's my heroine's name again? Oh, yeah. Mims. Lily Mims. She typed lazily: *Mims is my name and tracking buttholes is my game.*

The phone rang. Criminy, Fay said to herself. Every time I get started, I'm interrupted. Who can be calling at four-fifteen A.M.? Don't they know this is my *literary* time?

When she finished dealing with the wrong number, she filled a bowl with yogurt, topped her cup with the eye-opener she'd learned to drink in London—black tea strong enough to temper the spoon—and resumed her place in front of Evie the Everex. Ten minutes later she was still sitting. Inert. Unproductive. Totally devoid of novelistic ideas. Nothing came to mind except a few words of Tagalog and the name of her landlord's parrot in the Dominican Republic. And . . . Gypsies.

MIDWAY THROUGH HER morning bike tour with the galloping Beans, the only living dog who ran with all four feet off the ground like a racehorse in an old French print, she squeezed her caliper brakes so hard that she almost pitched over the handlebars. A flattened cat lay five feet ahead under a shroud of bluebottle flies. Fay had a morbid fear of any-thing dead—she thought it might be called "necrophobia," or would that be fear of dying?—and she'd canceled more than one excursion after spotting roadkill. She whistled Beans to her side, made a U-turn and biked three blocks out of her way to avoid the awful sight.

Back in her office she was surprised to hear from Inspector Dan Yawczak. The Fraud Unit seldom contacted her; usually it was the other way around. He told her they were still having trouble identifying the substance that was being sifted into the old men's food. He said it was crucial to the bringing of charges and they might have to walk away from the case.

Fay was surprised by the give-up attitude. "Walk *away?*" she blurted out.

"I hate to see you getting so involved," Yawczak told her. "I mean, some cases just fall through the cracks, ya know?"

She put down the phone in a slow rage. Maybe it was time to take Jerry Lama's advice. Kicking ass wasn't a specialty of the Rat Dog Dick Detective Agency, but something had to be done. The Fraud Unit seemed totally unconvinced about the case. But why? Orders from above? Does some deputy chief prioritize his investigations by age, with elderly victims at the bottom of the list? Or is the DA at fault, demanding evidence for a slam-dunk conviction instead of accepting a challenge and rolling up his sleeves?

She was haunted by the fear that the two old Sunset residents, Richard Nelson and Harry Glover Hughes, weren't the only victims-in-progress. She tried to decide which public agency would know the most about the elderly, perhaps maintain a log of recent hospitalizations and deaths. She ran a fingernail down the government listings in her phone book and came to "Adult Protective Services." They had a mandate to protect the abused and the injured. Maybe they could help. Maybe they cared. It was just a hunch.

A voice said, "Glen Billy," and she launched into her request. After listening for about thirty seconds, the man interrupted in a weary voice to explain that APS had so many cases of elder abuse that "we can't get to 'em all." Lucky me, Fay said to herself, I've reached another energetic bureaucrat, phone in one hand, cigar in the other, half asleep on the job. I wonder if he's getting a pedicure.

The man seemed to perk up when she mentioned Harry Glover Hughes and Richard Nelson. "I was just looking at their cases the other day," he said.

"Why?" Fay asked.

"Because those old guys *never* answer the door," Billy replied. "And . . . we're worried about them."

Fay complimented herself on her hunch. As tersely as possible, she explained that she suspected they were being poisoned.

Billy asked, "Aren't the police on this?"

She said, "Oh, yes," and felt like a liar. *Were* they? It wasn't easy to tell.

The social worker informed her that his own specialty was elder financial abuse and "I'll get right on the case."

"Do you have time?" Fay asked.

"Thanks for the tip," he said. "I'll *make* time."

FAY DID A short background check and learned that she'd accidentally recruited one of the city's more useful bureaucrats. Glen Billy turned out to be a part-Indian ex-hippie who'd worked as a bartender and street artist before returning to USC and earning a bachelor's degree in social work in his forties. Now he was trying to make up for years lost to alcoholism by recovering money for elderly victims of scams. And he was said to be good at his job.

34

The Sick Old Man

ON A THURSDAY in late September, Billy called back to report that he'd found no signs of life at the home of Harry Glover Hughes. "Rats!" Fay said. She wondered if he was lying dead in the bedroom.

"Relax," the social worker told her. He said that neighbors had advised him that the affluent old gentleman frequently drove off with a friendly young couple and stayed away for days.

Fay felt both alarmed and relieved. "How about Mr. Nelson?" she asked.

"Breathing," Billy said. "Barely." He said he'd driven straight to the Nelson home and was surprised when a haggard old face appeared at the front window in response to his insistent loud knock.

Billy told Fay that he'd called out, "What's the matter?"

"Please," the man replied in a weak voice that barely carried through the glass. "I'm too sick. I feel like I'm gonna die."

"Well, if you're that ill, Mr. Nelson," the social worker replied, "you really need to talk to me. I'm from Adult Protective Services. I'm here to help in any way I can. I think I might know what's making you ill."

"Please, *please.* Come back tomorrow and I'll feel better."

The frustrated Billy told Fay that he'd driven straight to the Taraval police station, displayed his credentials, and told the desk sergeant that state laws against elder abuse were being violated at 2266 Forty-sixth Avenue.

"We know all about it," the officer told him. "We'd appreciate it if you didn't disturb our investigation."

"Well, I'm upset that Mr. Nelson might be dying."

"I *told* you. We're on it."

Billy told Fay that the next morning no one answered his early knock on the Nelson front door. "I wanted to kick it in," he said, "but we're not the police and we don't have the authority. If people don't let us in, there's nothing we can do."

"I can't believe this," Fay grumbled, more to herself than the social worker. As far as she could tell, Billy had accomplished more in two days than the Fraud Unit had accomplished in a year. He'd confirmed that the danger wasn't only in the mind of a hysterical female PI. At least one old man was showing symptoms of poisoning. And the police were still asleep. She felt as though a nightmare was coming true.

"Huh?" she said dumbly. She'd almost forgotten that Billy was on the line.

"Mr. Nelson's so labile," he said. "They could talk him into anything."

"*Labile?*"

"Social-worker jargon. It means suggestible."

They talked for twenty more minutes and couldn't figure out a sensible approach to the problem. Finally Billy said, "Here's my last resort whenever I hit the wall." He read off a phone number.

Fay thanked him and dialed. An answering machine advised her that the assistant mayor would be back in her office Monday. It was

Thursday morning. By Monday the ailing Richard Nelson could be dead, if he wasn't already.

She poked out the phone number of her friend Maggie McCall, publisher of the *Marina Times*. An authority on the byzantine ways of city government, Maggie was on a first-name basis with everyone at City Hall.

Fay told her story in bursts: "Cops won't move—Old man half-dead—Adult Protective Services, nothing—Who next?—*Anybody?* Your father? My father?—Oh Maggie, what can I do? *He could already be dead!*"

Characteristically, it took the plainspoken publisher about thirty seconds to come up with an approach. "The police know what's happening and they're deaf and dumb, right? And two San Francisco citizens are gonna die and leave their money to con artists, right? Think about it, Fay. What happens when the legitimate heirs find out?"

"They get . . . mad?"

"They sue the city's ass off!"

Fay said, "I don't—well, I, uh—"

"Stop sputtering, Fay. Who's in charge of protecting the city from lawsuits?"

"The police? The . . . mayor?"

"Think! Who defends the city in court?"

"The city at—"

"—*The city attorney!* Right. You're so *quick.*"

Fay explained that she knew Louise Renne by her good reputation, but she'd never met the city attorney herself and was reluctant to call her cold. Maggie said, "Leave that to me."

Ten minutes later the city attorney was on the line to the Rat Dog Dick Detective Agency. When Fay started to describe the problem, Renne interrupted. "Maggie briefed me," she said. "You'll hear from our investigators. And, thanks, uh—Rat Dog."

35

"Nobody's Gonna Die"

LATE THAT AFTERNOON Timothy Armistead phoned. Fay had crossed cases with the city attorney's chief investigator and knew of his overqualifications. In a job typically filled by a political hack, Armistead was a hard-driving academic with degrees in psychology and sociology and a doctorate in criminology from Berkeley. She'd read his essays in journals of forensic science. He was perceived locally as part social scientist, part bloodhound.

He was polite but asked if they could put off a meeting till morning. Fay said, "Tomorrow's Friday. If we wait till then, nothing'll get done till Monday. By then the old men might be dead." She said she wanted to drive straight to his office and lay out the case.

Armistead promised that he and his fellow investigator Alex Kline would be waiting. She remembered Kline; he'd taken her to lunch to congratulate her on the publication of *A Private Eye's Guide to Collecting a Bad Debt*. In his spare time, he was an author himself. Thank God, Fay said to herself. These old pros will know what to do.

TWO U-TURNS AND a near sideswipe later, she sat in the investigators' office on Market Street reciting details of her story. She was careful to hold her criticism of the SFPD to a brief observation that the Fraud Unit seemed overworked and demoralized. For all she knew, it was the sad truth—or a part.

She soon realized that she could talk to Armistead and Kline in shorthand. Whenever she started to overexplain, they waved her ahead. She realized that she should have taken her case to this office months ago. Maybe it wasn't too late. By the time she'd stopped talking, the two investigators seemed as irritated as Jerry Lama.

"For a start," Kline said brusquely, "we gotta get into the houses. But . . . it's gotta be legal."

The sleuths agreed that the basic problem hadn't changed: the victims didn't want to know what was happening to them and wouldn't file complaints. Under the circumstances, neither Adult Protective Services nor the city attorney could make a forced entry.

"Wait!" Armistead said, pointing a finger at Fay. "You say you've been making trash raids. Do they put it out every week?"

"Mr. Nelson, yes," she said. "Mr. Hughes, never. I think he eats his trash."

"Health code!" Kline said.

"Huh?" Fay said.

Armistead explained, "If he's not putting out his trash, we can go in on a health code violation."

The two investigators thanked her and said they would take over. As Fay was leaving, Armistead touched her arm and said, "Nobody's gonna die."

At home, Fay called two of her girlfriends to cancel a sour-cream-and-onion-potato-chip vedge-out extravaganza at Lake Sonoma so she could track the weekend events by phone.

TWO EMPTY DAYS passed. She wondered again if the old men were already dead, their bodies putrefying in their homes. Then her new allies called and told her what had happened.

36

Wedding Plans

ON MONDAY MORNING, while Fay was still waiting for word, Timothy Armistead and Alex Kline had met with Glen Billy, Dan Yawczak and Greg Ovanessian to set up a rotating watch on the two houses. As long as Angela or George didn't arrive with more food, the elderly occupants would be safe. Billy grumbled about his failed attempt to talk to Richard Nelson and said he urgently needed to perform a welfare check on the sick old man. But the social worker agreed with the lawmen: a forced entrance would be illegal and might blow the whole case. The posse had to handle the matter from the outside.

JUST AFTER NOON, Kline and Yawczak were on station near the Harry Glover Hughes house when a blue BMW pulled up and parked. A dark-haired young woman carrying a small package admitted herself with a key. After a while she escorted a gimpy old man out the front door and helped him into the front passenger's seat. The BMW disappeared in traffic on Taraval.

THREE MILES AWAY on Forty-sixth Avenue, other observers watched Richard Nelson's home from an old Chevy van. They'd been on station for an hour when Glen Billy complained, "How do we know he's not dead?"

"He's okay," Timothy Armistead said emphatically. He explained that he'd watched the house over the weekend and seen stirrings.

"When did you sleep?" the social worker asked.

Armistead yawned.

BY 1:40 P.M. Glen Billy had lost patience with the niceties of the law and decided to walk up and knock. He wouldn't try to force his way inside, and the worst that could happen would be another rejection. He was joined by Armistead, Ovanessian and a policewoman from SFPD's Psychological Liaison Unit.

The elderly man looked in better health than a week earlier. "Mr. Nelson?" Billy said. "May we come in?"

"What's this all about?"

"We're very concerned, sir. We'd like to do a welfare check."

The old man hesitated, then guided the foursome into his neat living room. After Billy asked about his health, Ovanessian asked if he was acquainted with a young woman named Angela who drove a blue BMW.

The lined face seemed to brighten. "Oh, yes," Richard Nelson answered. "She's here a lot. She lives with her brother George, but she's moving in with me and we're gonna get married."

"*Married?*" Billy said.

"Oh, yes. I love her and she loves me."

He showed his visitors to a second-floor room with the lemony smell of new furniture. Some of the pieces bore price tags. "This is where she's gonna live till we get married," he said. "See how I fixed it up?"

Ovanessian nudged Billy into the hall and whispered, "Why don't you just tell him the truth?"

Billy said, "I don't want to break his heart."

The detective pressed the point, and the social worker said, "I'm sorry, Inspector. I'm just not gonna do it."

After the delegation convened in the living room, Billy asked, "May we look around the house?"

Nelson nodded. "Be careful in the kitchen," he called out. "Angela just waxed."

The searchers opened the refrigerator and found takeout food from the French Market Deli. They bagged samples and stepped into the dining room. A tabletop was covered with financial records; evidently the retired accountant had been going over his books. A deposit slip from a joint account at Great Western bank was imprinted with the names Richard Nelson and Angela Bufford. Another slip bore the same account number, 0618160172, but was in Bufford's name alone. It appeared that checks for some $60,000 had recently been cashed.

Ovanessian noticed a $200 check on a table. It was made out to Angela Bufford.

"What's this?" he asked.

The old man said, "Angela needed more money. I try to help her out."

My God, Glen Billy said to himself, the meter's still running. She's got his thousands; now she's grabbing his hundreds. If this isn't elder financial abuse, I've never seen it.

37

Regeneration

FAY MARVELED AT the activity that followed the city attorney's entrance into the case. Unofficial reports seemed to arrive almost hourly. Donald Nelson was contacted in Atherton and agreed to make a formal intervention on his uncle's behalf. The most exciting news was that the phlegmatic Yawczak had tracked down the pharmacists who'd provided the "magic salt" to George Lama. They were Edmond Lim of the West Portal pharmacy and his employee Allen Leong, a young druggist. Both men admitted that they knew Lama and his girlfriend Angela but denied dispensing any heart medications. Leong admitted that he'd given George a supply of the hair restorative Rogaine without a prescription, but only as a one-time trial. Apparently George's pate hadn't responded. The pharmacist also recalled selling him some penicillin.

Yawczak told Fay that he'd asked Leong to name the heart medications stocked by the pharmacy. The druggist mentioned Lanoxin, digoxin (synthetic digitalis), and Endoral and insisted that all required prescriptions. He said, "I didn't give George any heart medicine," and added a curious comment: "And if I did, I'm not into anything, you know?"

The next day, according to Yawczak, the young pharmacist's memory seemed improved. He reported that he'd checked the store's computer and found a 1988 digoxin prescription for Antone Lama, George's father. Leong said that his boss, owner Edmond Lim, had been the first to fill the senior Lama's prescription but that he, Leong, had refilled it later. Altogether, the two druggists had given the Palestinian immigrant some six hundred tablets, ending in 1990. After still more introspection, Leong admitted that he'd been mistaken again. He sounded nervous as he explained that he and his boss hadn't actually dispensed the drug to Antone Lama but to his son George. Leong agreed to show the detective the pharmacy's computer file on the prescription.

* * *

LATE ON FRIDAY afternoon, three days after the welfare check of Richard Nelson, Yawczak returned to the pharmacy in West Portal. A computer file showed that a prescription for synthetic digitalis at 125 milligrams strength had been written for Antone Lama and was dated 1987 through 1989. Druggist Leong refused to provide a printout because, he said, "George Lama will sue me."

Several days later, the young pharmacist did still another turnabout, this time promising to cooperate completely. He said that the medicine had been given to George Lama twice by him, four times by his boss, and once by another pharmacist. It was understood that George was mailing the pills to his ailing father in Palestine.

Store owner Edmond Lim remained intransigent. He said he vaguely remembered the prescription but couldn't recall which member of the Lama family had picked it up. He said that it hadn't been filled in years and the entire transaction was routine. When Yawczak asked for copies of the records, Lim demanded a search warrant. The detective asked if he would consent to a tape-recorded interview. The pharmacist declined.

38

The Noose Tightens

AS INFORMATION ABOUT Yawczak's aggressive sleuthing reached Fay, she tried to make sense of the abrupt mood swing and concluded that the City Attorney's Office must be pushing hard from backstage. Both of the assigned inspectors seemed energized. Not content to take the pharmacists at their word, they'd checked with female members of the Lama family and learned that the patriarch Antone had never been treated for heart trouble. Nicole Lama insisted that, contrary to the two pharmacists' stories, they'd filled the Digoxin prescription for her brother George as late as 1991. An uncle, Nabib Atalla, told family members that he'd watched George sprinkle the "magic salt" on takeout food in

1992. George had bragged about "really messing around with something" in front of Uncle Nabib and his sons.

To tighten their case, the detectives interviewed Jerry Lama by phone to New York. In his supercharged style, George Lama's older brother advised them that his father's personal physician was a cousin named Jacob Lama, and he had never prescribed digoxin. Jerry informed the officers that his father and his brother George hadn't been on speaking terms for years. He said that the idea that George was providing his father with intercontinental shipments of heart medicine was fucking ridiculous, and if they'd just be patient for a while, he would fucking prove it.

FIVE DAYS LATER, the detectives received a tape recording of a transatlantic phone conversation between Jerry and his father. In Arabic, Antone Lama confirmed that he had never received packages of any kind from his son George in America. If George was buying synthetic digitalis from a pharmacy, it was for a purpose known only to George.

Satisfied that they'd finally identified the poison, Yawczak and Ovanessian took their information to Dr. Boyd Stephens. The chief medical examiner showed them a picture of the digoxin pill in his *Physicians' Desk Reference*. In the 125-milligram strength, it was small, yellowish and round, exactly as described by Nicole Lama and other members of the family.

WHEN FAY LEARNED of the latest discoveries, she phoned an expert pharmacologist and charter member of Friends of the Rat Dog Dick Detective Agency. "Digoxin," she said breathlessly. "Synthetic digitalis. Bad stuff, right?"

"It can be," her friend said with aggravating calmness. "It's a heart regulator, quirky as hell. The toxicity varies. The dosage has to be tailored to the individual."

"How would it affect ninety-year-olds?" she asked.

"Give 'em enough, it might induce a heart attack. But . . . who the hell knows?"

"Would they just drop dead?"

"No way to tell without knowing the patient. Some old crocks, it might only make 'em sick."

Fay said, "If a person died of digitalis poisoning, how hard would it be to prove in court?"

"It takes a special test. The lab could detect its presence, but then the questions are just beginning. How much digitalis was in the body? How long was the victim taking it? How much is toxic in this individual?" He paused. "Say, Rat Dog, what's going on?"

Fay told him that the information was confidential at the moment, but after the bad guys were safely locked away in San Quentin—which shouldn't be much longer—she would take him to lunch and tell the whole story. She promised it had enough angles to hold his professional interest.

"If the bad guys are trying to use digitalis as a poison," he told her, "don't bet they'll ever go to jail."

"Why?"

"It's the toughest substance to prosecute. And you can get it in any drugstore."

"Thanks," Fay said. "We found that out."

AT THE SAN Francisco Public Library she learned that *Digitalis purpurea* was extracted from the dried leaves of the common purple foxglove. Synthesized, it bore names like digoxin and digitoxin and was used to regulate the heartbeat, increase cardiac strength, relieve swelling and improve circulation. Some doctors prescribed it for weight loss, but the *Complete Drug Reference*, published by Consumer Reports Books, warned that the drug "can cause serious problems," including vomiting, fainting, depression, exhaustion, blurred vision, diarrhea, nausea, hives and rash. Every now and then some hapless experimenter brewed tea from the big grainy leaves and became seriously ill. Some died. The stuff had been used in suicides, but it was an undependable killer compared to old reliables like arsenic, strychnine and cyanide.

Fay grabbed a stack of murder anthologies and almanacs and perused the indexes for "digitalis." Apparently it hadn't been popular with the classical poisoners of literature and history. She found a single reference. In the early thirties, a Belgian woman named Marie Becker had used a brew from the stately plant to murder her husband, a lover and eight others. She was sentenced to life in prison. Fay wondered how she'd been caught, but the information was missing.

* * *

THE NEXT DAY she learned why Ovanessian had needed the name of old Mr. Nelson's cardiologist. At police request, the physician, Richard Levy, had drawn a sample of his elderly patient's blood under cover of a routine examination. Fay asked Ovanessian how long the tests would take.

"Not long," he said.

The terse answer was reminiscent of childhood in Arizona. *How long till dinner? Not long, honey.* She wondered how long the cops would treat her like a child.

39

Positive Poison

ANOTHER WEEK PASSED before she heard the test results. At a meeting in his offices, Dr. Boyd Stephens reported that Richard M. Nelson's blood tested positive for digitalis. The reading of .09 milligram per milliliter was nontoxic and even below therapeutic levels, but the chief medical examiner emphasized that digitalis didn't appear naturally in the body and wasn't absorbed from any known external source. It appeared that someone was trying to hasten Uncle Dick Nelson to the grave.

When Fay heard the news, she asked Greg Ovanessian two questions: "What time is the bust?" and "Can I come along?"

He advised her to sit tight. She tried to remember how many times she'd heard the same advice from the Gypsy cop and his confreres. Ovanessian explained that the District Attorney's Office and the Fraud Unit were cooperating on the case, but she should bear in mind that Rom criminals were the hardest of all to prosecute. They seldom did prison time or even took a hard fall. On the rare occasions when they appeared at a booking desk, they yelled, sobbed, tore at their clothes, smudged their fingerprints, made faces at the ID camera, and created so much chaos that jailers couldn't wait to get rid of them. And on those rare occasions when Gypsy miscreants were brought into court, Ovanessian explained, they hired the best lawyers in town and the whole *familia* shared the expense.

Fay was disturbed by her friend's nonchalance. He didn't seem to see the difference between Gypsies in general and the Gypsies who'd made elder abuse a paying business. It seemed to her that criminals should be brought to justice without compromise, regardless of their ethnic origins or the trouble they might cause the system. She was sure that law-abiding Gypsies would feel the same. If she had her way, black-and-whites would already be speeding toward Fourteenth Avenue on lights and sirens. And en route to arresting Angela and her boyfriend, they would pick up Mary Steiner and Danny Tene. Let the whole scam unravel. No case was ever tight enough to suit the DA's Office. When it came to the need for additional evidence, prosecutors were insatiable. Sometimes it didn't hurt to file charges and take a chance on losing.

"So what happens now?" she asked.

Ovanessian said that the Nelson blood would be checked in a week. If it tested positive again, they would . . . reassess.

Fay shrieked, "Reassess? Are you gonna keep reassessing till he's dead? What about Mr. Hughes?"

He told her that Yawczak was working Hughes. "Nothing to worry about, Fay."

"You've got an elderly citizen who's been poisoned. *That's nothing to worry about?*"

Ovanessian told her to leave the heavy lifting to the police. "We can handle it." Fay said she hoped so.

SIX DAYS LATER, on October 21, 1993, Richard Nelson's blood was tested again. The digitalis level was unchanged.

40

Angela Revealed

THIRTY MILES SOUTH of the Hall of Justice, Donald Nelson and his wife Gerry were also troubled by the pace of the investigation. Over the last several months they'd stayed in contact with Inspector Ovanessian, providing updated social notes on their uncle and his Gypsy girlfriend. Angela now had her own key to the house on Forty-sixth Avenue. She visited often, ran errands, chauffeured the old man in her BMW, and occasionally slept over. She seemed more sure of his affections, as indicated by his grimy windows and dusty furniture. Instead of acting as a helpful housekeeper, she was becoming his personal banker, steadily infiltrating his accounts. At Great Western Bank, "Angela Bufford" had been listed as coholder at his address, then coholder at *her* address, and now as sole holder. The old man's account at Wells Fargo and his portfolio of stocks and securities seemed intact, but the Nelsons couldn't be sure. They warned police that their uncle's exchequer was under frontal attack and there was no way they could protect him without professional help.

ON SUNDAY, OCTOBER 24, three days after the second digitalis tests proved positive, Don Nelson was relieved to learn that the police planned to take action. Ovanessian called to report that under California law, the authorities were required to warn Richard Nelson of his danger. An intervention was planned for the next afternoon. The watching and waiting would soon be over.

"Do you want me and Gerry to come along?" Don Nelson asked. "This'll be traumatic for Uncle Dick. He's already had a stroke."

Ovanessian agreed.

"Who's going in?" Nelson asked.

"A whole party," Ovanessian replied. "Me, Yawczak, Tim Armistead, the chief medical examiner, your uncle's cardiologist, maybe one or two others."

Don said, "He'll be plenty upset when you barge in on him. And he'll be more upset when he finds out what that woman's been doing to him. He thinks they're gonna get married. Maybe Gerry and I shouldn't be seen with the rest of you."

"Why?"

"Uncle Dick thinks you're ganging up on Angela. She's convinced him you're the bad guys. Gerry and I don't want to lose his trust. How about if we just park down the street and observe? After you leave, we'll go in and see how he's holding up."

Ovanessian said it sounded like a good idea.

AT FIVE THE next afternoon, the Nelsons eased into a parking space a half block from their uncle's house. They saw Timothy Armistead watching from his car across the street. A dark sedan slowed as it passed the Nelsons' car, then made another pass a few minutes later. The Asian-American driver parked and took a seat on a flight of stairs across the street. He carried a radio and flashlight and had the wiry look of a Kung Fu master.

The Nelsons had been on watch for ten minutes when a blue-white BMW performed a neat semicircular tuck into the parking space in front of their Uncle Dick's house. A woman briskly climbed the stairs. "Look, Don!" Gerry exclaimed. "Our party guest."

After Angela used a key to enter, Greg Ovanessian and a man in civilian clothes drove past the house and parked their old white Chevrolet at the corner. Don stepped out of his car for a better look and noticed Ovanessian's partner walking rapidly toward him. "What're *you* doing here?" the man asked.

Don was surprised at his brusque tone. "Who're you?" he asked.

"Inspector Dan Yawczak. Who're *you?*"

"Donald Nelson," he said. "I'm Mr. Nelson's nephew. This was all arranged. You guys *wanted* us here."

Yawczak said, "The DA's gonna be real upset that you showed up."

Don was annoyed. "Wait a minute!" he snapped. "I took time off from work to be here at your pleasure."

After a few more hot words, Yawczak walked away.

Five minutes later, Uncle Dick's cardiologist, Dr. Richard Levy, arrived in a VW convertible and huddled with the Fraud Unit inspectors in Ovanessian's parked Chevy. The Asian plainclothesman walked to the back of the Nelsons' car and made a note of the license number. Don thought, I hope they're as concerned about Uncle Dick as they are about us major criminals.

Armistead climbed into Ovanessian's car, and a conference appeared to be going on. Forty minutes passed. The Nelsons couldn't imagine what the lawmen were talking about. Had the intervention been thrown off by their arrival? By *Angela's* arrival? Didn't they have contingency plans?

At six-ten, Ovanessian's old Chevy pulled sharply from the curb and lurched to a stop in front of 2266. Two patrol cars pulled up and disgorged more officers. Everyone clomped up the stairs. Don thought, This looks like a speakeasy bust in an old movie. Where's Al Capone? He wondered what was happening inside the house.

After five or six minutes, Gerry said, *"They got her!"*

Uncle Dick's party date stood at the top of the landing, her back to the wall. Ovanessian and several of the others circled her and made emphatic gestures. A third police car arrived and a uniformed officer guided the Gypsy woman into the backseat. The old man stepped back inside and shut the door. He looked bereft.

Don checked his watch. "There she goes!" he said as the car pulled away. It was 6:17.

OVER BEERS IN a neighborhood deli, the Fraud Unit inspectors debriefed the Nelsons on events inside the house. The cops sounded like athletes discussing a big win. Don felt ashamed that he'd doubted their sincerity.

The detectives reported that Drs. Levy and Stephens had officially warned Mr. Nelson of his danger and asked him where the digitalis might have come from. The old man had insisted that Angela never cooked for him or brought him food.

"That's not true!" Don Nelson said. "Poor Dick. He's still in denial. He told me she brings his breakfast and she's a great cook. They go out for coffee and Danish every Saturday morning. She's had *plenty* of opportunities to spike his food."

Ovanessian said that there'd been times during the intervention when Mr. Nelson didn't seem to comprehend what was happening. He couldn't remember his visitors' names or titles and was under the impression that Dr. Boyd Stephens, a coroner with a national reputation, was a patrolman.

"Once I referred to Angela by her real name," Ovanessian told the Nelsons, "and your uncle said, *Theresa?* I said, Yeah, her name's Theresa Tene and she's a member of a Gypsy family called the Tene Bimbos. Of course she denied it."

"What happened when you took her in?" Gerry Nelson asked.

Ovanessian said they'd told her that they knew exactly who she was—"Chuchi's your father. Mary Steiner's your mother. Danny's your brother. You're from the East Coast and you've been hustling old men for years. The party's over."

"How'd she react?" Don Nelson asked.

"She said, Anything you want to know, call my attorney. She was totally unshook."

"Why'd you guys all go inside the house at once?" Gerry asked.

Yawczak said they hadn't wanted to give Angela time to poison the old man while they sat in their cars. He was already involved in one lawsuit.

Don asked what charges they'd brought against Angela Bufford or Theresa Tene or her name of the moment.

Ovanessian looked quizzical and explained that no charges had been brought. "It was just an interview."

The Nelsons exchanged glances. Gerry said, "She's . . . out?"

Yawczak told her not to worry. "She'll never go near your uncle again."

The detectives seemed to feel that the problem was solved. The Nelsons were staggered. Why jump to such easy conclusions? Did anybody expect the pushy "Angie" to give up the golden goose she called "Rich"? To Gerry and Don, the police attitude seemed lazy or naive—or both.

THE NEXT MORNING Richard Nelson's phone number didn't answer, and Don decided to drive up to the house in the Sunset. Before leaving Atherton, he tried one more call. This time Uncle Dick came on breathing hard. He said he'd just returned from brunch with Angela. He especially enjoyed the salad bar at Lucky's.

"Did you make your own?" Don asked.

"Angela always makes it for me. She knows what I like. She's good that way." He was quiet for a few seconds, then said, "Don, what would I do without her?"

FAY FARON BLEW up when she heard the details of the Nelson intervention. "Now Angela knows she's being watched!" she railed at Ovanessian. "She went right home and cleaned her house. There won't be a *shred* of evidence left."

"It's the law," the detective insisted. "We had to warn him."

"But you had Angela *cold* and you let her walk, Greg. How're you ever gonna make a case?"

"That's our job. We'll do it."

"You think Mr. Nelson is safe?"

"Sure. His family's moving him away."

"What about Mr. Hughes?"

Ovanessian said that the other old man was scheduled for an interview.

"You haven't talked to him yet?"

"He's never home."

"How do you know he's alive?"

"Don't worry," he repeated. "We know."

Fay wondered how they knew. She still liked Ovanessian and trusted him, but she felt a chill at the possibility that Harry Glover Hughes was being fed a slow but steady poison and the cops didn't care. She wouldn't rest till she'd made a hard check of her own.

41

Return of the Jerry

JERRY LAMA SOUNDED excited when he phoned to tell her that the Fraud Unit was flying him west at the expense of the city and county of San Francisco. "My phone bills are two hundred, three hundred a month, talking to these assholes by long distance," he complained. "This'll be cheaper."

She asked, "What've you been talking to these, uh—what have you guys been talking about?"

"Same shit. Giving 'em information, blah blah blah, whatevuh." Calling from his home in New York, he sounded more Northeastern than ever, even though she'd learned that he was born Jalil Antone Lama in the Holy Land and was fluent in Arabic as well as English. Whatever the subject or language, Jerry Lama seemed an instant study.

He informed her that he'd taken a desperate call from his nephew, Roland Dabai, his sister Hilda's son. Roland knew more about George's activities, Jerry said, than any other member of the family. "And he doesn't hear it through the fucking walls, like my mom and my sisters," Jerry told her. "He gets it straight from George, blow by blow."

"I don't think you ever mentioned Roland," Fay said.

"I nevuh mentioned a lotta things."

"Enlighten me." Fay thought, This is like playing games with an angry cat. I'm glad he can't bite through the phone line.

Jerry explained that Roland went "way fucking back" with his uncle George. "He was on George's payroll, used to do dirty tricks for him. What did Roland know about right and wrong? He was just a kid. He's only twenty-two now."

"Roland phoned *you?*" Fay said, wondering where this conversation was headed.

"Yeah. He's in trouble. He's a good kid but he's fucked up, ya know what I'm saying? He's very intelligent, lazy, claims he has psychological problems. Blames his parents for everything."

"Like every other kid."

"He's going to school at Berkeley and he says Hilda and his papa never send him enough money. So he's always broke. That's his story, anyway. He lives in a fucking closet, claims he has to steal his food."

"Is that what got him in trouble?"

"A store cop busted his ass for taking a loaf of bread."

"Jean Valjean," Fay said. "Les Miserables."

"Huh?"

"Never mind."

"He says, Uncle Jerry, I want you to make sure the security officer doesn't show up in court. Then they'll have to dismiss my case."

Fay thought, Why would a nephew ask an uncle three thousand miles away to intimidate a rent-a-cop unless he knew the uncle had . . . special skills? No one seemed to know what Jerry Lama did for a living. Someone had said he worked as a bartender and someone else said he'd won a big lawsuit against a hospital and lived off the proceeds. He certainly hadn't been forthcoming about his personal bio.

Jerry was still talking. ". . . So I say, Jesus Christ, Roland, you want me to put the muscle on a security guard? What're you, nuts? He says, I heard you're gonna be in town. I say, Yeah, but I don't know when, and anyway this is *not* the way to do things. So we talked. Blah blah and fucking blah. He starts telling me some stuff about my brother George, and I'm saying, Wait a minute, kid, lemme get my tape recorder. He asks why do I want to bug him, and I tell him, Look, if I'm gonna help you, I need all the information I can get."

"So you've got Roland on tape?"

"The whole fucking story, and it's a legal tape 'cause I got his permission. I told Ovanessian, This kid knows *everything*. Maybe you can work a deal for him. It's his first offense. Ovanessian calls me back and says he's got an okay from the DA to go easy on him in exchange for information. Then Roland says no deal!"

"Why?"

"Roland hates the fucking cops. That's something else he picked up from George. Roland says he's not gonna talk to Ovanessian or Yawczak or the chief of police or *any* fucking cop. I argued with him for an hour and he finally says, Okay, I'll talk to 'em, Uncle Jerry, but only if you go with me. He says, I don't trust those assholes."

"So the Fraud Unit's flying you all the way out here to baby-sit your nephew?" Fay said. She was thinking about the refreshing change in atmosphere since City Attorney Louise Renne had called in her constabulary. Three or four weeks ago the city cops were ignoring the case. Now they were acting like real investigators.

Fay offered to meet Jerry at the San Francisco airport and chauffeur him into town. She picked up so many friends and relatives that she sometimes wondered why she didn't install a taxi meter.

"Don't bothuh," he said in his sharp tone. He explained that Ovanessian and Yawczak intended to drive him from the San Jose airport to Berkeley for the interview with Roland Dabai. "Why are you landing down at San Jose?" Fay asked.

"Is that all you do, Rat Dog? *Ask questions?*"

"No!" she said, a little stung.

"Answer one for a change. Did you burn that stupid hat?"

She was surprised that he remembered her baseball cap. She guessed that his choice of airports had something to do with security. She didn't ask.

42

Delivery Boy

TWO DAYS LATER Fay met with God's angry man at a coffee shop on Telegraph Hill. From their last meeting, she remembered that he seemed to have a Turkish capacity for tobacco and caffeine. I don't want to act unsociable, she said to herself, but if I try to match him cup for cup, I'll vault Coit Tower in the pike position. She looked around for a potted plant.

"I just came from the cops," Jerry said. "I don't know what to make of those fucking guys. Right in front of me, Yawczak tells Ovanessian, Hey, dude, I think we shoulda busted Angela for attempted murder.

Ovanessian says, I don't want her on attempted murder. I want her on *murder*. I says, What's the difference? He says, There's three types of murder in California: attempted murder, plain murder and murder for profit. Murder for profit gets the death penalty."

The explanation was a little simplistic, but Fay didn't bother correcting it. "What happened with your nephew?" she asked.

"Roland spilled." Smoke curled from Jerry's mouth and disappeared into his nostrils. My, she thought, what a great party trick! She checked his ears but they were smoke-free. "Now," he said, "we gotta hope he don't get reached. Lemme tell ya, Fay, he's a pretty unpredictable kid."

"Where'd you guys talk to him?" Fay asked.

"The Berkeley cops gave us an interview room—me, Ovanessian, Yawczak and Roland. At first, Yawczak did the questioning. Don't ask me why. It went a little slow till I jumped in. I said, Hey, Roland, tell the inspectors about Uncle George getting you a new driver's license in the name Ronald Ware. Tell 'em how Uncle George can do things like that. So Roland says, When I was an altar boy, Uncle George paid me fifty bucks to steal a church seal and some blank baptismal certificates so he could use 'em for new driver's licenses. Then Roland dummies up again. I said, For Chrisakes, Roland, tell the officers what *else* you did for Uncle George. Roland says, Well, I hassled people on the phone. I broke a guy's car windows for hitting on Angela. He says, George paid me twenty bucks for that and fifty bucks for breaking the window next door to the deli."

"George *faginized* him," Fay said.

"Whatevuh," Jerry said in his New York accent. "I says, What else, Roland? *What else?* He says, George paid me to deliver food to some old guys. Then he dummies up again. I say, *Which* old guys? He says, Well, old man Storvick, for one."

Fay plumbed her memory. "Was he the . . . longshoreman?"

"Yeah," Jerry said. "They drugged him till he couldn't see straight. He was the first one George and Angela did."

"How long ago?"

" 'Eighty-seven, 'eighty-eight. It was two, three years after she cashed in on old man Bufford."

Fay thought, That's about the same time Angela's mother was exposing her breasts to Konstantin Liotweizen and her brother was snuggling up to Hope Victoria Beesley. Victimizing defenseless old people—

it looked as though the Tenes had created a cottage industry. She wondered if they had a small-business license.

Roland's version of the Steven Storvick story, as related by Jerry, was notable for its bloodless ending. Angela had first spotted the retired Norwegian stevedore while serving him coffee in the French Village Deli. One afternoon she followed him to his address on Monterey Street and offered to take him shopping. Soon he was comfortably ensconced in the apartment above the deli and enjoying frequent deliveries of takeout food from the restaurant below. George also intercepted his mail, retaining the financial information, discarding the rest, and convincing the eighty-five-year-old man that his relatives had written him off. Then the couple began slipping him Halcion, grinding the blue-gray sleeping pills into food which Roland delivered. Uncle George scored several credit cards in Storvick's name and charged $5,000 on one card alone. Roland said that George had learned such manipulations after stealing a credit card from the previous upstairs tenant, an elderly gentleman named Arthur Brian Fish.

After several months of mistreatment, Steven Storvick confided to Roland that he was becoming suspicious of George and afraid of Angela. When Roland passed the word, George asked his nephew to help develop the old man as a "client." Roland quoted his uncle: "If you can hang out with this guy and he dies and leaves us a hundred grand, I'll give you twenty-five thousand dollars."

Roland said he continued to deliver contaminated food till one day he found the apartment empty and the old man gone. Uncle George was enraged when he heard the news. He bribed the movers and traced Storvick to a room in the run-down Mission District. "I found that son of a bitch!" he told his nephew. Roland said that Angela set right to work calming the old man in bed.

When Storvick again became suspicious a few weeks later, George threw up his hands. "I've been working on this guy for a year and a half," he told his nephew. "He's freaking out. He's gonna leave. I'm gonna get this guy outa here. *I'm gonna get this guy outa here.*"

Roland had taken the emphatic phrasing to mean that his uncle planned a final solution. He watched as Angela and George ground orange pills into his food instead of Halcion. They admitted that they wanted Storvick to die so they could grab his bank accounts. Then one day the old man moved again. Roland said they'd lost track of him after that, and turned to easier new clients.

Roland also confirmed that George and Angela often bragged about their scores: valuables taken from senile males whom Angela kept busy while George ransacked their homes; envelopes bulging with cash contributed by elderly "friends"; a luxury car that a victim had bought for Angela; scams on banks; joint tenancies and joint accounts they'd established; on and on. They didn't seem shy or ashamed or nervous about arrest. Roland confirmed that George kept a shotgun, a rifle and a silencer in his and Angela's half of the house on Fourteenth Avenue. He still used a computer and a camera to create fake ID cards and driver's licenses. Between his clients, his household activities and his clerking job at the car rental agency, Uncle George stayed busy.

IT WAS NEARLY midnight in the coffee shop, and Jerry Lama had been recounting his nephew's tale for two hours. Beans sat obediently outside the window, licking his lips as Fay poked at her second helping of carrot cake, the first food she'd eaten since lunch. She shook a finger at her canine partner and transmitted a telepathic message: *You wanted to be a detective, didn't you?*

Jerry looked red-eyed and tired. Jet lag, Fay decided, compounded by coffee, nicotine and anger. A waitress emptied their ashtray for the third time. Fay asked how well his nephew's story squared with his own memory and knowledge.

"Right on," he said hoarsely. "George feuded with the woman next door to the deli for years. He stole the vanity license plates off her Mercedes. I found 'em in his garage and turned 'em in as evidence. The woman got so pissed about the vandalism, she installed a video camera. The first week it was there, George ripped it off the fucking mounting! It's in his house right now, under the spiral staircase. The camera was outside but the actual recorder was inside where George couldn't get at it. The woman circulated his picture around the neighborhood. Remember what happened when George left his fake driver's license at the bank? *Nothing*, right? Well, this turned out the same fucking way. George laughed his ass off. He'd worn a disguise. Nobody recognized the security picture."

"He admitted all this?" Fay asked.

"I *told* you, Rat Dog. I'm his big brother." He lit another cigarette, blew a jet stream of smoke toward the window, and said, "George is a funny guy. He doesn't drink or do drugs and he's very intelligent. Working as a clerk is just a front. Right now him and Angela's main income comes from old men. And they're making *plenty*. How many people do you know that work at Budget fucking Rent-a-Car and drive a fucking Mercedes and belong to the Olympic Country Club?"

Fay asked, "Are they . . . in love?" Mating scorpions came to mind.

"Who the fuck knows?" Jerry said through the haze. "I asked him what she does with the old men. He said she gets naked and they go to bed. I said, George, how the fuck do you touch her after she sleeps with other men? He said, At ninety years old, what do you think they're capable of? They feel her, they play with her, they fall asleep. They're happy, she's happy. He says, It's just business, Jerry."

Business, Fay thought. The all-purpose rationalization. *It's just business.* So is vivisection. So is child pornography. So is the Mafia.

She asked if nephew Roland would stick to his story in court.

"He's told it on tape in front of three witnesses," Jerry answered, suppressing a yawn. "We got him locked in."

Fay didn't want to sound negative, but she couldn't help remembering her own courtroom experience: the repudiated confessions, the disavowed statements, the eyewitness identifications that changed into "maybe" and "perhaps" and "I can't be sure" on the witness stand. In the present state of the justice system, nothing was graven in Silly Putty, let alone stone.

After a final sip of cappuccino, Fay collected Beans and offered to give Jerry a ride, but he refused to enter the underground parking garage. "It's a good place to get hit," he explained.

43

Two Georges

IN THE MORNING Fay breakfasted on a brimming bowl of oatmeal and cranked up Evie the Everex. If Roland's story about his Uncle George checked out, the DA should be convening a grand jury to consider murder charges. She ran an "address profile" check on the Lama address on Fourteenth Avenue and came up with nothing on a George Lama. She tried minor variations and failed again. If Roland had told the truth, his evil uncle should have at least one listing and maybe more.

She punched in "60 West Portal," the address of the French Village Deli, and waited while Evie's inner organs moaned and groaned. At last two lines of information flickered into sight: George Antone Lama of the West Portal address possessed a valid California driver's license, and so did George Enzo Luccisanto of the same address. She asked a trusted DMV contact to pull the two licenses and compare the ID photos. The longtime member of the Friends of the Rat Dog Dick Detective Agency called back to report that the pictures appeared to be of the same man.

Fay phoned another networker at police headquarters and confirmed that official vandalism complaints had been lodged by the clothing store adjacent to the French Village Deli. Owner Simin Barjesteh had replaced her vanity plates—SIMIN—after the originals were stolen from her 1974 Mercedes in October 1990. Fay thought, You get a gold star on your chart, Roland! Ms. Barjesteh had a videotape that showed a masked man emerging from the deli and striding toward her shop. The picture went black after the man flung a hood over the outdoor camera. When the owner arrived in the morning to open up, the unit had been ripped from its mount and stolen.

FAY BEGAN TO wonder if it was time-effective to back-check Jerry Lama's information. So far she hadn't caught him in a lie or even an exaggeration. He seemed to have a photographic memory, and except for an occasional F-word he laid out his facts like a skilled lawyer addressing a jury. She was glad they were on the same side. What an enemy he would make in court!

But she still lacked verification on the Storvick case. If Roland Dabai's story was true, the retired stevedore had caught on to the scam and escaped the predators. Surely he'd complained to the police at some point? What had the cops done about it? Their usual nothing?

At the Federal Building she found immigration records showing that Steven (originally Sverre) had come to the United States from Norway. Through other sources she learned that he was a childless widower with a sixth-grade education and had worked on the San Francisco docks for twenty years. In a bank questionnaire he'd listed his interests as "Plays horses on weekend. Reads carpenter book. Current events." He kept a $120,000 certificate of deposit in a safe deposit box at First Interstate. He'd written a new will naming Angela Bufford as his sole heir but ripped it up after complaining to a lawyer that he was "being harassed by certain persons." Other records revealed a cryptic entry in neat block printing, written by his attorney: "Called Mr. Storvick who cussed me & told me that I had given out his phone # and that my friends were after his money. I suspect Angela & Co. Anyhow called PacBell and arranged a total block in that allowed Mr. Storvick to call out." Under a final revised will, the old man's estate was to go to relatives in the old country.

AT THE HALL of Justice, Fay learned that she'd guessed right; Steven Storvick *had* gone to the police, but with an unexpected companion. The files showed a "possible fraud/confidence scam report" prepared by an officer named M. Gallegos in March 1991. As suspects, the patrolman listed "Angela Bufford alias Angela Ciampa WF born 4/10/60 5'5 140 lbs brown hair blue eyes very attractive, possible Eurasian (Gypsie) background." It was confusing. If Angela had accompanied the old man to the police station, how had she wound up as a suspect?

SFPD report # 910329970 noted that Steven Storvick and Angela Bufford had complained to Mission District police that someone was trying to steal his life savings. The retired stevedore informed Officer Gallegos that he'd written a new will naming his dear friend Angela beneficiary. His story changed in the recounting and he seemed scattered, claiming at one point that he'd received phone calls from a male who said, "I hear you have lots of money. I'm going to get your money."

The Gallegos report noted, "I asked Bufford what was her relationship to Storvick. She stated she had known Storvick for two years and does errands and provides transportation and companionship for Storvick as friends."

The conscientious officer had checked with Fraud Unit detectives and learned that Angela and her boyfriend George Lama ("WM 5'9, 145 lbs, brn hair, brn eyes") were suspected of running a confidence scheme in which "Lama rents an apartment to elderly people gaining their confidence by providing errands, transportation and companionship whereby they learn about the elderly's financial and social status in return for monetary gain." They were also suspected of feeding Storvick dangerous drugs.

A few days after preparing his report, Gallegos had visited Storvick and his lady friend in their run-down apartment on Guerrero Street. The officer separated the couple by asking Angela to step into another room. After the frail old man was fully briefed about his companions, he recalled that on several dark nights a male jogger had bumped him from the rear and almost knocked him down. He also complained that he'd awakened one morning almost paralyzed, confronted Angela, and accepted her explanation that she'd accidentally overdosed him with sleeping pills. He told the officer that whenever he charged Angela with trying to take his money, she cried to regain his sympathy. Gallegos reported:

> Approximately (15) minutes into this interview Bufford entered Storvick's apartment and stated she had to leave. I asked Bufford if she could stay (5) minutes longer and if she had her California Drivers License and other ID with her. Bufford stated she had lost her identification. I then asked Bufford if she could supply a birth certificate at a later date and she stated she would. At this time I showed Bufford the photo of [George] Lama and she stated she did not know him but it looked like the man who rented the apartment to Storvick. Bufford then asked if there was something wrong and asked why I was asking questions. I then told Bufford

that the information I was asking for was necessary for the police report I was preparing. At this point Bufford stated she wanted to talk to her lawyer. Bufford then left the apartment after being told her lawyer could contact the police department regarding this incident report. . . .

After Bufford left, Storvick told me Bufford had found Storvick a new apartment to live in and was planning on moving Storvick to this new apartment during the evening of 3/12/91. Storvick stated to me he was not going to move and would stay on Guerrero until this matter was resolved. Also stated he wanted to change his will and reinstate the original family members to the will.

AFTER DIGESTING THE police reports, Fay ran Steven Storvick on the death index, ordered the corresponding certificate, and learned that he'd died on August 10, 1992, four months after his ninetieth birthday, of respiratory failure, pneumonia and lung cancer, compounded by "asbestos emphysema." It didn't sound much like poisoning, but Storvick's personal physician confided that the old man had seemed in good health a month before his death.

Fay checked with Jerry Lama and learned that George had bragged about bumping into the retired stevedore in an attempt to knock him down, break his hip and immobilize him, thus putting him at the mercy of his two young friends. Clearly the Storvick adventure had ended up as a nonprofit deal for the hustlers. Fay decided that George and Angela must have been refining their techniques at the time. Every business had start-up problems, and some old folks were just too cussedly mean to lie down and die on command. Jerry said that George and Angela had simply turned their attention to other targets, as Roland Dabai had already reported. Now one of the marks, old Richard Nelson, was under the protection of his family. But . . . what about the other old man, the retired transit engineer?

She dialed the Fraud Unit and asked if anyone had interviewed Harry Glover Hughes. She was told it was "still on our list of things to do."

She lowered the phone with a sick feeling. She thought, I told them about Mr. Hughes and Mr. Nelson *last spring*. Jerry's sisters gave them the same information even earlier. Now it's November, and Mr. Hughes is . . . "on our list of things to do"? She thought, These old men aren't dead and gone like Mr. Liotweizen or Mrs. Beesley or Angela's husband Nicholas Bufford. They can be interviewed. They can testify. They're *alive!* Or are they?

She shuddered at the thought that the SFPD had left the old man to his fate. She sped to the 2500 block of Twenty-third Avenue and knocked on his door. There was no answer, as expected. Glen Billy had told her that Hughes was seldom at home. From neighbors Fay learned that the ninety-three-year-old pensioner was a familiar neighborhood sight, trudging along with buckets of clay that he dug to thicken the sandy soil in the mini-garden behind his house. He was described as a debonair, self-sufficient and courtly old man who was shaped like a pencil and wore flannel shirts buttoned to the top in every temperature. He'd fought in World War I, retired comfortably after a long career with the California Department of Transportation, and become a net-worth millionaire through shrewd investments. He was an amateur photographer and still hiked to the zoo to shoot pictures of elephants and giraffes and big cats. He enjoyed spinning long yarns without endings.

Lately, neighbors said, the old gentleman had been having problems with disorientation, especially at night, but he always managed to find his way home, sometimes with the assistance of others, including police, whom he invited in for tea. The consensus on the block was that Mr. Hughes was competent but failing—but definitely alive. Friends said he retained the old-fashioned social graces, stood up when women entered the room, pulled out chairs, said "thank you" and "please," and smiled benignly when introduced. But he drank a little too much and tended to forget names, phone numbers and addresses, including his own. A near neighbor reported that Mr. Hughes was a proud founder of the California State Employees Credit Union, attended meetings as far away as Carmel, and was angry with himself on the frequent occasions when he forgot.

Fay thought: *Union?* She remembered the note from the Fourteenth Avenue trash can: *Papa forgot his union meeting. I'll be sure he goes,* or something similar. Unlikely as it had seemed at the time, the well-fixed Harry Glover Hughes was a union man of sorts. Everything was clicking into place.

The neighbors shared an admiring attitude about the old man's two friends, Angela and George, and felt he was lucky to have such companionship. He'd always been gregarious, and his visitors seemed to match his personality. "Hi!" the young couple would call to friendly neighbors as they ascended his front stairs. "How ya doing today?" Sometimes they stopped to discuss gardening and complain about their own brown thumbs. The guy with the thinning hairline admired the 49ers and the Giants and the woman with the curvy legs disliked cold and fog. The couple visited so often that they almost seemed a part of the neighborhood.

FAY SNAPPED A few pictures of the Hughes house in the middle of a prime block of the Sunset. The lovely old district always reminded her of something she'd read to the effect that San Francisco's homes were "flung across her forty-two hills like wash drying in the sunlight." From his rooftop, where neighbors said Mr. Hughes spent part of every sunny day, he could see two miles to Ocean Beach and ten miles to the Farallon Islands. Just to his south lay Stern Grove, twelve square blocks of eucalyptus, rhododendrons, camellias and other greenery, including a few specimens that grew nowhere else in northern California. In summertime, music from outdoor concerts echoed off San Bruno Mountain with its winking transmitter towers. Morning sun highlighted the turquoise dome of St. Cecilia's Church, whose chimes called the faithful to worship, and farther to the east the big illuminated cross on Mount Davidson served as a landmark for ships at sea and an aggravation to freethinkers who thought its concrete base should be ground up to fill potholes. The ambiance was bucolic European, except for an air raid siren that sounded every Tuesday at noon for reasons that no one could explain.

Residents told Fay that hardly a morning passed on the block without the appearance of the pretty woman in her blue-white BMW or Mr. Hughes' male friend in his white Mercedes, delivering food in Styrofoam containers which they usually carried away later. The couple seemed to personify the wholesome concept of "random acts of kindness." They hauled off Glover's garbage and trash in plastic bags, sparing him a neglected chore that had become painful with age.

Fay said to herself, No *wonder* I never found trash cans at his curb.

She realized that she should have banged on the old man's door months earlier and interviewed him on the spot, but she'd been nervous about interfering with the police investigation. Next time, she said to herself, I'll interview first and worry about the cops later.

44

Loving Friends

FAY RETURNED TO the neighborhood a few mornings later to talk to a close Hughes friend who'd been out of town during her original canvass. Someone had said that the woman was the only person on the block who'd ever expressed doubts about the elderly man's companions.

Fay knocked and was invited into the vestibule by a handsome fortyish woman with the bearing of someone accustomed to giving more orders than she took. "What's your interest in Mr. Hughes?" the woman asked.

Fay handed over her card and immediately wished she hadn't. If the woman behind the designer spectacles wasn't put off by the name Rat Dog Dick, she surely would hate the sexy-female logo. *When will you ever learn, Fay, you silly person?*

As the woman studied the card, she asked, "Are you Rat Dog Dick?" When Fay nodded, she said, "Do people call you Rat Dog? *Dick?* Or what?"

"It's . . . Fay." She quickly explained that she'd been investigating an old client's death when she stumbled on information that Mr. Hughes and another elderly man were in danger.

"Stumbled?"

"Well, I didn't mean I actually stumbled. I mean, my dog and I drove out to these people's house early one morning—"

She cut herself off. Why had she mentioned Beans? And surely there was no point in trying to explain freelance trash collection. Yawczak and Ovanessian had already made it plain that her gumshoeing techniques wouldn't stand up in court, and the police department didn't sanction much of anything she did, least of all sneaking around at 5:00 A.M. collecting used grapefruits.

She decided to change her approach. "Let's just say I have contacts," she said. "That's my job. I, I—find things out."

"What did you find out about Mr. Hughes?"

"He and another old man are being cheated. And maybe . . . poisoned." She plowed ahead. "They might die. And nobody cares."

The woman smiled. "Somebody cares," she said. "I thought I was alone in this. Please, Fay, come in and sit down."

THEY TALKED FOR the rest of the morning. The woman apologized for her cool greeting, but she said she was tired of being the only person who was convinced that George and Angela were criminals. She seemed in deep fear of the couple. "Please," she said, "don't use my name in your reports." Fay thought of listing her as Deep Throat, but settled on the pseudonym Margaret Buchanan.

The woman was a business executive and had functioned as informal adviser to her neighbor, viewing the goings-on from close range, sometimes from inside the old man's house. She was the first to notice that his telephone had been changed and unlisted.

"Glover would never have done that on his own," she said. "You could check phone books back to 1926 and find Harry Glover Hughes with basically the same number. He *never* would have isolated himself. How would his beloved union get in touch with him?"

"Did you ask George and Angela about the new number?"

"They played dumb. I said, Okay, then, if you don't know why the number was changed, I'll change it back. I found out later that George had given Pacific Bell a password to keep anyone from changing the number back. I got it changed, but it was a hell of a job."

"A password?" Fay said. "I'll have to try that." She'd had several threatening calls from a man who sounded like a TV wrestler. *Listen, bitch, I know where your kids go to school.* She'd have been more frightened if she had children.

"Margaret Buchanan" said she'd been concerned about her friend Glover's new pals for months. "They act so *loving*. They hug him, take his arm, help him into their car. I sensed from the beginning that they're too damned good to be true. Glover has a pacemaker and they were in his house when he had his third heart attack. He was playing the piano and went all cold and clammy. George drove him to the hospital in his Mercedes."

Fay thought, Heart attack! *Digitalis?*

She asked, "How'd they meet?" even though she was fairly sure she knew the answer.

"He was eating a sandwich at the French Village Deli. At first they called him Papa, but he thought that was a little too personal. He's very polite and formal. And *strong* for his age. Repainted his house when he was ninety! They went on a cruise last summer."

"Cruise?"

"Yep. The three of 'em, Glover, Angela and George. To Alaska. Glover said he enjoyed the ocean but wished he had more privacy. They shared a cabin."

"Does he talk about them a lot?" Fay asked. She was thinking of Konstantin Liotweizen and the way Mary Steiner had carefully separated him from his circle of friends.

"Yes, but they're not his favorite subject. The other day I said, Glover, who *are* these people? He said, They're cousins, but they live in the same house. I said, Have you given them any money? He said, You know I'm too smart for that. I said, Well, I'm nervous about your accounts. Let's check your balances and see where you stand. I looked them over and I was *aghast!* I asked if he was getting financial advice from George and Angela and he admitted he was."

"It's a wonder he admitted anything," Fay said. "Another victim did the denial number and lost a bundle."

"I don't think they've cleaned Glover out. Not yet, anyway."

"They've been busy with a man named Nelson. They just got caught in his bank accounts."

"*Really?* Will they go to jail?"

"Let's hope so." Given the lethargic state of the police investigation, she didn't know how else to answer.

"I hope somebody helps poor Glover," the woman said. "He's defenseless. I phoned the cops, but they always seem busy. I try to warn him that he's being taken for a sucker, but he says, George is my friend, he calls me every morning, he saved my life. He says, They bring me breakfast and take me out. Besides, he says, they owe me money. I asked him how much and he had no idea."

"Isn't there anything you can do? He obviously trusts you."

"He trusted me enough to take my advice and cut them out of his life—for about ten days. But then George sweet-talked him on the phone. Angela started coming over again, and Glover would entertain her on the piano. He drinks too much and he always plays ragtime when he's had a few. They resumed bringing food. Just this morning they brought his breakfast. Right now the three of 'em are out on a drive. I can't believe the nerve."

"I can," Fay said.

45

Dependency

EN ROUTE HOME, she willed herself to ignore the grinding noise from under the Frog Prince's bilious green hood and gave silent thanks that at least one endangered elder had an intelligent friend to take an interest in his health and finances. She wondered how Richard Nelson was doing and put in a call to his nephew Donald in Atherton. She wasn't surprised to learn that Angela was still in the picture, despite her involuntary visit to the Taraval Policy Station.

"We've warned Uncle Dick again and again," Don Nelson said, "but he doesn't want to hear about it. Angela's created such a dependency. He says, I need her. I can't get to the store anymore. She drives me to the doctor, cleans my house, makes my meals."

"That's the way the scam works," Fay said.

"Gerry and I drove up to his place and she was sitting on the arm of his chair, stroking his cheek. Uncle Dick looked awful. He'd taken another spill, and they were comforting each other. He was in pain and she needed money. He'd just finished writing her checks for fifty-five hundred and fifteen hundred. A nice afternoon's work for a salesclerk, huh? When she stepped out of the room for a minute, I said, Well, Dick, maybe it's time for a nice retirement center."

"Good move," Fay said.

"He didn't think so. So Gerry said, Tell ya what, Uncle Dick, come to Atherton and live with us for a while and we'll look at some places for you. If that doesn't work, we'll bring you back here. We didn't think he'd go for it, but as soon as the girlfriend left, it took him fifteen minutes to pack. That's how suggestible he is."

"He's living with you now?" Fay asked.

"He's in a very nice retirement home. But that doesn't keep him from phoning Angela every day. I asked him why he was staying in touch, and he said it was about a hundred-dollar check he'd given her to cash. And he wondered what she'd done with his disabled-parking placard. He said she has an attorney now and they promised to visit."

"Criminy," Fay said. "That's all he needs—two crooks and a lawyer."

"We enlarged one of her photos from our lawn party and gave it to the retirement home manager. Told him to alert us if that woman tries to get in. So far she hasn't."

Well, she *will*, Fay thought. If there's one thing Angela Ciampa, Theresa Tene, Angela Bufford, Mary Steiner, Mary Tene, Bessie Tene, Danny Tene, Danny Bimbo, Sal Lamance and the whole darned Tene Bimbo family have in common, it's nerve.

46

Terminal Amnesia

A FEW MORNINGS before Thanksgiving, 1993, Fay was working on a fresh and original way to describe an old San Francisco neighborhood in *Lily Kills Her Client*, her detective novel that was proceeding at the rate of about a paragraph per day. She reread her total output from the week before:

> North Beach is bordered by the green lawn of Washington Square to the north, Broadway's flesh parlors to the south, a boulevard of cafés to the west, and the sky along the top.

Within this vertical slice of heaven sits a quiet neighborhood of expensive condos, run-down bohemian flats and practically no parking spots. The place Lily's rich client called home was the top third of a trilevel which hung off the winding street that led to the city's only 360-degree view you could walk to without having to stop to throw up along the way.

Something bothered her about the passage, but she couldn't decide whether it was the reference to a disagreeable body function or the fact that the last sentence was overlong. She gave up and turned to the latest questions from "Ask Rat Dog" readers about identity theft, adoption searching, collecting bad debts, checking up on wandering husbands, and how to achieve orgasm. In this newest batch of letters she found three with jailhouse postmarks. Prisoners' letters were frustrating because there were so few questions she could answer. How to tell if your cellmate is cheating? How to break out? Every convict had been railroaded by a vicious prosecutor and Rat Dog Dick was the only living human who could prove it. She wondered how she'd managed to become the private eye of last resort. Maybe it had something to do with the sexy picture that King Features insisted on running with her column.

"Dear Ms. Rat Dog," she read. "I have nothing left except my name and a desire to clear it before I cave in to total depravity."

After referring to John 3:16, the inmate launched into a two-page elegy of total depravity. She jumped ahead to the ending: "I will give you voluptuous amounts of chocolate, bushels of flowers, and perhaps even a diamond or two if you come to visit."

She was trying to imagine the effect of voluptuous amounts of chocolate on her dress size when the splenetic Jerry Lama phoned with news that catapulted her back into the world of poisons and Gypsies and callous cops. It seemed that his nephew Roland Dabai was wavering about testifying against George and Angela. Roland had gone to court on his theft charge and was enraged by the result. Jerry, not the world's most patient Palestinian himself, was trying to keep the young man in line.

"What went wrong?" Fay asked. "I thought he had a deal."

"Roland got *no* fucking deal," Jerry said on the phone from New York. "After all their promises, the Fraud Unit did nothing. I called Ovanessian and said, What the fuck are you guys doing? You promised to help the kid. He said, Well, we gotta be careful how we deal with informants. They give us a little information and then they want favors and favors and favors. I said, *Favors?* You guys didn't do him favor *one*! He's your most important witness. You got no serial murder case without Roland! He said, Jerry, calm down. We already got his statement. I said, You got his statement, Inspector, but if you keep fucking with him you're not gonna have *Roland*, ya know what I mean?"

"What'd he say to that?"

"He told me not to worry about it."

"That's their slogan."

"I said, Roland's statement ain't worth shit if he ain't there to back it up. I said, Ya know what I think? I think Roland's gonna develop terminal fucking amnesia."

Fay asked, "Did that reach him?"

"You kiddin'? Those cops, it's fuck me and fuck Roland. Every night, I'm wet-nursing the kid by long distance. Funny things are going on. His mother found him a place to live—no more studying in a closet—and all of a sudden she's giving him a big fucking allowance. Then I hear George is slipping him big bucks. I'm thinking, What is Roland, the United fucking Fund? I call up and say, Hey, Roland, what is this I'm hearing? Are you gonna change your story to get more money out of Uncle George? Roland says, Never mind what you're hearing. The bottom line is I'm gonna testify under oath, and I'm gonna tell it straight."

"Do you think he'll keep his word?" Fay asked.

"No. I think he's outa here. But . . . maybe I got somebody else to take his place."

"Who?"

"I'll see you tomorrow. I'm heading for the airport."

47

The Magic Salt

THE NEXT MORNING Jerry phoned her from the Hall of Justice. She wondered who'd paid for the transcontinental round trip this time. He told her that his brother-in-law Nabib Atalla had chatted with police and now was willing to be interviewed in depth, but strictly on his own terms: no taping, no visits to his home, just a friendly talk in a restaurant. And Jerry had to be present. Apparently no male member of the Lama family would go near a cop without Jerry.

"What's Nabib told 'em so far?" Fay asked.

"Nothing much they don't know already. He told about the magic salt. Said George used it to slow the heartbeat, make it irregular, get things done faster instead of waiting for God's will. He said George told him the idea came from Angela's family. Danny Tene took over a big mansion and his mother inherited twelve condos. Angela got a car from Mr. Nelson. And he told 'em how George was listed on Harry Glover Hughes' ID card as the person to call in an emergency. That's about it. But Nabib knows a lot more. So . . . we're on our way to Citrus fucking Heights, California."

"You and who else?"

"Ovanessian and Yawczak."

Fay groaned.

BUT WHEN SHE saw the police write-up on the visit to Nabib Atalla, she felt a touch of optimism. Would the case be broken after all? She typed the crucial new information onto a floppy disk labeled "tne.cse."

1. George and Angela first drugged Steven Storvick so they could steal his valuables and use his apartment for sex.
2. George showed Atalla a burrito that he'd prepared for Harry Glover Hughes and told him it was spiked.

3. Mr. Hughes gave George his power of attorney and willed him his million-dollar estate. To allay suspicion, George prepared a new will that left a small amount to two Hughes nephews and a charity.
4. Mr. Hughes was losing his memory and Angela held his hand every night as they watched TV.
5. Angela and George stole his Masonic ring and square-faced Bulova watch.
6. George intended to file harassment charges against Ovanessian and Yawczak.

Jerry told Fay that the fraud inspectors seemed inspired by the interview with his brother-in-law, but as usual they'd needed guidance to draw him out. "When Nabib mentioned magic salt," Jerry said, "they bore down. They asked if he'd seen it himself. He said no, and they acted like they couldn't bring charges unless they knew what color it was, how it went into the victim's mouth, through his intestines and out his ass. I could see Nabib getting pissed. Pretty soon I was running the show and the cops were taking notes. Just like the interview with Roland."

"Terrible technique," Fay said. "That could hurt when the case goes to court."

"Maybe so, but Nabib wouldn't talk otherwise. When we were walking out of the coffee shop, Ovanessian said they let me ask the questions because I was on a roll. He said they don't usually operate like that. We got back to San Francisco at two o'clock in the morning and him and Yawczak had to punch the time clock. We're walking into the Hall of Justice and another inspector says, Hey, what're you guys working on? Ovanessian says, You know that bitch that's burying old people in her backyard in Sacramento? Well, this case'll make her look like a Girl Scout."

"Signs of life!" Fay exclaimed. "Signs of interest! The SFPD returns from the dead."

"Maybe they weren't dead," Jerry said. "Maybe they were just on their break."

Fay said they'd certainly had her fooled.

48

Alaska in January

THE YEAR-END HOLIDAYS came and went, and 1994 arrived with no further signs of activity by the Fraud Unit or any other branch of city government. Fay still presumed that they were working quietly behind the scenes, checking Harry Glover Hughes' blood for digitalis, keeping an eye on George and Angela, studying bank records and in general helping the DA make the complex case.

On Wednesday, January 5, "Margaret Buchanan" phoned to tell Fay that she hadn't seen Mr. Hughes since New Year's Day. "It's probably nothing. He's independent, crawls into his shell, doesn't like to be bothered by well-wishers."

"What about the cops and . . . his blood?"

"His *blood?*"

"Yawczak was supposed to arrange a blood test."

"Never happened. There hasn't been a cop around here in a month. I called Inspector Ovanessian a few weeks ago and told him George just arrived to drive Glover down the peninsula for lunch. He said, Well, there's nothing I can do about that. I said, Didn't you ask me to call you if they showed up? Didn't you tell me these people are killers? He said, There's no law that says you can't have lunch with anybody you want."

Fay thought, Here we go again. Inertia, indifference. "Rats," she said. "What are the cops *waiting* for?"

"I'm worried, Fay," Margaret confided. "Glover's becoming delusional. He thinks he's been named executor of a friend's estate and chatters about it constantly. He thinks he went to Lake Tahoe with George and Angela, but I'm sure he's confusing it with someplace else. He went for a drive with Angela and came back and told me they'd been on a business trip to Daly City or maybe it was Berkeley or San Jose. His short-term memory is shot. He pays the same bills two or three times and ignores others, gets into big fights about late charges, forgets—"

"Have you checked his bank accounts?"

"As best I can. He thinks he has a downtown savings account but he closed it out years ago. He forgot a live account that goes back to the forties. It's been dormant for so long the state was getting ready to confiscate the balance. He has three joint accounts with George Lama, including one at the Stonestown branch of Wells Fargo, but he's not aware of any of 'em. None of his checkbooks balance, and for the first time in his life he's got tax problems. He said George had him write out a ten-thousand-dollar check and promised to deliver it to the IRS, but it never arrived. Fay, I'm worried sick. Glover's too fine a person to end up like this."

AN HOUR LATER, Margaret Buchanan called to say that she'd found a note pinned to the Hughes door. "Gone to Alaska on rather short notice."

"Alaska?" Fay said.

"He must be with George and Angela. They cruised there before."

"Cruising to Alaska?" Fay said. "In January?" She thought of the punchline of one of her dad's old jokes: "The second prize is *two* weeks in Fairbanks."

She wondered if the sudden decision to go to sea might be related to the latest revelations about the "magic salt." By now, George and Angela knew that Richard Nelson's blood was being closely monitored. The Fraud Unit was being silent about Harry Glover Hughes, but his tests couldn't be far behind. A voyage outside the continental limits of the United States would separate the intended victim from police while purging his bloodstream with alcohol and lavish meals. Could that explain the "rather short notice"?

A WEEK LATER Margaret Buchanan reported that Glover was back and ditsier than ever. He barely remembered the trip. The vessel had made three stops, but he wasn't sure of the locations. "I asked him how he'd enjoyed Alaska in the winter. He told me it was too damned hot."

FAY FOUND THE cruise data easy to track. Six months earlier, in June 1993, H. G. Hughes of 2526 Twenty-third Avenue had paid a travel agency $2,155 for three round-trip fares to Alaska. The same individual paid $2,376 for the January 1994 trip, again for three passengers, but this time the destination was Mexico. The old man had simply confused "northbound" with "southbound." No wonder Alaska had seemed so hot.

Fay called Buchanan to share the information. They agreed that the old man, teetering through his tenth decade of life, was beyond caring about latitude.

49

The Hughes Intervention

WITH HARRY GLOVER Hughes back home in San Francisco, Inspector Dan Yawczak finally got around to the intervention that had been ordered months earlier. Fay learned the details from Margaret Buchanan, who'd gone along with an assistant DA as witness. She said that Yawczak had carried a box of documents to help make his points to the old man. Speaking slowly and distinctly, the fraud unit inspector had said, "Mr. Hughes, we think you're involved with some bad people."

He showed driver's-license photos of George and Angela and asked if they visited often.

"Not very," the old man said.

"Oh, Glover," Buchanan put in. "They're here all the time!"

Yawczak handed over a picture of Angela and old Richard Nelson arm in arm at the Nelsons' lawn party. "Mr. Hughes, I want you to take a good look at this, so you'll know I'm not making up this story. You see, you're not Angela's only boyfriend. This is Richard Nelson. He's in love with Angela too, and she claims she's in love with him. He fixed up a room for her at his house. We have it in writing."

The detective produced a picture of the lovebirds beaming from the front seat of her BMW. "Did you know Mr. Nelson bought her this car?" he said.

The old man glanced at the picture uncomprehendingly. Yawczak slowed down even more. "Let me ask you something, Mr. Hughes," he said as though talking to a child. "Do you know any *good* people who carry two driver's licenses? With two different names? What would you think of someone with two licenses? *What would that mean to you?*"

Hughes stared back.

"Look at this," Yawczak said, and handed over copies of driver's licenses issued to George Antone Lama and George Enzo Luccisanto, both with the same address and picture.

The old man finally admitted that he'd given Angela $70 for "house money." He said that George had suggested opening a joint account so that emergency funds would be available if he had another heart attack, but he'd rejected the suggestion. "Do you have *any* joint accounts with these people?" Yawczak asked.

"No."

The detective produced statements from the three joint accounts, and Hughes acted surprised. He suggested that someone check the signature cards on file at the bank "and if it's my signature, it's a forgery."

"Did you ever sign a joint tenancy agreement with George or Angela?" Yawczak asked.

"No."

"Did you marry her?"

"Oh, no," the old man said. "We're just good friends."

"Do Angela and George bring you food?"

"It tastes funny. Too bland."

"Did you ever make out a will naming George or Angela as executors or beneficiaries?"

The old man shook his head.

"Or a codicil?"

"No."

"So if we found your signature on a new will or codicil, it would also be a forgery?"

"Or . . . a trick."

Hughes was asked if he'd listed George or Angela as beneficiaries on life insurance policies or bought any real property with them.

"No," he replied.

"Did you give them your power of attorney or cosign any loans?"

"No."

"Did you cosign for this car?"

Hughes blinked behind his glasses as the inspector handed over a copy of a registration certificate issued to a Mercedes 380SL, license number 2KKR420, jointly owned by Harry Glover Hughes and George Antone Lama. "Did you buy this car with George?"

The old man said he hadn't owned a car in years. "Isn't this your address on the registration?" Yawczak asked.

Hughes didn't seem to hear. "Funny, I never got any mail from the DMV about this," he mused.

Yawczak asked for permission to check his bank statements and tax returns. Hughes rummaged in his drawers, but nothing came to hand. "That stuff might be in my safe deposit box," he said.

"Where do you keep the key?"

"It's been, uh, missing for about a year."

The old man couldn't remember if he'd made out a will. If he had, he said, it was probably in his safe deposit box at a bank in West Portal. That was also where he kept his gold coins.

The detective said, "Do you mean the First Commercial Bank on Taraval?"

Hughes said he wasn't sure.

When Yawczak informed him that Angela's other elderly boyfriend had tested positive for a dangerous heart medication, Hughes looked alarmed and said, "Should I have my blood checked?" and added as an afterthought, "Maybe I should stay away from George and Angela."

Yawczak shook his head and said, "Maybe you should."

After a while the threesome adjourned for an afternoon drive, first to a notary public, where Hughes signed a consent form authorizing the police to examine his bank accounts, then to the Wells Fargo bank branch in the mall where his friend Angela Bufford worked as a clerk.

"Mr. Hughes, did you sign this?" Yawczak asked when the signature cards for account 6049-575533 were produced. The old man said the signature looked authentic but he didn't remember signing. At the inspector's suggestion, the account was canceled. When Yawczak suggested that they review his stock holdings, Hughes said he had a broker but couldn't remember his name. The odd trio—Buchanan, the old man and the detective—ended the day at the offices of Hughes' personal physician, where a sample of blood was drawn. Yawczak said he would deliver it by hand to the medical examiner.

* * *

"GLOVER'S STILL IN shock," Margaret Buchanan told Fay after briefing her about the intervention. "He keeps saying, How could Angela possibly do something like this? He vacillates between anger and hurt. He doesn't know what the hell to think. I've never seen him so upset."

"Is he gonna break things off?"

"I'm not so sure. I didn't realize how much he's deteriorated. I honestly don't think he gets the picture. When I left, he was saying over and over, But she's so *pretty*. . . ."

Fay remembered the word she'd learned from the social worker Glen Billy: *labile*. It was a perfect fit for Glover Hughes. She was sure it would also fit the others who'd fallen into the predators' web: Philip Steiner, Nicholas Bufford, Konstantin Liotweizen, Hope Victoria Beesley, "Uncle Dick" Nelson. Steven Storvick had been suggestible, too, but he'd wriggled away in time to die a natural death.

WHEN THE HUGHES blood tested negative for toxic substances, Fay was angrier than ever at the way the case was being handled. What would they have found if the tests has been made before the sea cruise? How would it have tested three months earlier, when they'd first checked Richard Nelson? Or a year ago, when the Fraud Unit had been warned about George and Angela? She'd never seen such unconcern about human life, whether young or old. It was as though the cops were investigating the demise of a dead seal washed up on Ocean Beach.

"George and Angela won't stop unless the cops clamp down hard," she predicted to Margaret Buchanan over the phone. She hoped she was wrong but was sure that she wasn't. In a high school biology class, she'd learned one eternal verity about hyenas: they never stopped acting like hyenas.

ANOTHER WEEK PASSED, and Margaret called to report that the hyenas had just entered the Hughes house to a warm greeting by the owner. It was their fourth or fifth visit in the last few days. "Where's his family?" Fay asked. "Aren't they protecting him?"

"His family doesn't know what's happening."

"The police haven't—?"

"Nope. They haven't informed the family."

"How's Mr. Hughes doing?"

"He's drinking heavier. Forgets his pills. He's reverted to the 1930s.

He thinks bread should be a quarter a loaf, and the other day he asked me what happened to the milkman. He still insists Angela's gonna marry him."

"Don't tell me she's still bringing food?"

"Not unless it's in her purse. I'm watching pretty closely. The cops want a sample real bad. Yawczak told me to dial nine-one-one if she shows up with takeout and he'll send a black-and-white to collect it. Jesus, it's getting like the movies around here!"

"Didn't the cops take food samples earlier?"

"Yeah, but I think there was a problem at the lab."

"They probably let it spoil," Fay said, "or misplaced it."

"Or ate it," Margaret said. Fay started to laugh and cut it off. With this police department, it could be the truth.

50

Exit Roland

FAY WAS PONDERING whether to contact the Hughes relatives herself when Jerry Lama burst into her office. "We lost Roland!" he blurted out.

"He *died?*" Fay said.

Jerry was breathing hard. He said, "My fucking nephew will *not* fucking testify."

"Sit, Jerry," she ordered. "What happened?"

As he talked, he chased his cigarette puffs from one side of her dining room/office to the other. "First my sister Hami tells me George blew his top. He's been running around the house saying, I'm not going down alone! Before I go I'm gonna take care of that fucking Jerry! Then Roland calls me and he says George is driving my mother crazy, telling her to sweet-talk me and Roland off his case. My mom tells him she can't control me and Roland, but she'll have no trouble testifying that nofuckingbody poisoned nofuckingbody."

"What'd you expect?" Fay said. "She's George's mother."

"Yeah, but what's Roland's excuse? He told me he finally met with George and he was sure George bugged the room. He goes in for that shit, ya know? George told him to deny everything he told the cops and say I coached him on everything the fuck he said."

"So Roland's siding with George now?"

"It looks that way. Remember, the kid hates cops."

He told her he was en route to the Fraud Unit and would call later.

THE PHONE WAS ringing that evening when she returned from her evening romp with Beans. Jerry said he'd had a long·talk with Yawczak, and it looked as though the investigation was dead and buried.

"Why?" Fay said. "Because Roland reneged?"

"Yep."

"They've got other witnesses. There's hard evidence. There's—"

"The cops don't give a fuck. Yawczak says he's tying up a few loose ends and then it's over."

"Isn't anybody worried about the old men?"

"Yawczak says, As far as I'm concerned, if George and Angela have any brains they won't do this anymore. They know we're on to them. The dead aren't gonna get any fucking deader. He says, Jerry, the problem is taken care of."

Fay flopped on her couch, legs akimbo, and almost dropped the phone. "What did *you* say?"

"I said, What about fucking justice? Yawczak gets right in my face. He says you wanna talk about justice, Jerry? He says, Look at the Menendez brothers. They blow their parents' heads off and they'll probably walk. He says, There *is* no justice, Jerry! I said. What'd you do about the Gypsy broad in Marin County? He said, That's outa my jurisdiction."

Fay was puzzled. "Gypsy broad?" she said.

"A coupla months ago I tipped him about a Gypsy mama scamming old men in Marin. I thought he'd pass it along to the Marin sheriff. How hard is it to pick up the fucking phone and tell 'em this sweetheart-scamming is going on in our jurisdiction and it's also going on in yours? Maybe Marin County'll fucking *do* something. Yawczak—never—made—the call."

Fay said, "I'll talk to Greg—"

"Forget Ovanessian. He's off the case. You ready for this?" He didn't wait for an answer. "They assigned him to a parking lot skimming investigation at Candlestick Park. Yawczak says, None of the top cops give a fuck about Gypsies. He says the chief of police put Ovanessian on the Candlestick case so he could get some press in the *Chronicle*." Jerry took a breath and added, "I think Ovanessian is glad to get away from that fucking Yawczak. Those dudes never hit it off."

"Which would explain a few things."

"Ovanessian is too nice a guy to complain."

"What about Mr. Nelson? Mr. Hughes? What about the Storvick case?"

"Do you think the cops give a fuck about these old men?"

Fay suggested that Jerry contact the city attorney or her investigators and bring them up to date on the latest nonevents. "I trust Louise Renne," she said. "I trust Tim Armistead and Alex Kline. Maybe *they* can do something."

Jerry said he'd just about given up on San Francisco officials, even the good ones. Fay couldn't blame him. The Fraud Unit was off the case. The DA's Office was silent. Nobody seemed to be doing much of anything. Ho-hum, she said to herself. I hope we're not disturbing their rest.

51

A Slight Hope

FAY PHONED OVANESSIAN and confirmed that the *jawndare Romano* had been reassigned. "I'm sorry," he said. "I don't want to let you down, but nothing's gonna happen on the Gypsy case." She thought of how considerate he'd always been, how friendly and cooperative. He was one of the few inspectors who treated female PIs as though they weren't brain-dead. And he was one of the few who seemed concerned about helpless old men.

"Look, Fay," he was saying, "we all know what's going on, but . . . we don't have enough proof to take it any further." She thought, He can't *possibly* mean this. Can he?

"You don't have enough *proof?*" she said.

"Not enough to satisfy the DA."

Fay thought back on the Fraud Unit's performance over the last year. They'd hemmed and hawed and dissembled and procrastinated till they were prodded by the City Attorney's Office and the Rat Dog Dick Detective Agency. It seemed to her that they hadn't originated a single useful line of inquiry. They'd ignored the imperiled Richard Nelson till Timothy Armistead warned them that the city could be sued. They'd let three crucial months pass before checking Harry Glover Hughes' blood. They'd finally warned him about his danger, and with what results? *This old man who can't tell Mexico from Alaska is still hanging out with his abusers!* She wanted to yell into the phone, What are you working on that's more important than this, Greg? *Parking lot skimming?*

But she held her tongue. He was such a nice guy.

JERRY LAMA CALLED to say that he'd recited his story to Louise Renne from the fucking alpha to the fucking omega. The city attorney had listened attentively and told him to expect a call from her chief investigator.

"That's Tim Armistead," Fay said. "He's our last hope."

"Does he know his ass from second base? Or is he like the rest of these fucks?"

"He's a pro. One of his jobs is to keep the city from being sued. I've talked to him. He cares. If he's willing to see you, take a cab."

SEVERAL DAYS LATER, Jerry reported back. "We met at the guy's office. The first thing I told him was that the Fraud Unit's a worthless piece of shit. I told him Yawczak is a gynecologist trying to do brain surgery. I told him most of the fraud cops should be checking dipsticks in the city garage."

"Nothing but compliments, huh?"

"I spoke highly of Ovanessian. And . . . you."

"What else did you say?"

"I told him the whole fucking story, but I don't think he believed me. He said he'd talk to his boss and get back. We'll see."

He didn't sound hopeful, but then he seldom did.

52

Alive and Endangered

DONALD AND GERALDINE Nelson returned from a vacation trip to Arizona just in time to learn by phone that their Uncle Richard was entertaining friends in the dining room of his retirement home. They covered the distance at flank speed.

The old man greeted his relatives with a big smile. "Hi!" he said. "Have a little ice cream with us."

Angela was accompanied by a young woman and a distinguished-looking man in suit and tie. All three visitors looked colder than the fudge ripple. Gerry asked the man, "Who are you and what do you do?"

"I'm Robert Sheridan, Mrs. Bufford's attorney," he said pleasantly, "and this is my assistant." He nodded toward the woman, whose pencil was poised over a notebook. "I wondered if we could have a little talk." The lawyer informed the Nelsons that his client was unfairly suspected of slipping drugs into their uncle's food. He asked if they knew whether digitalis or other heart medications had ever been prescribed.

Gerry said, "Definitely not."

"Could you give us a list of his doctors so we can look into his medical history? We're sure there's a digitalis prescription somewhere."

Both Nelsons got the impression that the lawyer sincerely believed Angela's story and was making a conscientious attempt to turn up proof of her innocence.

"I understand your view," Don said, "but we see things differently. We *know* what's been going on. And we're pretty reliably informed that digitalis has never been prescribed."

Uncle Dick wore a fixed smile. The Nelsons realized that he probably hadn't heard a word. "Come to my room, Angie," the old man said. "I've got magazines for you."

"Sure, Rich," she said as she took his arm.

The lawyer's female assistant trailed after the lovebirds while Don and Gerry made small talk with Sheridan. After the trio returned and the visitors filed out of the building, Richard Nelson seemed upset. "That girl?" he said. "She went through my medicines. I told Angie to get her out of my bathroom! Leave my things alone!"

Gerry asked if he'd signed anything. "No," he said. "They wanted me to sign a paper saying that Angie never brought me any food, but I wouldn't do it." He hesitated. "Not now, anyway. I'll write 'em a letter later. Angie's coming back."

It was all too plain to the Nelsons. Even in the security of the retirement home, their uncle wasn't out of danger.

NOT LONG AFTERWARD, an investigator from a TV station tracked Richard Nelson down as part of a probe into elder abuse. An observer later recounted the conversation to Fay Faron:

"Can we talk?"

"Sure. What do you want to talk about?"

"Well, we'd like to talk to you about Angela Bufford."

"I don't want to talk about that."

"Well, we just wanted to ask you a few things."

"No. You didn't hear me. I said I don't want to talk about that."

"We're just—"

"Please. Just leave. Let me eat my lunch in peace."

THE SAME TV crew found the SFPD equally uncooperative, leading one of the producers to comment, "We've never been treated so shabbily, Rat Dog. What's going on?"

Fay said, "I wish I knew."

53

Task Force

FOR A CHANGE, there was good news from Jerry Lama. In his customary mix of words and smoke, he told her, "Tim Armistead called this morning and said, We're back on track. I said, What the fuck does that mean? He said, We're putting together a task force from the Fraud Unit, the DA's Office, city Homicide."

Fay asked, "How many members?"

"Sixteen, eighteen. Vehicles, surveillance equipment, secure radio channels, everything. He said they'd kick some major ass."

A FEW MINUTES later, Ovanessian phoned in an equally upbeat mood. "Fay," he said, "I don't know what Jerry told Tim Armistead the other day, but it worked. I'm back on the case, and we're finally gonna have enough manpower."

"I heard. How can I help?"

"You've done enough. We'll wrap this up in a month."

THE NEWS THAT trickled back from the task force's organizational meeting was less encouraging. Deputy Chief Fred Lau, head of the SFPD Inspectors Bureau, had admitted to the assembled lawmen that he'd never heard of the poisoning cases. "We didn't want to bother you," a fraud inspector piped up.

Another police official wanted to know if there was a pony buried in all the manure from Jerry Lama and the Rat Dog Dick Detective Agency, or was this just a bunch of theory and hearsay? "Who are the victims and who are the complainants? *Is digitalis really a poison?*" A sergeant mentioned that Rat Dog Dick seemed to know a lot about the case and someone else responded that she was a money-grubbing publicity hound looking for headlines.

* * *

WHEN FAY HEARD about the accusation, she was hurt but not surprised. *Headlines?* What headlines? There hadn't been a peep in the Bay Area press. She reminded herself that there would always be cops who felt that woman's place was in the bed. Whenever she'd been approached by the media, she'd insisted that nothing could be aired until the investigation was completed and the case closed. She didn't lack for personal publicity; her book on collecting bad debts was selling steadily, her newspaper column appeared in more newspapers than ever, and she was scheduled to appear on an Oprah Winfrey show to track missing persons before the eyes of a national audience. She didn't care if her name was *ever* mentioned in connection with the elder scammers as long as the cases were prosecuted and the old men were protected. That was the issue and the only issue: *old men's lives.* Why couldn't the top brass get that through their heads?

As for the accusation about money-grubbing, whom was she grubbing it *from?* Konstantin Liotweizen? Philip Steiner? Nicholas Bufford? *The mayor?* If she was such a hustler, how come the Rat Dog Dick Detective Agency was running deep in the red because of unbillable hours spent on the elder-abuse cases? She consoled herself with the remembered words of the empowerment guru, Jocelyn Nash: "You do some things because of what you are." If I go broke, Fay said to herself, it won't be the first time. I can always buy seconds at Levi Strauss and start over. Pro bono or otherwise, it was the case of a lifetime. And she didn't intend to quit.

ON THE SECOND day of the task force's existence, Fay found out that the members were still biting one another's backsides in a boring old tradition of law enforcement. Every cop she'd ever known, including some of the best and brightest, seemed to possess a visceral aversion to sharing information or glory with anyone else in uniform. Territoriality, she decided, must be a required subject at the police academy.

Some members of the task force were complaining that the district attorney should have brought charges ages ago; now the trail was cold and the suspects had plenty of time to destroy evidence. A DA's Office spokesman argued that the SFPD hadn't done its job. The city attorney's representative said it didn't matter who was to blame and repeated the warning that the city of San Francisco was at serious financial risk if old men died of poisoning long after the authorities had been informed of what was happening.

After more discord, one of the police representatives dropped his own personal bomb: he'd done some research and learned that digitalis couldn't be reliably detected in human blood. Therefore, homicide charges were out, leaving nothing but chippy cases like elder abuse and theft, hardly the business of a massive investigative agency.

After more squabbling, the police contingent withdrew and the task force toppled of its own weight. It had lasted three days. "For admittedly rational bureaucratic reasons," a member observed, "you get an insane result."

FAY LEARNED THAT Inspector Dan Yawczak was left to work the case solo. He was tasked to warn Harry Glover Hughes of his peril, interview him in depth, arrange for another blood test, collect financial records on Hughes and Richard Nelson and their interlocking bank accounts with Angela and George, and continue surveillance of the suspects to see if they were developing more clients.

Fay wondered how Yawczak or any other detective could handle such a load. His federal civil rights suit was slated for trial after a year and a half of preliminary wrangling, and in the next several months he would be forced to spend long hours under oath on the witness stand, explaining why he'd found it necessary to kill one young man and wound another while chasing them for the crime of purse-snatching, hardly a capital offense. Trial preparation alone would take weeks. How much time and energy would that leave for the poisoning cases?

Next to none, Fay feared, and hoped to God she was wrong.

54

The Gypsy News Network

FEBRUARY OF 1994 produced a continuing silence from the Hall of Justice. Fay kept checking in with Ovanessian but stopped when she began to realize that nothing churned up his stomach acids more than the names Lama, Bufford, Steiner, Tene, Bimbo—and Yawczak.

She consulted with Jerry Lama often even though she was afraid that the two of them had begun to resemble the last survivors of a great war, passionately orating about something that no one else cared about or even remembered. She felt a brief spasm of encouragement when she learned that the IRS was considering tax charges against the Tene Bimbos and George Lama, but later she heard that they'd dropped the matter when the Fraud Unit refused to cooperate. She wasn't surprised.

IN THE FIRST week of March, the hang-up calls began. She wished she had the new Caller ID feature, but the innovative service was still months away. One night a whiskey-voiced female said, "Rat Dog Deek person? I put on you a curse." Fay said, "Hello?" and got a dial tone in return.

After a while the tenor of the calls changed from threatening to informational. Still without identifying themselves by name, the mystery callers began passing hints and tidbits of information "for your own good," usually derogatory information about other *vitsas* and *kumpanias*.

"Gypsy crooks waste a lot of time screwing each other," a Rom expert explained. "They must've seen your name in the papers and now they're trying to use you for their own purposes."

"Like what?" Fay asked.

"Like—who knows? It's an old pattern. They use the *gaje* to get back at one another. They'll call nine-one-one and say, I think I just heard shots fired in that *ofisa* down the street. Or they'll say, Some dark-haired guys are running a crack house next door! The cops bust in with guns drawn. Not too great for business! The criminal element of Gypsies, they love to snitch each other off. There's constant turmoil between the *familia* that runs Chinatown and the one that runs Fisherman's Wharf. And your Tene Bimbos, well, they fight *everybody*."

Fay remembered a passage from Anne Sutherland's *Gypsies: The Hidden Americans,* researched and written in the 1970s: "San Francisco, the most open *kumpania* in the area, also has this reputation for a great deal of fighting, and during the whole period of my field work, the families there were embroiled in one *kris* [Gypsy court] after another."

Now Fay was becoming embroiled herself.

AS HER TELEPHONE traffic increased, she began to think of her sources as GNN, the Gypsy News Network. Now that she was in touch with blood members of the Rom, she thought she detected the slightest foreign accent, which she attributed to centuries of cultural isolation. Some of her informants seemed to forget that she was a *gaji* and burbled on so fast and intimately that she could hardly take notes: "Yvonne's a Machwanka, from L.A. She used to be married to Louie's brother—but she just married Louie's other brother John! They took up a *kidemos* for ten thousand bucks' *daro*. She walked away with two mil! That *beng*, he went to L.A. to arrange the settlement, said, Okay, you get half, Sammy gets half—but she took it *all*. Louie told her to suck his *kar.* . . ."

Similar dark tones colored most of the conversations, and Fay began to realize that the Gypsy underworld might be more dangerous to itself than it was to outsiders. An informant told her about a beating administered to Steve Tene, handsome protagonist of *King of the Gypsies* and grandson of the clan's original strong man: "They put a doorknob in his mouth and taped it shut, tied him up, handcuffed him, and beat him off and on for twenty-four hours. Then they poured whiskey on him, threw him in the street, and called the cops to pick up the drunk."

NIGHT AFTER NIGHT, Fay scribbled notes as she listened to a mix of street language, macho profanity and threats from Gypsies who were involved in crime: "So as soon as he finds out I'm talking to the cops, he says, I'll hand you your cock, motherfucker. His brother calls and says, You the tough guy? Listen, I'll stuff your nuts in your mama's mouth. I says, Fuck *your* mother, Dicky-Blue. He says, You're dead in my eyes. Later he calls back and says excuse him, he was drinking. He says, You know me, I never hurted nobody. The next day he calls and says, You gonna lay in the earth wit' Big Joe, awright, creep? Let's see if you can blow each other underground."

FAY HAD TO keep reminding herself that the underground reports from the Gypsy News Network originated in a world she would never know or comprehend. Everything she was hearing went against the Rom stereotype of lighthearted, joyous travelers dancing in front of campfires. Underneath the messages, she detected an agenda of bitterness, despair, rage. She knew that her callers were feeding her information for a purpose, and the purpose wasn't to be friendly and helpful to the Rat Dog Dick Detective Agency. The news tidbits could be true or false, straight or exaggerated, but if she listened long and patiently enough, she might pick up an item or two of value.

As expected, the Tene Bimbos turned out to be the hottest topic on GNN. The *familia* didn't seem popular even within its own culture. A vociferous informant told her, "Miss Rat Dog, if you can throw some of them Bimbos in jail, every honest Gypsy in the country will kiss your ass, pardon my French. Those people were trouble even before King Tene Bimbo or whatever title he gave himself. There's very little intermarriage between them and other Gypsies—nobody wants to be associated. Listen, I'm not saying Gypsies are perfect, okay? We do what Gypsies have to do. The difference is, too many of the Tene Bimbos hurt people. My God, one of 'em took a shot at a Massachusetts cop! They threatened to break my son's arm—and they did it! My other son, they shot off his knee. We don't even take the Tene Bimbos before a *kris* anymore. We just throw the *bola* on them without a hearing. That's like the eight ball. Because they won't listen and they won't change. Hey, they've hustled old men for years. This poisoning, it's just—what's the word? A refinement."

HER CURIOSITY AROUSED, Fay reached out to amateur and professional Gypsiologists, sometimes through third parties, and soon was on speaking terms with *jawndari Romani* in several cities. The lawmen spun tale after tale about Rom crime, how it was almost never violent, usually involved cheating or trickery, and dated back to the days when pariah Gypsies either worked their scams or starved. Most "Gypsy cops" admitted that they'd learned to settle for restitution instead of wasting time with futile charges. One of them quoted San Diego Deputy District Attorney Thomas Hardy: "No one wants Gypsies. They create so much havoc in jails when they're arrested that they've always been let go after they pay their bail and fines and return stolen property."

Prosecutors like Hardy found the criminal Gypsies eager to adapt to an improvised system that had worked to their benefit for years. When they were caught cold, their technique was to do whatever was necessary to survive, even to confessing and overpaying restitution. Fay remembered how quickly Angela Tene had walked away from dotty old Helen Mitchell as soon as her motive was exposed. The ancient technique of yielding an inch to gain a foot had enabled Angela to survive to plunder the personal treasuries of Richard Nelson and others.

"Just to give you an example of how it works," Fay was told by a frazzled New York City cop, "the Gypsy moneyman in the East is a guy named Two Bones. He travels up and down the East Coast posting bail and making deals. Restitution—that's his game. The victim recovers his money, the Gypsy skates, the cop clears his books—it's everybody's favorite way to close a case. But how do you end up? You don't prosecute, you don't get fingerprints, you don't take an ID photo, and the perp is free to do the next scam. Wouldn't a bank robber love to rob a dozen banks and just repay the money from the last job? Then go out and rob another dozen? That's the system, and lemme tell ya, Rat Dog—it works bigtime."

FAY FOUND SOME of the *jawndari* resigned to reality, others demoralized. "The thing you gotta remember," she was told over lunch with a visiting expert, "is that crooked Gypsies see the world as victims. They're contemptuous of you and me. Their culture is our culture tipped upside down. We value honesty; they value deceit. We teach our kids not to lie; they teach 'em to lie their ass off. There's nothing Gypsy criminals respect more than a major liar. They use their kids as diversion, decoys, then reward 'em for it."

Fay said, "Be fair. Haven't you met plenty of honest Gypsies?"

The officer crinkled his nose, shut his eyes, and appeared to be drawing on reserves of memory. "Not in the usual meaning of the word," he said at last. "I've met personable Gypsies, smooth, intelligent, interesting to be around. But would I trust 'em? *Never.* They are what they are, what they've always been. They may play the fiddle for you and do their little dance, but believe me, Fay—to a lot of Gypsies, it's all a game."

Fay recalled a passage in Joe Gores' comic novel *32 Cadillacs*: "If you sentimentalize Gypsies, you run the risk of ending up with a car that won't run, a roof that won't stop the rain, or a driveway that comes up on the sole of your shoe." Yes, she said to herself, and if you sentimentalize the ones I've been dealing with, you might end up drinking a digitalis cocktail. She'd thought Gores was exaggerating for effect when she first read the book. Now she wasn't so sure.

ONE AFTERNOON SHE sat enthralled as a Florida deputy sheriff named John "Nick" Nicholas Jr., one of three full-blooded Rom in American law enforcement and the only one willing to give up the trade secrets of the Gypsy Mafia, delivered an animated lecture about the problem.

"Most Gypsies consider me a rat, an informant," the swarthy lawman told an audience of police and private investigators. "They're used to dealing with another kind of cop. In every major city, Gypsy crime is controlled by one or two families, and in every major city they try to have a cop in their pocket. Sometimes he's on the pad, sometimes he's just professionally interested. My people can't understand why I took a different route."

Deputy Nicholas, directly descended from the Gypsy *familias* Nikolayevich and Markovich, described the techniques that had been a part of criminal Roma existence ever since they'd rattled around the Balkans in brightly painted wooden wagons pulled by spavined nags. "They say, Why should I eat the whole loaf at once when I can eat it slice by slice? A palm reader will work a mark for a year, slow and easy, to not attract the law. Then she'll hit 'em for ten, twenty grand."

Someone in the audience asked, "How do they find their marks?"

"They're always looking," Nichols answered. "They say, If the bear don't hunt, the bear don't eat. If they're in an airport and see a chance to do a slip-and-fall, they go for it. If they see an extra bag, they grab it. They'll vacation in Vegas and set up an insurance scam to pay for it. My own mother—God bless her, she's eighty-five and can't do full-time scams anymore—when she visits me and my wife in Palm Beach, she begs me to let her go out and work a scam or two. She says, I don't want the money. I don't *need* the money. She says, I'll do it for *you*. After eighty years, it's inside her. I say, No, Mom, please. Please *don't*.

It's embarrassing. Don't ever get the idea that Gypsy crime is nickel-and-dime stuff. The average income is in six figures. It's as organized as the Mafia, and it's nationwide. We can make an arrest in Florida and fifteen minutes later they're talking about it in a San Francisco *ofisa*. Their attitude is, It's us against the *gaje*. They take good care of their own old people, but they rip off yours. I know other Romani that've left the life and become jerks like me, working for a living. The criminal Gypsies think we're stupid. It's so easy for them to work their scams. They go to states like Wyoming and Alabama and Vermont where they can get driver's licenses easily. They thrive on how simple it is to get birth certificates, credit cards, library cards, Triple-A cards. Every crooked Gypsy has a walletful."

Someone asked Nicholas where his native people stood politically. "They don't care about politics," the *jawndare Romano* replied. "They don't care about having a homeland like Israel. They don't care what's going on in the world, who's in the White House, who's liberal and who's conservative. They don't care about Social Security, because most Gypsies don't go broke and don't retire. They consider the United States a great big fruit tree, and they take that fruit and eat it."

As FAY HEADED home in the Frog Prince, she was thinking how little she or any of the other *gaje* knew about Gypsy criminals. The more she learned, the more she didn't know, or didn't understand. She couldn't wait to brief Jerry and the others.

THE ANGRIEST ARAB-AMERICAN in San Francisco was in no mood to discuss Romani sociology when Fay met him at the Marina's latest shrine of creative espresso. "I'm through with the fucking cops," he snapped before she could decide whether to order the Tanzania Teaberry dark roast or the Cafe Oro de Ometepe from Nicaragua. "I'm seeing Melvin Belli and we're taking this whole thing to the newspapers and TV. We're gonna bust some balls."

"You're seeing *the* Melvin Belli?"

"How many fucking Melvin Bellis are there?"

"You have an appointment?"

"In two days."

* * *

WHEN FAY MET with Jerry a week later, he confessed that the deal
with San Francisco's most flamboyant lawyer had fizzled. He didn't seem
interested in explaining why. "Who needs Melvin fucking Belli?" he
said. "I'll plant the story myself. Gimme a name to call."

"Whoa!" she said. "Slow down." In her mind's eye she saw him
barging into the *San Francisco Chronicle* newsroom and ordering everyone to stop the fucking typing and listen up. Security would take him
down with pepper spray. She laid her hand on his wiry forearm and said,
"Before you take this to the media let me just check around."

55

Skulking 101

SHE TRIED TO decide who would be the best journalist for the job
and ended up calling the *San Francisco Chronicle*'s Dan Reed, a longtime
admirer of her newspaper column, which was now appearing in the *Dallas Morning News*, the *Denver Post*, the *Philadelphia Daily News* and thirty
other newspapers. Reed had always seemed impressed with her eclectic
mix of talents and booked her to address the Contra Costa Press Club
during his term as president. He was thirtyish, a big rumpled man who
seemed indifferent to clothing styles in an older journalistic tradition.
He enjoyed jazz and rock despite high-end hearing loss from eight years
as a drummer, a minor disability that he claimed had no effect except
in his dealings with rodents. His reportage revealed a sensitive nose for
misbehavior, especially among politicians. He also had the skilled reporter's knack of making interviewees relaxed and comfortable so they
would blurt out more than they intended.

"Dan," Fay said, "I've got a guy with a story you'll never believe.
But I swear every word is true." *Gypsies,* she babbled. Dying old men.
An undetectable poison. Indifferent cops.

She stayed on the phone until long after Beans gave up on the
game of fetch he'd forced her to play as she talked. She described the

activities of Angela Bufford and her boyfriend and their two current clients, and that led back to Mary Steiner and Konstantin Liotweizen, and that led back to Danny Tene and Hope Victoria Beesley, and that led back to an ex-fighter named Chuchi, and that led back to a Rom clan named Tene Bimbo that seemed to come from the northeast or Canada or Russia or the moon. When she was finished, her mouth felt like the inside of a clothes dryer. She promised to call him later.

"When?" Reed asked.

"Soon."

"Would you mind if I did a little research on my own?"

"Quietly?"

"I took Skulking 101."

Fay said, "Take these addresses."

SHE CALLED JERRY Lama and advised him that a star reporter was working on the story. He asked, "Will he print something this week?"

She thought about her long hours with computer and microfiche, the trips to City Hall and the Public Library and the Hall of Justice, the interviews and surveillance and confidential informants. If she knew Dan Reed, he would walk in every one of her footsteps and then some. "It'll take a lot longer," she said.

"I don't know how long I can wait," he said. "That fucking George is breaking my chops."

"Threats?"

"Every day."

"Watch your, uh—"

"Watch yours."

56

A Piece from the Middle

IN MID-MARCH, 1994, almost a year and a half into the case, Fay came across a fresh affidavit in City Hall files. Dr. Doris So, a mental health counselor, had made a routine evaluation of Harry Glover Hughes and noted:

> Client has very poor memory and confabulates. He forgot his appointments even though he was reminded in the morning of the same day. His refrigerator was filthy and the food in there was bad and not edible . . . Client is a prey to a couple, Angela Bufford and her boy friend George. . . .

Fay was confused. *Mr. Hughes still isn't safe?* She wondered why a mental health counselor would be interviewing him at his old address in the Sunset. Surely he was tucked away in a retirement home by now? Like Mr. Nelson?

In the same file she came across a statement by the old man's nephew, Dr. David Payne: "Mr. Harry Glover Hughes is 95 years old and unable to take care of himself or provide for his own physical or financial welfare. I visited him at his house and saw very little food in the refrigerator. His home was dirty, the kitchen and the bathroom were filthy and his clothes soiled."

Payne added that his uncle had started drinking heavily and was losing his memory. "He failed to recognize my wife whom Glover has known for almost 25 years." The old man had told Payne that he had a young friend named Angela, didn't especially like her, but was considering marriage.

Fay dialed Margaret Buchanan and learned that Mr. Hughes was again enjoying the breakfast deliveries that once had been as regular as the morning chimes from St. Cecilia's. Fay realized that the stubborn George and Angela were still defining themselves by their gall.

"The cops haven't been around?" she asked.

"Hell, no," said the outspoken neighbor.

"They were supposed to take a food sample. That was the next thing on their list."

"They botched it. When Angela showed up with a takeout container I called nine-one-one, and the dispatcher didn't know what I was talking about. I said, Didn't Inspector Yawczak tell you I was gonna call? And they said, Who's he? So I called Yawczak and said, Get your ass over here. Angela's back with the poison! He told me he couldn't possibly get away, and I said, Well, send a cop from the Taraval Station, for God's sake! That's two blocks away."

"I can't believe it," Fay said. "They could've sent a clerk, a crossing guard."

"Yawczak says, Hey, can you do us a favor? Could you just go over and get a sample? He says, Get a piece from the middle. That's where the poison'll be."

"Don't tell me you did it?"

"God's sake, somebody has to do *something.*" Fay thought, How many times has that same thought gone through my mind?

"I go over and Glover's eating a burrito," the woman continued. "He's showing *zero* interest in sharing. Very unlike him. I don't know if he was hungry or just thrilled to get another home delivery from his honey, but I sat and sat and he didn't offer. So I had to ask. He cut a little piece off one end and I said, Glover, could I, uh—could I just have a middle piece? When he wasn't looking, I tucked it in my shirt pocket."

"Smells like a setup," Fay said. "Did Angela take the empty container when she left?"

"Nope."

"That's a first. They're slick. Maybe they *wanted* the food analyzed. To divert suspicion, I mean. They're murderous, but they're not stupid."

"Never thought of that. I called Yawczak and said, The sample's here."

"How did it test?"

"*Test?* What test? He never picked it up. I called and called. It sat in my freezer for weeks. I finally threw it out and—I gave up on the San Francisco PD. Totally. Forever."

Fay gulped, sighed, slapped her forehead and emitted a word she hadn't learned at Baptist services. Margaret Buchanan concurred. Fay finally summoned enough poise to ask, "How's Mr. Hughes now?"

"Oh, Fay, I thought you knew! Isn't that why you called?"

"What happened?"

"Glover's in the hospital. A stroke. It happened after he came back from Fort Bragg."

"Fort Bragg?"

"I finally got in touch with his family last week and told them what George and Angela were trying to do, and they hid him out at Fort Bragg. While he was away, George called, all excited, and he says, Where's Mr. Hughes? I'm thinking, Where the hell did this creep get my phone number, but then I realized he probably had Glover's address book."

"What'd you tell George?"

"What *could* I tell him? I said I thought Glover was away on a visit. He said, You don't suppose he's had a heart attack and he's lying dead inside the house? He said, We had plans for Glover for the weekend. I said, Yeah, I bet you did. I found out later that George and Angela were calling everybody in the neighborhood. They were *desperate*. They were afraid they'd lost their cash cow."

"What's happening now?"

"The relatives are setting up a conservatorship to protect the estate. Last week they changed the locks and moved Glover back into the house with three full-time guards. They call 'em caregivers, but they're guards. Angela showed up—"

"No!"

"—and got bounced. After that, the mystery phone calls started— we need to install this, install that, check your wiring, get some credit card information. As subtle as a kick in the crotch."

"You said Mr. Hughes is in the hospital?"

"St. Mary's. I'm on my way now. I hope he's alive."

A WEEK LATER Fay pulled up the final records at the Department of Health. Harry Glover Hughes had died at 8:29 A.M. on Wednesday,

March 30, 1994, just short of his ninety-fifth birthday. Most of his $1.2 million estate would go to relatives after his will was probated. Under "cause of death" on the certificate, Chief Medical Examiner Boyd G. Stephens had entered "Pending further investigation and/or testing." An addendum confirmed that an autopsy had been performed and the final cause of death was "hypertensive intracerebral hemorrhage," medicalese for stroke. How sad, Fay said to herself. Another old man spared in time to die.

SHE RAN INTO Margaret Buchanan as the neighbor was returning from a visit to Olivet Memorial Park cemetery in Colma, a few blocks from Konstantin Liotweizen's resting place in the Serbian Cemetery. Mr. Hughes' best friend said she felt better now that she'd visited his grave and reached the realization that George and Angela had probably lengthened the old man's life.

"All those trips to Mexico, Alaska, Lake Tahoe," she explained. "That was stimulating for an old man. They brought him food, took him to fancy restaurants, dressed him in coats and ties. He came home so happy and told me about it. He was impressed that George always paid the checks."

"Part of the con," Fay said.

"Well, sure! It was Glover's own money. But he never knew. He loved the way Angela fussed over him. It gave him something to live for."

"Good Samaritans," Fay muttered. "I wonder how many others they helped."

57

Bad News

WITH THE ARRIVAL of spring 1994, Fay tried to push the case from her mind and concentrate on her agency's dwindling accounts receivable. She started writing one of her newspaper columns but quit after a single cutesy paragraph. She enjoyed whimsy, irony and even sarcasm; she hated being cute. She turned to her novel but couldn't sustain the proper mood. *Lily Kills Her Client* was supposed to be a waltz, not a dirge. Each new take was gloomier than the others.

Lately she hadn't known herself and wondered if she might be entering early menopause. She snapped at Beans and made him whimper, then hugged him till he yelped. Her mood wasn't helped by a hint from a GNN source that San Francisco wasn't the only city where opportunistic Gypsies were hastening old men to the grave. She saw dying patriarchs in her dreams and jumped whenever the phone rang. It was usually bad news.

The phone rang. It was bad news.

"Yawczak lost his case," Jerry Lama said in his sharp New York accent. "The jury nicked the city for two hundred and fifty-nine thousand."

"Payable to—?"

"The kid he shot's family. Must've wrecked his day. He pissed off my sister and she quit the fucking case for good."

"What?"

"Don't ask the details. All I know is, Nicole says, I'm gonna get on with my life. She says, Nobody's ever gonna be charged, Jerry. This case is a joke. I say, Hey, Nicole, what happened? You're an important witness. You heard 'em bragging about the poisoning. I says, You can't give up now. She says, I don't care if I'm a witness or not. Yawczak made a pass at me and called me a liar. So I tell her, Look, Nicole, fuhget about it. I'll take care of Yawczak. She says, I *already* took care of him. Then she says, I'll never talk to another cop. I'm outa this thing for good."

Fay tried to remember if Yawczak was married. She had a vague memory that he had a family in L.A. "Not too professional," she said.

Jerry rattled on: "Yawczak promised to protect Nicole, said he'd put her name on a high-priority response list. But it never happened. She called one time and they said, Who the fuck are *you?* Yawczak also insinuated that Nicole was in on George's action. Cute, huh?"

"Where's this leave us, Jerry?" Fay said.

"Fucked" was all he answered.

SHE PONDERED THIS latest blow and realized that if the case wasn't dead, it was barely on life support. For reasons unknown, unfathomable and perhaps even unthinkable, someone's wish was being fulfilled; she wished she could figure out whose. Was it a higher-up in the SFPD? Or . . . City Hall? The DA's Office? Nothing made sense. What would anyone have to gain from sabotaging a strong prosecution that might save lives, both present and future? She shook her head as she thought back on the days when the police had had a solid list of witnesses who'd seen George and Angela sprinkle the magic salt, watched them deliver the adulterated food, and even helped them make the deliveries. They had statements from the pharmacists who'd put the digitalis into George Lama's hands. They had copies of the prescriptions—hard evidence, not circumstantial. They had tape-recorded assurance from old Antone Lama that his son George was lying; the heart stimulant hadn't been for the father, nor did anyone in the family recognize the name of the doctor whose name appeared on the prescriptions. They had toxicology reports showing the presence of the poison in Richard Nelson's bloodstream: more hard and damning evidence. And they had the solemn word of Lama family members like Jerry, Nicole and Hami that George and Angela bragged openly about their murderous techniques. In short, the police could show means, motive and opportunity, the three main requirements for a successful prosecution. Weaker evidence had sent criminals to the gas chamber.

But now vital links were snapping, one by one. Roland Dabai was angry with police for double-crossing him in court. Nicole Lama swore she wouldn't testify. Nabib Atalla had useful information, but Jerry said his brother-in-law was wavering. The matriarch Gloria Lama refused to speak any evil about her younger son. As for Jerry, he would walk through a crocodile pit to testify against his brother and Angela, but after building up such a rage against the local authorities, God's angry man would be iffy in front of a jury. Fay wondered which witnesses the cops would alienate next. *What are they up to?*

She wondered if a basic disregard for life might be at the heart of the problem. She could imagine the jaded fraud detectives chattering among themselves at Liverpool Lil's: *What the hell, these old crocks are gonna die in a year or two anyway.* No one except herself and Jerry and a few noble warriors like Glen Billy and Timothy Armistead had ever seemed truly disturbed by what was happening. Were old men discardable simply because they were in their last few years of life? She thought of Al Faron, successful businessman, public official and world-class parent, her personal cheerleader from birth, now lying terminally diabetic in Arizona, blind, helpless, dependent for his needs on her sainted mother. Fay shuddered as she imagined her father reduced to banging on the radiator pipes for help. The mental images made her sick to her stomach, and it was hours before she fell asleep.

58

Task Force Redux

A FEW WEEKS later, Fay learned from contacts at the Hall of Justice that there had been renewed activity behind the scenes after the death of Harry Glover Hughes, and now the poisoning cases were top priority. "I hear it's balls-to-the-wall CYA," a friendly sergeant told her.

"Catholic Youth Agency?"

"Cover—Your—Ass."

With a few confidential calls, she learned the details. Police Chief Anthony Ribera had heard the bare bones of the case, apparently for the first time, and summoned Ovanessian, Yawczak, an assistant DA, the head of the Homicide Unit and his own personal deputy to an emergency meeting. The chief ordered the dignitaries to form a new task force from Homicide, Fraud, the DA's Office and anywhere else they could find loose bodies. Their assignment was to cut straight to the core of the case, no matter whose backsides were scarred in the process. Otherwise, Ribera promised, he would melt a few badges into babbitt metal.

The elite new group was assembled with the deliberate speed of a flotilla of warships forming up to steam past the Presidio. Ranks and egos had to be considered, turf allotted, vacation time coordinated and off-days canceled. Despite the firmness at the top, the usual interdepartmental warfare continued. The Fraud Unit considered the homicide inspectors to be prima donnas, and the Homicide Unit considered the Fraud Unit to be the last refuge of incompetent, herniated and hemorrhoidal old-timers. From Fay's perspective, each side had a point.

Six weeks after the tumultuous meeting with the chief, the new operation was still limping along in the planning stage. Then the Hughes death sent the lawmen into a panic. Were senile old men being poisoned under their noses? *A year and a half after the original tip?* It was the stuff of nightmare lawsuits.

By the time the Hughes blood tests came back negative, the elephantine police group had roused itself. Easter season was at hand. Cadavers were about to rise from the earth.

59

Garden Work

NEWSCASTER VIC LEE of KRON-TV had just clocked in on the morning of Monday, April 18, 1994, when a cameraman briefed him about an overheard conversation at the Hall of Justice the night before. "This captain was bitching, Vic. He says, Jeez, they cut back on our overtime and now they're stealing my men to dig up stiffs. And we're not even Homicide!"

"Digging up . . . *bodies?*" Lee said, savoring the phrase. Like most journalists, his nose twitched at a hint of the macabre. Normal humans yearned for peace and quiet; Lee looked forward to plane crashes, multiple homicides and shipwrecks. For twenty years, his twitchy nose had brought him star turns on local and network news programs. He was as much a San Francisco fixture as the columnist Herb Caen or the quarterback Joe Montana, and just as connected.

Lee phoned a friendly source in Homicide and asked where the hell they were digging.

"Digging?" the inspector said.

"You know. Uh—bodies?"

"You got the wrong shop, Victor," the inspector said. "I heard some talk at Fraud, but I don't know what those assholes are up to."

Lee called the Fraud Unit and was told that everything was quiet.

He asked, "You guys aren't doing a little, uh—garden work?"

"For God's sake, Vic, get a grip!"

Lee pushed back his chair and considered the situation. Why such an emphatic response? He knew from long experience that the more vigorous a cop's denial, the more likely that his nose was as long as a telephone wire. The newsman wondered: Is another Zodiac killer in action? Did Juan Corona break out? Are more winos being strangled in the Tenderloin?

He wondered how to pinpoint the action. Where could the cops be exhuming bodies? The answer was . . . anywhere there's dirt. How do you check *that?* There were bodies in cemeteries, of course, and cemeteries could be checked. Sillier hunches had paid off. He pulled out a phone directory and began punching numbers.

"This is Vic Lee, Channel Four News," he said. "We've heard that the police are working on something at your cemetery."

It took only a few minutes to exhaust the San Francisco listings. He considered checking the entire Bay Area, but it would take all morning, and he had priority assignments on his clipboard, including a remote for the network. He settled on a few spot checks. He'd just about given up when he reached a custodian at Mountain View Cemetery in Oakland.

"Hey, Vic," the man said, "great timing! Your coroner's coming over with a crew. It's a high-profile thing."

"What's high-profile about it?" Lee asked.

"Gee, I dunno. He's bringing a homicide captain and some other cops."

"That's high-profile," Lee agreed. "When is this gonna happen?"

"I think they said tomorrow morning."

AT 8:00 A.M., Lee and a camera crew drove across the Bay Bridge to the cemetery. Backlit by thin morning sunlight off the peaks of the Sierras, a group of men appeared to be worrying the ground at the bottom of a slope. Lee recognized several heavy hitters, including a captain from Homicide and Chief Medical Examiner Boyd Stephens.

"Drive past," he instructed his driver.

They stopped at the top of a rise and set up behind a tree. Fifty yards downhill, a backhoe puffed a plume of blue-gray diesel smoke and began taking divots. After a while a casket came out of the earth like a rotten tooth. As the KRON-TV videocamera whirred, the oblong box cracked and broke in half. Cops in street clothes lifted the shattered coffin by hand and placed it alongside the open grave while a few of the dignitaries hastily applied handkerchiefs to their noses. One lit a cigar.

All at once a member of the exhumation party detached himself from the group and speed-walked uphill toward the filmmakers. Lee recognized Inspector Daniel Yawczak of the Fraud Unit. The detective had been in the news for shooting a juvenile and involving the city in a costly lawsuit.

When he was still ten feet away, Yawczak called out, "What're you guys doing?"

"It's a wonderful day for a picnic," Lee answered. "Isn't it, Inspector?"

"How much do you guys know?" Yawczak's manner seemed more disappointed than angry. Apparently the gravedigging operation had been a well-kept secret.

Lee decided to run a bluff. "I know *this* much, Inspector," he said. "You're exhuming bodies. There's poison involved. And . . . well . . . that's as much as I want to tell you."

Yawczak glanced over his shoulder toward his superiors, then said, "Okay. You can come on down."

As the TV crew arrived at the graveside, a detective was studying what looked like a thin slab of damp cardboard while the others peered into the cracked casket. The scent of old mushrooms was in the air. One of the men snapped, "The bitch buried him in fiberboard."

A homicide captain said, "Okay, Vic, we'll make a deal. Please don't air this tonight. You'll ruin a fraud investigation. In return we'll keep you clued in."

"I'm listening," Lee said.

"We think a Gypsy family is poisoning old men for their money. It goes way back. There's a pattern."

"In San Francisco?"

"Maybe in other places, too."

"How many victims?"

"We don't know yet. Three, four. We're just getting into it. When we know something we'll fill you in."

Lee thought about his tedious sessions on the telephone and the man-hours expended on the drive from San Francisco with a full crew. Shouldn't there be some kind of payoff for beating hell out of the competition? On the other hand, the case had sensational elements—Gypsies, mummies, poison, secretive cops wearing bandannas. Maybe it would pay to wait now and be on the inside later.

"Fair enough," he said, extending his hand. "When you make an arrest, let us know." He'd made plenty of such compromises. In the long run, most of them paid off.

Before leaving, the veteran correspondent peeked into the coffin. It looked as though the contents had steeped in the porous container like an old tea bag. A plastic ID bracelet and a remnant of hospital gown clung to a blob of jellied tissue. Nothing human was easily recognizable.

"Somebody was in a hell of a rush," an inspector observed.

"They must've took him here by cab," said a uniformed cop.

A small marker memorialized "Philip Steiner" and noted the date of his death: April 23, 1987. Lee counted backward; the cloth-covered casket had lain in its shabby container for seven years. He thought, This is how the homeless are buried. No wonder there isn't much left.

60

Old Man in Aspic

FAY FARON SOON learned the details of the disinterment and more. It turned out that three other bodies had been exhumed before Vic Lee became the first member of the media to catch on. On March 28, three weeks before the scene at Mountain View Cemetery, Nicholas Bufford, Angela's husband and first big score, had been dug from the earth at the Fernwood Cemetery in Mill Valley, a short drive north of San Francisco. Like Philip Steiner, the Mark Hopkins Hotel janitor had been buried in a cheap casket, but his body was better preserved.

A few days later Steven Storvick had been exhumed at Cypress Lawn Cemetery in Colma. The wide-eyed corpse was nattily attired in a dark blue polyester suit, wide tie and white shirt, and Fay's informant commented that the dead man looked like a salesman.

The remains of Konstantin Liotweizen had presented special problems. Graziana Gandolfi's beloved landlord had been buried in a sealed coffin, but there wasn't enough passageway for a backhoe or tractor in the densely packed Serbian Cemetery at Colma. Three pick-and-shovel laborers had sweated through the job on the late afternoon of Monday, April 11. The cemetery custodian, who remembered pleasant talks with the czar's former captain at his wife's grave, commented later, "It was nice to see the old gentleman again."

The original plan was to remove the Liotweizen organs for testing and then rebury the Cossack veteran with the framed picture of his wife, but the coffin was defective and the lid wouldn't reseal. Greg Ovanessian's friend John James Nazarian, a private detective, former deputy sheriff and onetime embalmer, stepped up to solve the problem.

"I could tell right away the worm gear broke on the crank that runs through the cap at the end of the casket," Nazarian explained later. "That's how you lock down the lid. The idea is to maintain a sanitized environment so the mice and rats don't get in and chew off Dad's nose.

That's what I always told the family when I was in the funeral industry. I told the inspectors this busted gear wasn't fixable. They're going, Jesus Christ, the chief's gonna shit when he finds out we gotta spend two grand for a new sealer casket. I said, These sealers come under an Eternal Warranty Plan. So we contacted the mortuary and the manufacturer gave us a new casket, no questions asked. The cops put the gooey mess inside and reburied it. Old man in aspic. It was a challenge."

NOT LONG AFTERWARD, Fay was formally introduced to Nazarian in Ovanessian's office. She found him an interesting study. Ovanessian explained that he and the former deputy had been tight for years. That explained why Nazarian seemed so comfortable in the Fraud Unit, leaning back with his feet on the desk like an insider.

"He's read your book, Fay," the Gypsy cop told her. "He thinks you're rich and famous."

"Oh, I am, I am," she joked.

At first the beefy ex-deputy put Fay in mind of an off-duty pirate. He had a sharp adenoidal voice with a New England accent and a slight lisp. He was friendly, personable, talky, and affected a dramatic look, with thinning black hair, a Fu Manchu goatee, heavy eyebrows and dark mischievous eyes behind tinted glasses. He was professionally profane, but not as profane as Jerry Lama, perhaps because he seemed more amused than angered by the passing parade. He wore black cowboy boots with tall heels, a gold Rolex, a diamond ring that reminded Fay of a cable car headlight, heavy gold bracelets and chains, and a shoulder holster. It didn't take him long to mention that he owned a Bentley. Gee, Fay said to herself, a PI with a Bentley! I'll have to learn his secrets.

Over a pleasant lunch at Meharry's restaurant and double-decker driving range under I-280, she learned that he was the son of a sea captain and had circled the globe many times on his father's ships, worked his way through college as an apprentice embalmer, run a San Francisco escort service, and eventually found his way into law enforcement. "It was something I'd always wanted. I tried the LAPD, but they wouldn't take me. I was too big of an asshole. I started as a corrections officer at a women's prison. Anybody could get that job."

Fay enjoyed his candor and panache. He was bright and quick, and if he was embroidering his stories, he was doing it convincingly. "Weren't you a San Francisco deputy?" she asked.

He nodded and said, "I resigned to go private."

"Didn't you like the work?"

"I had a simple approach," he said. "If I liked a person, I'd do anything for 'em. If I didn't, I'd zap 'em every chance I got."

He seemed to have a low opinion of lawmen in general. "To this day," he said, "I haven't met any people that are more dishonest and criminal. This is a hard thing for people like you to understand, Fay. There's no such thing as an honest police officer, not the way the job has to be done. Of all the beasts of the world, a cop can justify anything." His voice fell to a low rumble. "I *know*," he said, "because of what I did and what the guys around me did."

"Like what?"

He launched into tales of what he called "my own special justice," including harassing especially evil perpetrators. Fay thought, What a simplified approach to enforcement: judge, jury and executioner in one beefy package.

She asked about his interest in the poisoning case. He explained that he'd done investigative work for a local *familia* and developed a rapport with Gypsies. "There's a lotta things to admire about them, even the criminal ones," he said. "They take pride in not physically hurting their victims. They have a strict code of honor. If I ever come back from the hereafter, I'd like to come back as a judge or a Gypsy."

"Why?"

"Just the way they do things. Like, some Gypsies might have a dozen identities."

"So I heard," Fay said.

"Cops can't touch 'em. Feds, IRS, FBI, nobody can consistently make cases against criminal Gypsies. They have their own banks, so they leave no paper trail. They use a Reno pawnshop where nothing gets written down. They take over the names of dead people, or they create aliases by putting two *gaje* names together: Sonny John, Ely Miller, Frank Adam, Tony Paul. They have to keep the names simple because they're mostly illiterate. They never pay a bill they don't have to pay. They rent a house or an apartment, fall six months behind in the rent, and move. You would have better luck finding the pot of gold at the end of the rainbow than tracking the average Gypsy perp."

"They seem to live pretty well," Fay said. She was thinking of

Danny Tene, his Corvette, his designer shoes. And his mother Mary's million-dollar apartment building. And his sister Angela's BMW.

"There's Gypsy millionaires, plenty of 'em," Nazarian said. "The Emil family in San Francisco, they're loaded, but they're discreet about it, solid citizens, as respectable as the mayor. The Marinos are big in San Jose and L.A. One of the richest landlords in Orange County is a Gypsy with twenty-five hundred rental units. The Marks family in San Diego owns millions in low-rent property and more in Dallas and other places, but their main income still comes from fortune-telling. One of their leaders got in trouble and they posted bond—a big house in Aspen, Colorado, free and clear. That's how the Gypsy aristocracy does things."

He paused for a gulp of coffee. "They eat at the finest restaurants. Most of 'em can't read the menu, so they always order steak. They drink out of paper cups and bring their own utensils—*gaje* knives and forks are polluted, unclean, no matter how hard they're scrubbed."

"And they drive big cars," Fay put in.

"*Love* 'em. If a Gypsy has twenty thousand dollars to his name, he'll put it on a Lincoln Town Car. That's from all those years behind the south end of a horse. Their palm readers bring in thousands, *millions*, but very few of 'em pay business taxes or apply for licenses. When their people die, they buy the best caskets. Mortuaries know some of the crooked Gypsies and make 'em pay cash in advance. Otherwise the cemetery statuary would disappear, the stone seats would be hauled off, and the funeral bill wouldn't be paid."

"Fascinating people," Fay said noncommittally.

"Some of 'em are amazing!" Nazarian said. "They live so well. They love hundred-dollar bills. This Gypsy guy I know, he owns apartment buildings, diamonds, drives a Rolls, wears a gold Rolex. He looks like Al Pacino. You gotta love the guy."

"Why?"

"Think about it, Fay. *He never held a job!*"

She sat spellbound as her new friend continued, "He won't let his kids go to school, but he teaches 'em how to survive. His daughter, she's a great kid. Sharp! Six years old, and she walks out of F.A.O. Schwarz with these great big packages—and never gets caught! She shoplifted a blow-up plastic castle, bigger than she is. It's *amazing!*"

Fay thought, The man certainly knows his subject. She was well aware that a certain element of Gypsies shared an antisocial mind-set and saw the world as Rom vs. *gaje*. And maybe they weren't being entirely unrealistic. Ancient animosities ran on their own momentum long after they stopped making practical sense.

". . . I can take you to a Gypsy house where the kid's six years old and he'll carry on a conversation like he's thirteen," Nazarian was saying. "Articulate, quick! The family's *so* proud of him. He makes me laugh like hell. Like I'll go to the house and I'll see six bikes. I'll go, Where'd you get all these fucking bikes? And he says, Down on the street—one at a time." He smiled and shook his head. "You gotta love 'em."

Fay couldn't bring herself to see thievery as lovable, but she enjoyed learning about the Rom Mafia from the inside. Nazarian seemed proud of his connection. "You know, Gypsies won't drink out of your glasses or eat off your plates," he told her. "They have separate dishes for the *gaje*. But I go over there and they use all the same stuff. I'm accepted. They respect me and I respect them."

Fay felt enlightened as she headed home.

61

Waffling

THE FIRST UNOFFICIAL report from the Medical Examiner's findings was that all four of the exhumed bodies had tested positive for digitalis. Fay thought about calling a celebratory meeting of the Friends of the Rat Dog Dick Detective Agency, but Jerry Lama warned that it was too early. "There might still be a way to fuck this up," he complained. "If there is, the cops'll find it."

Jerry said he had bet Ovanessian a dollar that the Storvick body would show traces of digitalis—"I knew I'd win because George used to brag about putting it in the old guy's food." According to Jerry, Ovanessian paid off his losing bet without argument.

* * *

IN LESS THAN a week, the stories from the Hall of Justice began to weaken. It was said that the tests were questionable as murder evidence against George and the Tene Bimbos because the digitalis level had been nonlethal. "So *what?*" Jerry Lama exploded. "Why was it there at all?"

Then Fay heard that the tests were being repeated by a different lab and the DA's Office was quietly minimizing the original findings. She checked in with her personal expert on pharmacology and was reminded of his earlier advice that digitalis was a quirky drug. He told her that anyone who expected quick and accurate results from digitalis tests on decomposed organs didn't know his toxicology. It was a tedious and sophisticated undertaking involving as many as sixty-five separate procedures. The tests could take years and produce skewed results.

"Finding digitalis isn't even positive proof of murder," the expert reminded her. "There's no scientific literature that says you can prove murder by digitalis based on tests of exhumed tissue. The most you could charge is attempted murder or conspiracy to commit murder, and then let a jury decide." Such a reduced prosecution, he said, might well prevail. "What difference does it make whether you try to murder somebody with cyanide or strychnine or digitalis or table salt, as long as you were trying to commit murder? It's the intent that matters." The theory made sense to Fay.

SHE FOUND JERRY Lama even edgier than usual. He'd already heard the new reports about digitalis and had other aggravations on his mind. He said his visits to his mother and sisters at the white stucco house on Fourteenth Avenue were becoming as relaxing as the family's ordeals in Mediterranean battle zones years earlier. Gloria Lama continued to back her mercurial son George despite mounting evidence of his misbehavior, but she despised his Gypsy girlfriend for her smart mouth, modish attire and overuse of cosmetics. Skirmishes were frequent. Gloria and her daughters would spot Angela's BMW approaching, disconnect the automatic garage door opener, and shower her with insults in English and Arabic when she climbed out to open the door by hand.

Jerry said that key information was still passing through the thin walls of the duplex. It seemed that Angela had been expelled from the Tene Bimbo clan by her biological parents, Mary Tene Steiner and Stanley "Chuchi" Bimbo. Several times Angela was heard sobbing out words that sounded like "Mary May." From her crash course in Gypsiology, Fay suspected that the listeners were hearing the word *marime*, which meant polluted or accursed and could be the basis for permanent exile from the Rom world. The *marime* stigma resulted from such offenses as wearing short skirts, consorting with the *gaje* (one reason why Gypsies almost never engaged in prostitution), showing disrespect to the family leader or Rom Baro, washing the upper and lower body with the same piece of soap, resting one's feet on a table, or eating with a utensil that had fallen to the floor. It was also considered *marime* for a Gypsy woman to expose herself below the waist. Her upper half, however, was regarded as *wuzho* or pure, and it was socially acceptable for Gypsy woman to flaunt their "ever ready treasure of pendant breasts," in Beaudalaire's phrase.

Jerry told Fay that it sounded as though the excommunicated Angela was feeling insecure and rootless and therefore trying to push the Lama family out of the house so she could regain ownership. "The place is still in joint tenancy between George and my mother," Jerry explained.

Fay nodded. "Joint tenancy?" she said. "Famous last words."

Jerry said that George seemed to be working himself into a homicidal rage and was armed to kill. Jerry had already removed a loaded shotgun and ammunition from their cases in the garage. "We got enough trouble," he told Fay between nervous drags at a cigarette. "We don't need any fucking whatta ya call it—fratricide. The crazy asshole, he's got a handgun and a silencer stashed away. I never know what to expect when I drive up."

62

Dinner Engagement

FAY'S FAVORITE REPORTER Dan Reed phoned to say that he'd quit the *San Francisco Chronicle* for the *Oakland Tribune* and taken his Tene Bimbo files with him. His new editor was fascinated by the case. But word of the recent exhumations was bound to leak out, and Reed worried about losing his exclusive. He told Fay that he'd followed the paper trail she'd laid out, confirmed every word, and turned up plenty more. Now he wanted to confront police and principals and run the story.

Fay thought, This is a big step, releasing this dirty business to the press. It's an irreversible lifetime decision. I may never work in California again.

She said, "I don't think you should confront the cops till you've talked to Jerry Lama."

"Is he cooperative?"

"Shake hands and duck. He has a tendency to bounce off the walls."

WHEN FAY AND Beans returned from their next morning's biking expedition to Ocean Beach, her phone was ringing. Before she could say hello, a familiar voice snapped, "Rat Dog?" She could imagine him calling from a phone booth, the outline of his dark face barely visible through the smoke. "Who the fuck is Dan Reed?"

"Hi, Jerry. He's a reporter on the *Oakland Tribune.*"

"What the fuck is the *Oakland Tribune?*"

She told him it was a respectable newspaper that was published across the bay.

"What do they care about a San Francisco story? We want the *Chronicle,* the *Examiner.*"

"Don't worry. If the *Trib* runs the whole story it'll be in the *Chronicle* and the *Examiner* and the *L.A Times* and . . . the *Yomiuri Shimbun.*" She advised him to take Dan Reed on faith. He was their best bet to build public pressure and force the police to take action.

"Best bet, huh?" Jerry snapped. "Like Ovanessian? Like Yawczak? Like the DA? I took them on faith. Now I'm expecting a bullet up my ass."

"Jerry, do you think I'd lie to you?"

He paused. "No," he said. "Not you." He paused again. "Not yet." She took it as a compliment.

FAY BEGAN TO wonder why Inspector Dan Yawczak started calling, and calling, and calling. He seemed obsessed by the chronology of the case. When did she first take on the Beesley matter? When did she first report her suspicions to the Fraud Unit? When did Angela marry Nicholas Bufford? When did the trash raids start, and what did she find, and how long did she continue collecting?

After a spate of such inquiries, Fay said, "Dan, I'm happy to help, but . . . what's going on? Are you writing a book?"

He told her he was preparing a report for the District Attorney's Office. She was impressed. Anything to help the prosecution.

"Call whenever," she said.

After fielding still more of his requests, she agreed to meet him in a bar before going to dinner with a girlfriend. She promised to show him some of the gleanings from recent trash raids and he promised to show her a picture of Angela Bufford gazing adoringly at her ancient boyfriend "Rich."

Yawczak ended up having dinner with Fay and the other woman, but seemed irked when one of Fay's oldest male friends arrived on the scene and offered to drive her home. After that, the phone calls stopped as precipitously as they'd begun.

63

Too Much Coffee and a Phone

DAN REED WAS forced to run a gauntlet of suspicions about his newspaper's pedigree before Jerry Lama opened up and began laying out the facts of the case in a long precise line. "He's like somebody with too much coffee and a phone," Reed reported to Fay. "He not only knows the facts but what everybody was wearing and what time the sun came up on the day in question. A reporter's dream. He knows police procedure, he knows California law, he—"

"He's a grump," Fay interrupted, "but he's *our* grump."

"What's his problem anyway?"

"He's angry, he's cynical, and he's *right*. He thinks the cops are incompetent and the city administration ought to be ashamed. Who can argue? Did he give you what you needed?"

"And then some."

"Is your piece scheduled?"

"Hell, no. I've got a million things to check."

64

The Silver Screen

ON A BRIGHT summer day, John Nazarian phoned and said, "Fay, this Gypsy story's gonna be *big*. TV. Books. Movies!"

Maybe so, Fay said to herself, if it's ever prosecuted.

"And . . . I own the property," Nazarian continued.

She was puzzled and asked, "Can you own a news story, John?"

"I registered the whole thing in Hollywood." He told her to meet him at Roosevelt's Tamale Parlor in the Mission District and he would explain their mutual good fortune.

"Mutual?" she asked.

"Trust me," he said.

By now she'd learned a little more about Nazarian, and their association was becoming unsettling. Unlike most PIs, he seemed to revel in notoriety. He flaunted his masculinity, boasting to one of Fay's colleagues that he'd been known to throw suspects over the hood of his police car to make a point. He said he handled the toughest cases and lived by the acronym AFAB: anything for a buck. When she heard that bit of biography, Fay realized how it happened that he drove a Bentley.

She was on her second tamale with salsa verde and sour cream when he walked in and dumped a thick document on the table. Across the top of a sheet of plain paper, she read:

AFFIDAVIT OF DANIEL J. YAWCZAK

She hefted the pages and glanced at the wording. The document looked as though it had been written at top speed by someone with a broken typewriter. It began:

AFFIANT, DANIEL J. YAWCZAK, GRADUATED FROM THE CALIFORNIA STATE UNIVERSITY AT LONG BEACH IN MAY 1977 WITH A BACHLOR OF SCIENCE DEGREE IN CRIMINALISTICS. AFFIANT WAS A POLICE OFFICER IN THE CITY OF REDONDO BEACH CALIFORNIA FROM FEBRUARY 1979 UNTIL NOVEMBER 1984 . . .

She interrupted her reading to ask, "What the heck is this?"

"It's the police chronological on the case," Nazarian said. "It's like an affidavit. *Read!*"

She counted forty-two pages and estimated that there were twenty thousand words, a fourth the length of a novel and more than she'd been able to write on *Lily Kills Her Client* in two years. Every word was in capitals, and the author's keyboard seemed to lack certain essentials. Most of the narrative was written in police doggerel, complete with misspellings like "post-mortum," "errythmia" and "Egeroff" and odd constructions like "the name of the man that owns the pharmacy was an Asian man named Edwin or something very similar." But the whole sordid story was there, in all its lurid detail.

Fay found her name in the fourth paragraph:

ON 3/21/93, AFFIANTS PARTNER INSPECTOR OVANES-SIAN RECEIVED A TELEPHONE CALL FROM A PRIVATE INVESTIGATOR BY THE NAME OF FAY FARON. FARON TOLD OVANESSIAN THAT SHE HAD BEEN HIRED BY AN ATTORNEY BY THE NAME OF KEN CHAN. CHAN IN TURN HAD BEEN RETAINED BY THE ESTATE OF HOPE BEESLEY. BEESLEY HAD DIED AND HER REAL PROPERTY AT 1045 BALBOA HAD BEEN INHERITED BY DANNY TENE BIMBO. . . . FARON SAID THAT CHAN FELT THAT HOPE BEESLEYS SIGNATURE ON THE JOINT DEED HAD BEEN OBTAINED FRAUDULENTLY, POSSIBLY BY TRICK OR DEVICE.

She scanned the rest of the document as Nazarian stared from across the table and Beans watched them both from the sidewalk. Her Rastafarian dog looked unsettled, but he'd always been dubious about her male companions.

Fay noticed that much of her agency's role, including the crucial identifications of the first victims, had been downplayed or omitted. There wasn't a word about the detention and questioning of Angela Bufford, or about the disinterments, in which Yawczak himself had played a part. Some of the most important dates were off. On first reading it appeared to Fay that the affidavit had beefed up the roles of the Fraud Unit inspectors, especially Yawczak himself. In parts he came off as a synthesis of Sherlock Holmes, James Bond and the two Joes, Friday and Wambaugh:

AFFIANT HAS BEEN A POLICE INSPECTOR SINCE JULY 1990 AND HAS BEEN ASSIGNED TO THE AUTO DETAIL, THE GENERAL WORK DETAIL, THE NIGHT INVESTIGATIONS DETAIL AND THE FRAUD UNIT. AFFIANT HAS CONDUCTED OVER THREE HUNDRED INVESTIGATIONS INVOLVING APPROXIMATELY ONE HUNDRED ARRESTS. INVESTIGATIONS HAVE INCLUDED AUTO THEFTS AND AUTO BURGLARIES INCLUDING VIN SWITCH CASES, FELONY ASSAULTS AND KIDNAPING CASES, ROBBERIES, FELONY HIT AND RUN ACCIDENT INVESTIGATIONS, CHECK AND CREDIT CARD FRAUDS, EMBEZZLEMENTS, FORGERIES AND OTHER THEFTS.

Fay thumbed to the end and was surprised to find that the account dribbled to a halt with no ending, signature or seal. What kind of affidavit was this?

Nazarian said, "I want you and Greg to be my partners in this."

"Partners in *what?*"

The gold glittered from his rings as he waved the papers. "*This,*" he said dramatically, "is a Hollywood movie. *This* is three or four million bucks. Nobody else can touch it. I told you: I own the rights."

Fay thought, Here we go again: it's the O. J. influence. The book and movie industries would never be the same. Anyone who ever sold Simpson a pair of shoes or bought him a drink intended to get rich by selling his rights. As a published author, Fay knew that most of them could earn more money squirting Windex on car windows at the corner of Market and Geary.

"John," she said, "where'd you get this, this—?"

"From Yawczak," he said.

"How?"

"Don't ask."

When she insisted, he told her that the Fraud Unit inspector had drawn up the chronological for Murlene Johnson, the assistant district attorney in charge of the case, who requested it for a search warrant. According to Nazarian, the young ADA had taken one look at Yawczak's draft and told him it was ten times too long. He'd dutifully prepared a shorter version and slipped Nazarian the original.

Fay was incredulous. "You registered this in *Hollywood?*" she asked.

"With the Writers Guild of America. We'll be equal partners, you, me and Greg. Of course, he can't be officially involved. We'll take care of him on the quiet. When the movie comes out, we'll buy him a house or something."

Fay thought, Equal partners with *you*, John? For what? You haven't worked this case for five minutes. She reflected on the long months of frustration. Where had Nazarian been? Until a few months ago, she'd never even heard of him. Now he was talking about brokering a million-dollar movie as though the whole investigation was his idea and the deaths of the old men were just a part of the plot.

"John," she said, "the bad guys have to be arrested and tried. That's a year away. I expect to testify. I can't get involved in profit-making schemes."

He assured her that it would take at least two years to begin production of the movie. By that time the perps would be serving their terms. The film project would have no effect on the case one way or the other, but it would help to alert old people to the Gypsy Mafia and their scams. "Somebody's gonna do a lot of good and make big bucks at the same time," he told her. "Why not us?"

Fay put him off and said she had to run.

* * *

WHEN THEY MET again, Nazarian pulled a cassette tape marked "confidential" from his briefcase. Even before Fay heard the word "fucking," she recognized the recorded voices. It was Jerry Lama being interviewed by Inspector Dan Yawczak. She knew about this conversation; Jerry had mentioned it several weeks earlier. ·

"John," she asked Nazarian, "is this a copy?"

"This tape," he said proudly, "is the *original*."

Fay wondered what a private investigator was doing with official police evidence. It was one thing to have friends at the Hall of Justice and another to remove material. She didn't know how deeply Nazarian was involved with Ovanessian and Yawczak, but whatever their relationship, she didn't intend to risk her license by having anything to do with SFPD tapes.

"John," she said, "you've got to take this back."

He told her she was acting silly and repeated his solemn assurance that no movie would be made until the offenders were behind bars. He asked if he could peruse her files and she said she had no objection. She couldn't imagine that it would do any harm.

65

Family Tree

FAY CONSULTED OFTEN with Dan Reed on his research. Between the two of them, they'd managed to flesh out a file on the elusive matriarch, Mary Steiner, née Bessie Tene, much of it via incoming phone calls from Fay's rapidly expanding Gypsy News Network. Distant relatives of the Tene Bimbo clan informed her that the woman had been born in New York in 1940 and lived in Chicago, Boston and other cities before migrating to San Francisco around 1975. Like most Tene Bimbos, she was poorly educated and could read only small words. Even within the clan, her genealogy was murky, but "Bessie" seemed to be perceived by all as a *gaji*, a sort of Gypsy Lite.

"By blood, half of Bessie is Gypsy and the other half is part Irish and part German," a GNN correspondent explained to Fay in a midnight phone call. "Her father was a *gajo* from Canada and her mother was a Gypsy named Sonia Wilson who lives in Florida. So we consider Bessie a *gaji* because of her father. Gypsies go by the father's side. When she was little, everybody called her *gajihuh*: American girl."

Another insider told a slightly different story: "Bessie holds herself out to be a Tene Bimbo, but she's a *gaji*. Her father was half Irish and half Gypsy and her mother was a *gaji*. So she's only a fourth Gypsy. That's a *gaji*. You can tell by looking at her. Her daughter Theresa, the one that calls herself Angela, she inherited the Irish skin."

There was a third variant: "Bessie had a Gypsy mother and a *boyash* father. A *boyash* is a *gajo* who lives with Gypsies. So she's—what? Half Gypsy? All the time she was growing up, her family considered her a *gaji*. They'd say, Don't trust her. She's different. She's the one that's gonna hurt the *familia*."

LIKE SO MANY members of the clan, Bessie-Mary's life seemed prefigured by the antisocial style of the legendary King George Tene Bimbo. A Boston member of the family explained: "The king bought baby Bessie from another Gypsy family as a pet for his wife. Queen Mary was a character herself, born in Argentina, smoked a long stemmed pipe. She miscarried a baby girl, so that's when they took in Bessie. The king and queen lived by the old Romani saying 'Many children, much luck,' and they ended up with thirteen, fourteen kids. They put little Bessie right to work—it's the Gypsy women that earn most of the money, you know? She always liked the boys. One day in New York, her older sister Fat Ann spotted her kissing an American boy on Fourth Street and beat the hell out of her. Bessie sold flowers, worked hard, grew up beautiful and smart, and as soon as she was big enough, King Tene Bimbo took advantage of her. He fucked every female relative he could get his hands on, including his own kids.

"Later he decided that Chuchi was the only man they could marry Bessie to because she was damaged goods. He didn't mention that he did the damage himself. Chuchi was a wild kid. Him and Bessie weren't blood, but they were raised in the same *familia*. So Bessie was sold to Chuchi for a forty-five-hundred-buck dowry. That's cheap. A young virgin with big earning power should bring thirty, forty grand, ya know? But there was no virgins around King Tene Bimbo unless they was seven or eight and ran like hell. Incest ran in his family. The king's son Al forced his son to fuck his own mother. Remember? The big scene in *King of the Gypsies?* Some people thought Peter Maas invented that story to sell more books, but it's true."

FAY ALSO LEARNED via her Gypsy contacts that the young Bessie had been close to a female cousin nicknamed Red who in later life developed the art of adulterating the diets of old men before handing them paper and pen. According to one of Fay's informants, "Red did her first old guy in the 1950s. She knocked him out with a drink, and when he was still in the twilight zone, she had him sign over his property. Then she fed him pills to make him sleep. In the middle of the night, he dies of a heart attack. Old guy in his eighties. She didn't intend to kill him, but he died anyway, so she made the best of it. Red turned the whole family on to doing old men, and they're still doing 'em all over the country. She's retired now, a millionaire."

The same source informed Fay that another Tene Bimbo cousin had employed a variation on Red's original system and also retired with millions—"She worked it out so she didn't have to fuck nobody, neither." The source didn't provide details. As for Bessie Tene, reborn as Mary Steiner, the informant said she'd been hustling old men for thirty years, dating back to her days in New York and Boston. The well-practiced technique was one of the signature activities of King Tene Bimbo's descendants.

AS FAY'S INFORMATION network grew, she began hearing increasingly dark stories about Gypsy crime. It didn't take long for her to realize that the rival branches and subbranches had their own bad-mouthing agendas and didn't mind spilling to a *gaji* as long as they were treated respectfully themselves. Fay schooled herself to say "yes," "uh-huh" and "I see" while cradling the phone on her left shoulder and scribbling notes. Snippets from her files began to resemble a joint effort by George V. Higgins, William Burroughs and Elmore Leonard:

That Isaac looks like a goddamn morphodite. Somewhere between man and woman. And they're saying he's not a man
in bed! But him and Gracia stayed hooked for fourteen years.
What the hell did they do at night if he's a morphodite? You
tell *me*! Now he's marrying Vera from Boston. Maybe she seen
his dick. . . .

The Tene Bimbos, they all fucking Machwaya. They the ones
with blond hair and blue eyes. Do the biggest scams. King
Tene Bimbo was a Russki. His wife was a Machwanka—that's
a female Machwaya. Same blood as him. . . .

The great-great-great-great-grandfather's name was Bim-Bye,
spelled B-I-M-B-A-I. That's Romany for tough guy. King
George's family name was Deenya—D-I-N-Y-A. That's where
Tene come from. So it should be the Dinya Bimbai family,
not Tene Bimbo. But Gypsies can't write, so the names
changed a little through the years. Did you know that "pal"
is a Romany word?

Sometimes Fay considered slipping some colorful Gypsy material
into her detective novel, now in its second glacial year of creation, but
she didn't have the time or patience to introduce a new set of characters
in long skirts and head scarves. And besides, she said to herself, if I
tried to publish this Gypsy stuff, who would ever believe me?

66

Hard Questions

DAN REED PHONED Fay to report on a visit he'd made to the Fraud
Unit to discuss his upcoming article with Ovanessian and Yawczak. He
said that they'd been joined by Sergeant Phil Tummarello, a hard-
driving troubleshooter who was close to Chief Ribera and was newly
assigned to ramrod the case.

"All three of 'em dummied up on me," Reed told her, "but that's what I expected. I basically gave 'em a chance to talk me out of running the story. I said, The *Oakland Trib* does *not* want to screw up your investigation. I said, If a story about Gypsies exploiting old men would hurt you in any way, in *any* way whatever, tell me right now."

"What'd they say?"

"The only fear they expressed was that George Lama might read the story and shoot somebody. He's such a crazy bastard. I said if you guys think he's such a homicidal lunatic, why haven't you arrested him for the murders of the old men?"

The detectives insisted they were working the cases full-time. Reed said he'd told them, "We're certainly not gonna kill a story because it pisses somebody off."

"Otherwise they didn't object?" Fay asked.

"All they said was, We can't stop you."

"Did you check with the DA's Office?"

"I went through the same drill with Murlene Johnson. I said, Talk me out of running the story. I don't want to mess up your prosecution. She didn't even try. So I guess that's it."

"Will your piece run long?" Fay asked.

"About a hundred inches."

"*A hundred inches?*" Her own columns ran ten to fifteen. "It'll be cut, right?"

"It's already been cut."

"When will it run?"

"I've just gotta make a few more calls."

THAT NIGHT REED reported on his final telephone interviews. First he'd called the house on Fourteenth Avenue.

"Hello?"

"Angela?"

"Yeah."

"This is Dan Reed over at the *Oakland Tribune*. There's some allegations out there about you. I wanted to run 'em by you."

"I don't want to say anything."

"Do you have an attorney?"

"If you can find *me*, I'm sure you can find *him*."

"Yeah, but I'd like to have your side of the story."

Reed heard the dial tone and redialed. "Angela, is George there?"

"You can talk to his attorney, too." She hung up again.

THEN THE REPORTER had called Mary Steiner's apartment on Funston:

"Hello?"

"Is this the Steiner residence?"

"This is Danny Tene. Who wants her?"

"This is Dan Reed at the *Oakland Tribune*. I was just talking to your sister Angela."

"Well, I don't know too much about that."

"I'd like to talk to your mother if I could."

"She's not here."

The reporter left his name and phone number.

REED TOLD FAY that after he'd completed his phone calls, a police source tipped him that an irate Phil Tummarello planned to arrest him for interfering with a police investigation. Reed described his reaction: "I'm saying to myself, Please, Sergeant, *do it!* You're threatening to arrest a reporter that's trying to expose murderers, but you're not arresting the murderers. This'll make my career!"

Reed said that the exposé was now in the final stages of copyediting and everyone at the newspaper was sworn to secrecy. He thought he still had a clean beat on the other Bay Area media, but he'd heard rumors that the *San Francisco Examiner* was sniffing around and the *Chronicle* had footage of a coffin being dug up. Like all good reporters, he wanted to break the story first.

67

A Doctor from Mass

FAY AND JOHN Nazarian began chatting back and forth, exchanging small professional favors, sharing office space for a while, but she still wasn't sure how to take this raffish man with the big ideas. Was he a blowhard or a Hollywood-savvy businessman? She hadn't been able to forget the matter of the tape recording he'd "borrowed" from the Fraud Unit.

More and more she found herself worrying about his movie deal. How could she enter into a working agreement with someone who seemed so relaxed about regulations? If he couldn't be trusted with official police files, how could he be trusted with the details of a movie or TV deal? Would he respect her solemn demand that nothing be shown on film till the case had worked its way through the courts—become a *res judicata*, as the lawyers called it? She couldn't be sure.

A FEW DAYS later, Nazarian slid a videotape into her VCR and said, "Watch this!"

A familiar-looking dark-haired female appeared behind a counter. "That's Angela," he said.

Fay asked, "How'd you get close enough to film her?"

"I went to Nordstrom's and convinced her I was a neurosurgeon from Melrose Mass. That's where I grew up. The Tene Bimbos lived next door in Stoneham Mass, but they were known all over the Boston area: Malden, Medford, Weston, Watertown, Braintree, Foxboro. Angela and me, we recognized each other's accents."

"John," she said, "aren't you afraid of interfering with the police investigation?" Phil Tummarello was already after Dan Reed, but reporters were protected by the California press-shield law. Butting into police business could cost a private detective his license.

"No prob," he said. "Remember? I'm connected."

* * *

FAY BROODED ALL day and half the night and finally decided to disengage. John Nazarian might be the best private eye on the West Coast and close companion of every producer and starlet in Hollywood, but he was one type of PI and she was another.

She phoned his office and politely asked him to include her out. He sounded disappointed, then angry. "You double-crossed me," he said. "Now I gotta do what I gotta do. I've got stuff that's worth a hundred grand to the defense." He clicked off.

Fay remembered something he'd said about zapping the people he didn't like. She wondered how long it would take her to become a zappee. She'd never been thrown across the hood of a car. It might be an interesting experience.

68

Arrested at Last

"HE'S IN JAIL, that crazy motherfucker!"

Jerry Lama was yelling at Fay over the telephone.

"*Who's* in jail?" Fay asked.

"My brother."

Fay exhaled and said, "It's about time."

"Don't get too excited," Jerry said.

He explained that he'd gone to the house on Fourteenth Avenue to drive his niece to the airport. "She wasn't quite ready, so I parked and went next door to visit the neighbors—an older couple, good people—and while I was there my mother phoned to say George needed to get his car out of the garage and I was blocking his way. No fucking problem, ya know what I'm saying? I pulled my car into the street and George comes out in new tennis shoes and hundred-dollar sweats. He backs his car into the middle of the driveway and stops dead. Now he's got *me* blocked. I'm waiting for him to drive away in the fucking Mercedes that he conned out of old man Hughes, ya know what I'm saying?"

Fay said she knew what he was saying but it would be helpful if he slowed down. He usually spoke clear English, but today he sounded like a Moroccan street vendor.

". . . He just sits there," Jerry continued at the same speed. "It's obvious he ain't fucking moving. He's sending me a message, right? Don't rat to the newspapers, asshole, and don't snoop around where you're not fucking wanted. So I yelled, Hey, Mr. Luccisanto, I need to park in the driveway!"

Fay said, *"Luccisanto?"*

"His alias."

"I forgot. I'm sure he was thrilled to hear you yell it for the neighbors to hear."

"He *loses* it! Says, I'm gonna blow your fucking head off. He runs inside the garage and grabs his gun case. Surprise *surprise!* I hid his shotgun in the house a long time ago. Now he's *really* pissed. He starts ripping open boxes and saying what he's gonna do to me. Remember, he's got a handgun with a fucking silencer. So I drive to a phone booth and call nine-one-one. While I'm on the phone to the cops, George is breaking down the door to my mother's place and yelling he's gonna kill the whole fucking family. My niece locks herself in the bedroom and calls nine-one-one herself. The two of us were talking to the dispatchers at the same time."

Fay said, "They must've thought it was a riot."

"It *was* a fucking riot! By the time I got back to the house, George was barricaded in the garage and the place was surrounded by cops. My mother runs out and says George isn't even home, she doesn't know what they're doing there, go away, go *away!* I'm yelling, He's a crazy motherfucker, officers, and he's hiding inside the garage. A cop says, The guy's not armed, is he? I said, Armed? How about a rifle, a shotgun and a handgun? *Is that fucking armed?"*

"What'd your mother say to that?"

"She's telling 'em I'm lying, there's nothing going on, the garage is empty, why are you picking on my poor son George? Two cops finally locked her in a police car to keep her from running back inside the house. I called the Fraud Unit and told Ovanessian, Explain to your cops why this isn't just another fucking domestic disturbance and this man is fully capable of murder. He radioed the cops at the house and pretty soon the door opens and George comes out with his hands up, all mild and mellow. They took him away in handcuffs."

FAY WENT TO the public access station at the Hall of Justice to see what charges had been brought. At the scene the incident had been treated as a domestic disagreement until officers heard George Lama shout, "I'm gonna kill you!" Under an urgent code, a sergeant and lieutenant had set up a perimeter and arrested "George Antone Lama DOB 5/23/58 alias George Luccisanto" and charged him with "making terrorist threats." Police seized a Browning Magnum Twenty shotgun, 450 rounds of .22 caliber ammunition, a Ruger .22 caliber carbine, a loaded ten-round magazine and six loose bullets. Fay noticed that George's handgun didn't appear in the inventory of seized weapons. Its absence was unnerving. Small-caliber pistols with silencers were the weapon of choice for professional assassins.

"THE CRAZY FUCKER'S on my ass," Jerry told Fay several days after his brother was released on bail. "He sees me on the street in West Portal and cocks his hand like he's gonna shoot. I think he's watching too much TV."

Jerry said he planned to seek a restraining order to keep George beyond the range of a handgun or longer, preferably five hundred yards. He also intended to take his message of police ineptitude to the mayor, the governor, the president, the United Nations and the World Court at the Hague, if necessary. When Fay counseled him to wait until the *Oakland Tribune* article appeared, he shook both fists and said, "We already waited too fucking long. We depended on too many dickheads."

"Don't you trust *anybody?*"

"Do *you?*"

"I trust you, Jerry. You've never lied to me."

He said, "These San Francisco cops are horseshit."

"What about Dan Reed?"

"He's been working on the story for three, four months now. What happened? Did he break his fucking pencil?"

IN LATE JUNE, God's Angry Man made good on his promise to carry the attack to the Mayor's Office. "I talked to this Marie fucking Mitchell," he told Fay through his usual nimbus cloud of smoke. "I said, I need to see somebody close to the mayor. She said, Well, sir, can you tell me what this is about, and I said, Yeah. I need to bring them up to speed on what the fuck is going on with their fucking police department."

Fay said, "Made a good impression, huh?"

Her sarcasm was lost in the smoke. "That was five days ago," Jerry said, "and I haven't heard one fucking word since."

"Jerry, how much do you know about Frank Jordan?"

"I know he's the mayor."

"Do you know he's the former chief of police?"

Jerry looked surprised. "He's—?"

"—Still a cop at heart."

JERRY PHONED THE next day and said, "You were right."

"You talked to the mayor?" Fay asked.

"His fucking holiness couldn't be bothered. Instead I get a call, guy says he's Michael Hughes of the San Francisco Police Department, calling about my complaint. I hung up and called that woman at the Mayor's Office. I said, Congratulations, lady, you did it again. I said, I have a major fucking problem with the fucking police department—and you have a *cop* return my call? I hung up on her, too. I should've realized they're not interested."

"As predicted," Fay said.

"So who the fuck *is* interested?"

"Dan Reed," she said.

69

Arsenic and Old Lace

FAY WAS APPROACHING her nine hundredth and final rope-skip on her sun-splashed balcony when a girlfriend burst in with a fresh copy of the Tuesday, June 28, 1994, edition of the *Oakland Tribune*. She could read the banner headline from twenty feet away:

A BIZARRE TALE OF MARRIAGE, DEATH
Police order exhumations in investigation of Gypsies

The article was copyrighted, and the Reed byline appeared in heavy black type. In a photo at the upper right, a pair of smiling lovebirds leaned against each other above the caption "George Lama and Angela Bufford, pictured at Lake Tahoe, are at the center of an investigation in a decade-old tale of marriage and death."

Fay scanned the article, then flopped on her couch to savor the words again. Like the best reporters, Reed had let the facts carry his story without inserting his own opinions or prejudices. She realized that she should be thrilled and excited, but she also felt a twitch of fear. *Now* I've done it, she said to herself. The article amounted to nothing less than a broadside attack on the SFPD, the district attorney and the entire city administration, and she'd been the driving force behind its publication. She'd never felt more naked and vulnerable. Could a private eye survive after "throwing the cat among the pigeons," as her Parisian boyfriend used to say? More than once she'd started to pick up her phone to ask Reed to hold off for a few more months. After so much hard work, he would have put up an argument, but he was a decent man and might have yielded out of a sense of obligation. Now that option was gone. She read the lead for the third time:

> The bodies of four elderly widowers have been exhumed and tested for poison in a police investigation of an alleged decade-old murder-for-profit scheme, sources told the *Oakland Tribune* this week.

The second paragraph noted that police had worked on the case for more than a year but "no arrests have been made." The article described how the suspects "befriended lonely old men and persuaded them to deed over their property and to change their wills, while feeding them food laced with digitalis, a heart medicine that is deadly in high concentrations."

John Nazarian was quoted as saying, "This case makes *Arsenic and Old Lace*, the Zodiac killings of San Francisco and several other major murder cases look like child's play." Nazarian described himself as "an expert on Gypsies" and explained that the technique of exploiting the elderly "is something that has been done for years in the Gypsy community. But in this case, I think it has taken a new twist. They've managed, I believe, to find a way to speed it up."

The article examined the case of Hope Victoria Beesley and gave date, time and place on the interplay among the various Tenes, George Lama and five of their intended victims: Philip Steiner, Konstantin Liotweizen, Nicholas Bufford, Steven Storvick and Harry Glover Hughes.

As she read, Fay realized that the enterprising Reed had dug up fresh information to reinforce what she and the Fraud Unit already knew. He'd interviewed pharmacist Edmond Lim and learned that some eight hundred digitalis pills had been dispensed to George Lama over a three-year period, not the six hundred cited in police reports. Fay was surprised to read Jerry Lama's charge that his brother had tried to poison their mother Gloria to regain control of the house on Fourteenth Avenue. "I started putting one and one together," Jerry was quoted as saying. "It hit me like a ton of bricks." The article included a brotherly appeal: "I want him to cooperate with the police department. I don't want him to get the bad end of the stick."

In her mind Fay could hear the sharp voice of the angry man spitting his story at the newspaperman. Surely Dan Reed or his editors had omitted an adjective or two? An Anglo-Saxonism here or there? She was grateful.

Reed had confided to her that his editors were nervous about giving the impression that they were trashing a race, a perennial problem in any discussion of Gypsy criminals, so she wasn't surprised to see a few lines of historical perspective:

Modern Gypsies are descended from people who originated in India. They historically have been nomadic, and often persecuted.

She looked for a reference to Ovanessian, Yawczak or the latecomer Tummarello, but no SFPD officer was mentioned or quoted. The article concluded:

Police argue that understaffing and the complexity of the probe have slowed and sometimes stalled their efforts.

Fay was perusing the story again when the phone rang. Jerry Lama sounded upbeat for the first time in months. "I already heard from the Mayor's Office," he said.

Great news, Fay told herself. Maybe we did the right thing after all.

Jerry said, "It was Georgia Dunn, the mayor's assistant."

"When're they gonna see you?"

"*See* me? I wouldn't go near them, Fay. What're you, crazy? I told her, When I wanted to talk to the mayor, he wasn't fucking interested. Now it's in the papers and he's covering his ass. I said, I got nothing to say to you *or* your fucking mayor. I'll communicate with him through the media."

Fay's heart sank. Our first chance to deal directly with the administration, she said to herself, and Jerry blows it. But then I'm not the one being threatened by a lunatic brother. She asked, "What did she say to that?"

"She said, Well, Mr. Lama, I've been assigned to make sure your needs are met. So I said, Let me tell you a few things, Miss Georgia Dunn. So I told her the whole story from day fucking one right up to George trying to kill me in the garage. I left out *nothing!* I said, If you're assigned to help me, ask your fucking mayor why hasn't there been a fucking arrest?"

Fay felt relieved. At the least, Jerry had ruffled the mayor's velvet curtain. For all anyone knew, it was the first he'd heard about the case. "Where'd you leave things?" she asked.

"She said she'd call me back."

Fay thought how well politicians played phone tag. "Don't hold your breath," she said.

"She just called!"

"She *did?*"

"Yeah. She's definitely on the case."

"What'd she say?"

Jerry gave a wry laugh. "She said the cops are working on it."

70

Through the Cracks

FAY WAS HAPPY to see that the afternoon editions of the *San Francisco Examiner* carried the poisoning story several steps further. Using local police contacts, a nine-man saturation team of reporters revealed that "a major investigation" was in progress and homicide detectives were "poised to enter the case." John Nazarian provided some philosophical background: "When old people die, nobody pays any attention to you—that's why they targeted people in this age group who didn't have family members. It's the perfect recipe. The death certificates are very similar."

Jerry Lama was quoted as saying that he'd told police about the poisoning scheme "almost a year ago. . . . All you have to do is cozy up to some old man, and—BOOM!—you get their entire inheritance in three ways. It's either by way of a fake will, or joint tenancy, or by marrying this poor old man and knocking him off. They target the very old. They're an easy target because at ninety years old, you're lucky you're breathing, and mentally you may not be all there. They refer to these people as clients."

The depth of the *Examiner* coverage made it apparent that the newspaper had been researching the case for some time. One staffer confided to Fay that both San Francisco dailies had known what was happening for weeks but held back at the specific request of police. Local editors were enraged that the story had broken in Oakland.

THE NEXT MORNING'S *San Francisco Chronicle* quoted Deputy Police Chief Fred Lau to the effect that the Fraud Unit was conducting an "investigation involving senior citizens who may have been victimized by people who have taken advantage of them after befriending them through business or personal ways."

Other lawmen seemed reluctant to discuss the matter with the

Chronicle, but the ubiquitous John Nazarian explained that he'd received a tip in July that certain San Franciscans were "killing old people and taking their money." His wording made it sound as though he'd been on the case ever since.

71

Foxglove

DAN REED'S SECOND-DAY story, again atop page one, described Fay's quest for justice. Under the headline STALLS IN INQUIRY FRUS-TRATE PRIVATE EYE, the article began: "What started as a routine back-ground check by a private eye into a property dispute in the fall of 1992 has spun out into a full-scale police investigation—complete with ex-humed bodies and allegations of murder-for-profit."

The *Tribune* credited Fay with discovering that two old men were being poisoned and complaining to "three different agencies before po-lice intervened." "Basically," the article quoted her, "Jerry is giving them a case, and I'm giving them a case, and all they're doing is sitting there and smiling and saying thank you very much."

THE AFTERNOON *EXAMINER* hung the tag "Foxglove" on the in-vestigation and provided vivid details of the victims' deaths. A two-column picture showed the Lama restaurant in West Portal and noted that "alleged victim Stephen Storvick lived above the deli."

Fay noticed that even in the friendly San Francisco press, the au-thorities seemed to be avoiding the opportunity to explain nearly two years of lethargy. The *Examiner* article noted that "police were inundated with inquiries" and added, "By day's end, police declined to discuss the case further and issued a terse one-paragraph statement through the pub-lic affairs office, which only confirmed that fraud inspectors were in-volved in a complex, lengthy investigation and that any further release of information could jeopardize the case, which is still under investiga-tion."

* * *

FAY SPENT THE day running from radio station to TV studio to newspaper office, answering questions and repeating her theme with the intensity of an evangelical preacher. "This is *serial murder* in our community, and nobody's doing *anything* about it." It was inspiring but uncomfortable work; the Frog Prince's shocks had given out, and she kept bumping her head on the roof as she negotiated the city's potholes. She'd been more comfortable on burroback in the Great Sonoran Desert.

She told one interviewer, "Now that this has become a public matter, we're sure the city government will want to make up for lost time. We expect them to call people on the carpet. We expect them to put the Gypsies on notice. Every San Franciscan should be ashamed of this disgrace. I know I am. We expect this to be resolved quickly."

SHE BEGAN TO hear from some of the more hypertonic national news shows, and a friend suggested that she peddle her personal story to Hollywood. It was true that she and Beans could use the money. She'd just moved the Rat Dog Dick Detective Agency into an old brick building in the gritty warehouse district, and the rent was steep for the single room decorated with pictures of her mother, Cagney and Lacey, Magnum PI, Charlie's Angels and Beans.

"I don't want to taint my testimony against these serial killers," she explained to an insistent tabloid reporter. "They've made people suffer too long. I want to see them convicted and the stolen property returned. That's the only agenda I've got."

TWO AFTERNOONS AFTER his story broke, Dan Reed called Fay to report that the presence of digitalis in the bodies had been confirmed, but he wasn't free to reveal his source, even to her.

"Are you gonna go with it?" she asked.

He said, "We're already on the street." She biked to the nearest newsstand and found his third consecutive page-one article under the headline TRACES OF DRUG TURN UP IN TWO EXHUMED BODIES. Reed had written:

> Laboratory tests confirmed the presence of digitoids, the products that indicate the presence of the heart medicine digitalis,

which allegedly was slipped to the men in concentrations high enough to speed their deaths, sources reported.

Reed again quoted Deputy Chief Fred Lau: "We can always do better. We strive for excellence. . . . I'm not going to criticize my investigators, because it's my overall responsibility."

Fay wasn't surprised to hear from Jerry Lama. "Fred Lau's job is to make silly excuses to the papers," he told her by phone. He read her a passage:

> "The police are a bunch of incompetent idiots," said Lama, who gave investigators an account of the alleged plot. . . .

"I was misquoted," Jerry told Fay. "I didn't say the police were a bunch of incompetent idiots. I said they were a bunch of incompetent *fucking* idiots."

"Jerry," she said gently, "they don't use that word in family newspapers. Listen to me. We can't keep bad-mouthing the police. Give 'em a chance. They're working hard."

"How can you tell?"

"Didn't they dig up the bodies? Didn't they find digitalis? Is that progress or what?"

"Didn't I tell you they'd find a way to fuck it up?"

She wished the angry man weren't always so negative—and so accurate.

72

Sell-out

THE *San Francisco Weekly* confirmed that John Nazarian was thinking about selling Yawczak's forty-two-page "chronological" to lawyers for Angela Bufford and George Lama. The former sheriff's deputy was quoted as admitting that he was close to a deal. "I'm basically a loose cannon," he explained to reporter John Roemer. "I'm trying to make a buck off this."

The newspaper described Nazarian as "a cavalier private detective" and noted that his asking price for the Yawczak affidavit was $60,000. Fay presumed that he must have encountered sales resistance; his original price had been $100,000. She was sorry that she'd ever allowed herself to deal with the man, let alone share office space and her files. Looking back, she realized that the mistake had been hers, not Nazarian's. He'd never tried to hide a touch of roguery from her or from the reporters who interviewed him. He seemed to encourage a reputation as a swashbuckler who wasn't afraid to cut corners on behalf of his clients and himself. She remembered something he'd told her about a private eye's responsibility—"You go out and get the evidence, that's all. *Any way you can.* Or you go to Napa Valley and pick grapes."

She wondered how his million-dollar movie deal was going and who would play Rat Dog Dick and her partner. Or would they both be written out of the script now that she refused to cooperate? It didn't matter to her, but Beans would be crushed.

TWO DAYS LATER, Jerry Lama called to tell her that his brother George had now read every line of the Yawczak document, plus other confidential police material, and the Tene Bimbos had placed a Gypsy curse on the Lama family, including the father Antone in the Holy Land.

"Now George knows what *every* witness said," Jerry told Fay. "He's already started the threatening calls. He said he wants to make a deal with my mother. If she won't testify against him and Angela, he'll sell her his half of the house and leave. Can you believe this? He'll sell her half of *her* fucking house. Is this a generous motherfucker or what? George never put a penny into it! My mother said she'll testify whatever George wants but she can't control what the rest of us say. George says, Mom, if you can't control our own family, then it's no fucking deal."

Fay asked, "Did you ever find George's gun? The one with the silencer?"

"No. Nobody's safe now. Not Nabib, not Roland, not my sisters, my mother or me or you."

"I thought you got a restraining order."

"Hey, it's not bulletproof." He paused. "Did I mention that the cops would find a way to fuck this up?"

FAY FELT DISTURBED, then dejected, then depressed, a rare progression in her busy life. Day by day she grew more sickened about her role in making the case public.

For a week she barely slept. She felt threatened, her apprehensiveness so finely tuned that she heard sounds that weren't made. The cops must *hate* her. She wondered what she would do if someone tried to break in. Beans would snore through a four-alarm fire. Nine-one-one would hang up when they heard her name.

She started each day by shoving the dog out of her way so she could sprint to the bathroom and throw up. Sometimes she made it. She brooded about Greg Ovanessian and what a good friend he'd been. She decided that she'd been too hard on Dan Yawczak. A fair person might even say that the junior partner had done his best. He'd had so much weight to carry from the first days of the case. Who was Fay Faron, a common skip tracer, to judge an experienced police detective?

She toyed with the idea of phoning Ovanessian to apologize, but she was too nervous about his reaction. They hadn't spoken for a month. How he must detest her for the terrible press she'd brought the SFPD in newspapers up and down the coast. She wanted to apologize for misreading John Nazarian's intentions—she owed it to Greg as a friend and colleague—but she couldn't seem to lift the phone.

SHE WASN'T SURE whether to feel glad or sad when she learned that Nazarian and Yawczak had gone public about the telltale affidavit, each blaming the other.

"They're telling entirely different stories," Deputy Police Chief Fred Lau commented in the *San Francisco Weekly*. "If the document was provided in violation of department procedures, we've got an administrative problem. If it was obtained without our consent and used to obstruct justice, we could have a criminal violation. Mr. Nazarian is very much aware of his professional ethics . . . I hope."

FOR A WEEK, Fay and her fellow readers were treated to a public dogfight. Yawczak claimed that the document had been stolen from his desk and that Nazarian had "forced" him to turn it over.

"What size gun did I hold on Inspector Yawczak?" Nazarian fired back in print. "If I was the accused inspector, I might have trouble sleeping at night." As an afterthought, he added, "I'm kind of big and burly, so you know what they call me around the Hall of Justice? They call me Nightmare."

Fay was acutely aware that "Nightmare" enjoyed controversy, but she also began hearing that he was genuinely hurt and angry. She hadn't taken him for the sensitive type. A mutual friend told her, "John claims that Yawczak used a police Xerox machine to copy the forty-two pages while John sat there and watched. He said it wasn't an official document because it came from Yawczak's personal computer and there was no letterhead. He's *livid* about Yawczak. He said, I've *never* been accused of anything like this. He said, If I was gonna steal, it wouldn't have been this goddamn affidavit. It would've been those bodies coming out of the graves!"

Mount Jerry erupted predictably. "All these news stories about how Nazarian got the affidavit—that's bullshit," he told Fay. "I don't care *how* he got it. I don't care the Pope gave it to him. He got his hands on a confidential police document when he wasn't supposed to fucking have it. And what is the city doing about it? Why is Nazarian still walking the street? Why is Yawczak still carrying a badge and a gun? Are we the only ones that give a fuck?"

Fay said it looked that way to her.

73

Redemption

GREG OVANESSIAN CALLED and invited her to his office in the Hall of Justice. Bumping along in her shockless green command car, she thought, I've finally reached bottom. All these months I've been blaming the cops for screwing up Foxglove. Ovanessian, Yawczak, Phil Tummarello, Fred Lau and who knows who else—they'll all line up against me. She wondered if she should have brought Beans to divert some of the heat, but in physical confrontations he usually tried to lick his opponents to death.

Ovanessian greeted her with his old Danny Thomas charm. He took her arm, led her to a chair, and slid a stack of documents across the table. There were photocopies of her files—every report, every contact, every interview, every street address and Social Security number and phone number and genealogy. She was looking at the results of twenty months of unpaid labor.

Ovanessian said, "Do you recognize these copies?"

"They're my investigative files, Greg. Where'd you get 'em?"

"Nazarian gave 'em to me. Did you tell him to?"

"No."

"Is John supposed to have this material?"

"No."

"How'd he get it?"

"I, I . . . don't know."

Ovanessian slid a tape recorder between them and pushed the record button. Sergeant Tummarello entered the room and asked if she intended to lodge a formal complaint against her fellow PI. She said she wasn't sure. With the tape recorder running, she related the story of their relationship, starting with the first meeting in this run-down police office and ending with Nazarian's implied threat to sell the police file to the defense. As she spoke, Tummarello glowered. She was glad they were on the same side, at least at the moment. He was known to be ambitious and authoritarian; some called him ruthless. Maybe, she said to herself, that's what's been lacking in this case.

After the formal interview, she lingered to chat. Ovanessian assured her that the Fraud Unit had always been aware of Nazarian's aggressive style. "That's just John's way," Ovanessian said. "He's an old-fashioned PI. Get the job done, and try to stay out of trouble."

As Fay walked down the hall, she felt pounds lighter. No longer did she have to take the heat alone. She went home and slept well for the first time in weeks.

A FEW DAYS later the *San Francisco Weekly* carried the latest pronouncement by Deputy Chief Fred Lau: "It has been brought to Mr. Nazarian's attention that if he has anything in his possession that does not belong to him, he should consider returning it."

Dear me, Fay said to herself. *Consider returning it.* That'll shake John to his socks.

Nazarian responded with a public hint that he would destroy all his copies of the Yawczak affidavit, presumably including the one he'd registered with the Writers Guild. Then he dubbed Fay "the evil of evils," started spreading the rumor that the wanton woman didn't wear a bra, and renamed his pet rats Tummarello and Faron.

Fay thought, How nice to be noticed.

74

"It's All PR"

DAN REED SPELLED out the case against the SFPD and Inspector Dan Yawczak in a long article in the July 18 *Oakland Tribune*. Under the headline SOURCES CONDEMN POLICE DETECTIVE'S ROLE IN INVESTIGATION, he noted that Yawczak had failed to collect the food that had been delivered to Harry Glover Hughes, allowed three months to pass before testing the old man's blood, alienated a key witness by making "an overt pass," and permitted a detailed account of Foxglove to fall into outside hands.

The police department had also been remiss, Reed reported, in not making arrests on Steven Storvick's complaint, in pulling its "Gypsy cop" off the serial murder case to work on a parking lot scandal, and in failing to follow through after Richard Nelson's blood tested positive for digitalis.

Once again Fred Lau didn't seem to get the point. "If [people] feel they have concerns about the officer's conduct, I would encourage them to file a complaint," he was quoted by Reed. "As of now, nothing has given me any indications that there are any problems."

Lau also complained that Nazarian was failing to cooperate. "We'd like to get to the bottom of this, [but Nazarian] keeps saying he's got [the chronological], and we keep saying if you've got it, let's see it, and he keeps referring us to his attorney." The deputy chief said it was his opinion that the affidavit wouldn't jeopardize the prosecution even if it fell into defense hands. Nor would he directly criticize any of the inspectors under his command, including Ovanessian and Yawczak. "I would not say there were mistakes. There were some issues that were brought up initially that need to be looked into again."

FAY AND JERRY Lama commiserated about the wheel-spinning at the Hall of Justice. "It's all PR," Fay commented in disgust.

"Worse," Jerry said. "When you go into any police office in San Francisco you see this yellow sign: Stop elder abuse. Stop it? They're *enabling* it."

WITH APPROPRIATE HOOPLA, the Fraud Unit turned Foxglove over to Homicide Unit inspectors, as though these masters of crime detection could wave their magic badges and bring the poisoners to justice. Internal investigators were assigned to dig into the conduct of the disgraced Fraud Unit. Police and coroner's records were sealed to prevent further leakage. Out-of-state toxicologists began more sophisticated tests for digitalis. The State Board of Pharmacy opened license revocation proceedings against Edmond Lim and his West Portal Pharmacy.

Mingled expressions of sincerity and frustration continued to flow from the desk of top police officials. "The bottom line on this thing is we really want to prevent the possibility of any additional victims," Fred Lau told the *Oakland Tribune*, "and to identify and eventually successfully charge and prosecute the people who are responsible for some of these crimes."

Jerry Lama mocked the statement. "The bottom line is George won. Angela won. The Tene Bimbos won. Everybody else got fucked."

DEFENSE ATTORNEYS ASSUMED the expected aggressive posture. Robert Sheridan, the former assistant DA who had accompanied Angela Bufford on a visit to old Richard Nelson, pointed out that the elderly men died "while under a doctor's care and while being attended by staff in the hospital. Some died long after contact ceased." The murder-by-poison story, he charged, was "missing only two things: poison and murder." Allegations to the contrary, he said, were "false and malicious" and "concocted by ill-motivated individuals who wanted to sell them or cause harm." The blunt reference to Nazarian's wheeling and dealing confirmed what Fay and the prosecutors knew too well: the case had been seriously compromised, and they would face crippling problems in court.

WITH THE ARRIVAL of fall 1994, two full years had passed since the first anonymous warning to 911 that elderly San Franciscans were at risk. It had been a year and a half since Fay identified two of the old men and began producing evidence of fraud and abuse. A year had gone by since Angela Bufford's old boyfriend "Rich" had tested positive for digitalis. One by one the dismal anniversaries were passing with no sign of action by the DA's office.

Media interest waned. Routine press releases from City Hall and the Hall of Justice were folded into airfoils and wafted toward receptacles known to reporters as "the circular files." A shamed truculence seemed to fall over the Fraud Unit and the hotshot homicide inspectors. The public tumult faded and died. Then Fay found out what was behind the Gypsy News Network's hints about poisonings in other cities. Foxglove leapfrogged three thousand miles.

75

One Dead Editor

JAMES VLASTO HAD been trying to solve the mystery of his elderly uncle's bizarre death for almost a year when a newspaper clipping made its roundabout way from San Francisco to Athens and then back across the Atlantic to Vlasto's one-man office in New York City. The words leaped like sparks from the flimsy fax paper: "exhumation," "four bodies," "suspected murder-for-profit scheme," "digitalis," and the most energizing buzz phrase in Jim Vlasto's lexicon: "Tene Bimbo."

My God, the public relations consultant said to himself, this is Uncle Andrew's case to the last semicolon! He turned to his computer and found a dozen other articles on the same subject, mostly in West Coast publications. His first reaction was surprise, then relief. It was gratifying to learn that he wasn't the only person on earth who suspected that members of a Gypsy clan had poisoned an elderly relative, and that New York wasn't the only city where the Tene Bimbos were suspected of elder abuse and murder.

VLASTO WAS A tall, slender, fine-boned New Yorker whose political connections went deep into the capitol building in Albany, the Mayor's Office in New York, and every newsroom in the state. He'd handled press relations for former governors Hugh Carey and Nelson Rockefeller and a dozen other city agencies. His father, Solon, had emigrated from Athens in 1918 to work for the family-owned newspaper, *Atlantis,* the first Greek-American newspaper in the United States.

For thirty-five years Jim Vlasto had been friendly with Selwyn Raab of the *New York Times,* and he immediately faxed the West Coast articles to the investigative reporter's office. Vlasto also sent copies to his old friend Robert Morgenthau, the Manhattan district attorney. The PR man was optimistic that someone would take an interest. One way or another, he intended to shake things up on his late uncle's behalf.

JIM VLASTO HAD vivid memories of the first indications that something was going wrong in the late years of the old man's life. On October 5, 1993, while the endangered Richard Nelson was in the process of being rescued from Angela Bufford in San Francisco, Vlasto had received a phone call from cousins in Athens. "We can't reach Andreas," he was told. "The phone's been busy for days. Have you heard anything?"

"Uncle Andrew and I aren't close anymore," Vlasto replied. "I haven't seen him in ages."

"Please, Demetrius, pay him a visit. This isn't like him at all."

FOR THIRTY-SEVEN YEARS Andrew George Vlasto, a small man with wavy gray hair and the strong profile of his ancient Greek forebears, had lived in a snug apartment a mile south of his nephew's public relations office in mid-Manhattan. He was a retired editor, lawyer, writer, banker, owner of a company that supplied candle holders for Greek Orthodox churches, and sole proprietor of extensive real estate interests in his native country. At eighty-five, he lived modestly, paid $252 a month for a rent-controlled apartment, and spent his time playing his piano, reading Greek-language publications with his one good eye, and taking short walks in his downtown Chelsea neighborhood. A lifelong bachelor, he'd always been self-reliant, a loner, more Hellenic than American, and local members of the prominent publishing family were accustomed to his self-imposed isolation. Since the death of his twin sister in 1987, his social life had consisted of phone calls to relatives in the old country, to whom he spoke the language of his childhood. Now, suddenly, he spoke no language at all.

IN RESPONSE TO the request from his cousin, Jim Vlasto had taken a taxi to the apartment building on Twenty-fourth Street between Fifth and Sixth Avenues and knocked on the door of 3R. A woman poked her head from a nearby doorway and reported that she hadn't seen her elderly neighbor for days. Alerted by Vlasto, two uniformed patrolmen from the nearby 13th Precinct attempted entry via the fire escape, but the windows were boarded.

As neighbors crowded around the apartment door, a team from Emergency Medical Services picked the lock and entered. The two-room flat appeared neater than Jim Vlasto remembered but still smelled a little like the lower-level men's room at Grand Central Station. Hot air rippled above a portable heater that was turned to high. There were a sink and toilet but no bathtub or shower, kitchen, refrigerator or stove. The only cooking appliance appeared to be an electric toaster. The closets were empty except for a few items of men's clothing, and the phone was off its cradle.

Jim Vlasto wanted to search for clues, but a patrolman barked, "This is private property, pal. Your uncle's not here, his body's not here, and our ass is out a mile. Let's *go!*"

The PR man handed his business cards to curious neighbors and said, "If you see Mr. Vlasto, please give me a call."

TWO DAYS LATER a tenant phoned to report hearing the old man's piano. No doubt about it—Andrew Vlasto was home. The cousins in Greece were relieved. Vlasto tried to phone his uncle, but the line stayed busy for hours.

HE LET A week go by and dialed again. A male answered and identified himself as a health care nurse. He said that Mr. Andrew had hurt his hip in a fall and was under medication. No, he wasn't in danger.

"Can my uncle come to the phone?"

"I'm sorry, sir. Not now."

Jim Vlasto thought about dropping in but decided to put off his visit until the old man was on his feet again.

ON THE EVENING of Thursday, October 14, nine days after his first unsuccessful attempts to reach his uncle, Vlasto phoned again and got no answer. He taxied to the apartment and found a note on the door in unfamiliar handwriting: "Andrew is at the doctor." A neighbor reported that technicians from Emergency Medical Services had rushed the old gentleman to Lenox Hill Hospital.

Vlasto hurried to a pay phone down the street. Lenox Hill and other local hospitals reported no such admission. He called Bellevue Hospital, the storied old institution on the East Side, and was told that a gentleman named Andrew Vlasto was in critical condition in the intensive care unit.

AT THE ADMITTING office, a clerk said, "He can't have visitors."

"I'm his nephew," Jim Vlasto said, sliding ID cards across the counter. "I'm his closest relative in New York."

"Sir, his closest relative is his wife."

"Wife? What wife?"

The clerk studied a slip of paper and said, "Sylvia Vlasto."

"He's been a bachelor all his life!"

"Mrs. Vlasto left strict orders. No one is to see him."

"This is nonsense."

"I don't make the rules."

Vlasto appealed to the hospital's Office of Risk Management and was turned away.

He went home to begin a phone search for his uncle's friends and finally located a Greek-American woman who lived in Uncle Andrew's building and sometimes joined him for dinner. Judith Zervas Deluca told the puzzled nephew that she would be glad to meet him at Bellevue to see what could be done. It wouldn't hurt that she was a retired lawyer.

At the admitting desk they were reminded that "Mrs. Vlasto" had ordered visitors barred. While Jim distracted the staff, Judith Deluca sneaked up a back stairway and found her friend unconscious in intensive care. Jim finally reached the bedside and whispered, "Andreas, this is your nephew Demetrius." When the old man failed to respond, Deluca leaned over and spoke to him in Greek, but there was no reply.

En route back to Chelsea by taxi, Vlasto told Deluca, "Something's wrong. This marriage happened too damned fast. Did he ever mention a girlfriend or a wife?"

"Never," the woman replied.

Neither was surprised when their knocks on Andrew's door went unanswered. Apparently the "wife" wasn't home. The telephone number didn't answer.

THE NEXT DAY Vlasto did a hurried search of his uncle's financial status and learned that between September 27 and October 5, nineteen withdrawals had been made in the old man's name on a Chemical Bank ATM card. The total amount was $8,500. His funds at Chase Manhattan had been transferred to the "joint account of Andrew George and Sylvia Sabrina Mitchell Vlasto" in the Bank of New York, and on Wednesday, October 6, the new bank had wired $70,000 from the joint account to the Trump Taj Mahal casino in Atlantic City. Three days later the account was closed. There the money trail ran out.

Now Jim Vlasto was sure that his uncle was being robbed. The old man had always banked in person, never owned an ATM card, and frowned on gambling. It had taken him eight decades to amass a respectable estate, and he never would have blown tens of thousands of dollars in Atlantic City or anywhere else.

Vlasto retained a lawyer and within twenty-four hours established a temporary guardianship, freezing his uncle's assets on the grounds that he was the incompetent victim of an illegal marriage. As far as the younger Vlasto could tell, something in the neighborhood of $80,000 had been lost, but the remaining balance of $170,000 was safely under court protection. The necessary papers had been served on old Andrew in the hospital and on "Sylvia Vlasto," a dark-haired, dark-eyed young woman, at the apartment on Twenty-fourth Street.

Jim Vlasto visited the open ward but found his uncle enfeebled and incommunicative, his memory gone. After a week of systemic detoxification and healthy food, the patient showed gains, and doctors talked about sending him home to convalesce. Then Sylvia exercised her conjugal rights and visited overnight. The next day, Jim Vlasto found his uncle unconscious. A doctor whispered, "There's something wrong here. We're concerned."

Andrew's blood tested positive for digitalis, phenobarbital, benzodiazepine, codeine and opiates, none of which had been administered by the hospital. He died at 11:44 the next morning. A preliminary report to the Manhattan chief medical examiner listed the cause of death as "severe intractable metabolic acidosis" and noted, "Patient reportedly was prescribed phenobarbital and Tylenol and codeine by outside MD prior to admission. Unclear how benzodiazepine or digoxin were obtained and/or administered." Under "name of person related to deceased who can provide additional information," the report listed Sylvia Vlasto.

NO WILL WAS found, which meant that under New York law the old man's $170,000 in assets plus $500,000 in Greek real estate would pass to his young wife. Over the new Mrs. Vlasto's objections, the hospital performed an autopsy, and the official cause of death was reentered as Alzheimer's disease with sepsis and pneumonia, complicated by acute narcotic intoxication. Under "supplemental case information," a physician scrawled: "Decedent's hospital course was remarkable for patient's serum digitalis level 24 hours prior to his death. At no time was digitalis Rx [prescribed] for decedent. (Level was 1.5—therapeutic level = .5 to 3) . . . As per reporting MD, decedent's wife who is 28 seemed somewhat inappropriate. As well, there are reports that decedent's wife made a number of phone calls to various hospital staff in which she made allegations that someone was attempting to murder her husband. Repeated attempts to contact decedent's wife Sylvia Vlastos have been unsuccessful."

The serum digitalis that had been detected in Andrew Vlasto while he was dying went unmentioned in the toxicologist's report, perhaps because the necessary postmortem tests for the famously quirky substance weren't performed. The final autopsy report noted: "Black charcoal-like material fills the oral cavity and is also present in the nasal cavities. . . . The stomach contains a bolus of charcoal material, admixed with about 100 cc. of black granular fluid." There was no explanation of how a fist-sized clump of a commonly available filtering agent had found its way down the dying man's gullet and back up his nose.

*   *   *

BY THE TIME Jim Vlasto and other family members learned of the death, Andrew Vlasto's body had been released to the sole custody of the new wife. Overnight Sylvia had changed the phone number at the Chelsea apartment and ordered it unlisted. The nephew canvassed local mortuaries and located the remains at a chapel on Spring Street in Manhattan. Repeated calls established that arrangements for burial services were confidential, and the undertaker was taking orders from the wife only.

A WEEK LATER Jim Vlasto learned that his uncle was in the ground in a New Jersey cemetery. Although hundreds of New Yorkers were personally acquainted with the deceased and his influential family, Sylvia Sabrina Mitchell Vlasto had been the only witness at the funeral. She'd paid $800 for the casket, $25 for a hired pallbearer, and $300 for security guards to keep out intruders. Before leaving for an unknown destination, she'd tipped the driver of the hearse $25.

OFFICIAL INTEREST BY agencies like the New York PD and the Medical Examiner's Office soon ebbed. Jim Vlasto's requests for his uncle's paperwork were ignored by every relevant agency, including Bellevue Hospital. After months of delay, he received copies of a few records under subpoena. He took them to the Manhattan District Attorney's Office.

"Mr. Vlasto," a young ADA told him in a preliminary meeting, "you have to face reality. Your uncle is just another old man who got ripped off by a Gypsy."

"He wasn't poisoned?"

"This is a case of elder abuse. We've got more of those than we can handle." The nephew brooded about the lackadaisical reply and responded in the arena he knew best: public relations. He drew up a bill of particulars under the eye-catching title 82 DAYS FROM MARRIAGE LICENSE TO DEATH CERTIFICATE:

> The Medical Examiner conducted an autopsy on Nov. 11, 1993. . . . The findings: Andrew Vlasto had Alzheimer's Disease. The cause of death was "sepsis and pneumonia complicating acute intoxication by the combined effects of benzodiazepines, phenobarbital and opiates." Manner of

death: "UNDETERMINED." This conclusion makes no sense, not only to me, but to outside experts whom we have consulted.

What is Bellevue Hospital hiding? Bellevue failed to allow Vlasto family members and lifelong friends to visit Andrew during his fatal hospitalization, yet allowed his "wife" to remain all night long without supervision, in apparent violation of hospital rules. Who knows what was administered to him at this time? Aware of my challenge to the validity of the marriage, the hospital denied us visitation rights, despite the fact that subpoenaed Bellevue Hospital records indicate their own suspicions of Andrew's situation.

The Manhattan District Attorney has done virtually nothing, despite assurances to me that the case has a high priority. . . . We have supplied him with a volume of evidence gathered through exhaustive personal effort and expense. . . . My uncle never wrote a check for more than $250.00 in the last three years of his life. Yet his personal banker at one of NYC's most prominent banks failed to stop a $70,000 check written on his account and deposited in another bank that wired the money to a casino in Atlantic City where it could be withdrawn in cash with impunity. A third major NYC bank was involved in the withdrawal of further large sums. More would have been taken from my uncle's account if I had not intervened and persuaded the banks that Andrew was the victim of a scam.

The PR consultant summed up:

Andrew was ripped off by a 28-year-old woman with a 7th grade education and a documented criminal record. His health, welfare and assets were unprotected by public and private institutions that ignored specific rules meant for cases like his. In death he is being ignored by an indifferent City government that is supposed to protect its elderly citizens. Andrew Vlasto is dead. His remaining assets are in jeopardy, his name and reputation smeared. My personal intervention with support of family members is the only reason the courts and investigators are involved.

A recent NBC-TV news segment on Gypsy crime had overloaded the network's switchboard with complaints from victims, and Jim Vlasto's press release attracted the attention of ABC-TV's newsprogram, *20/20*. Reporter Dan Sturman and producer Richard Greenberg started their research by going door to door in Chelsea and talking to tradesmen, waiters, mailmen and anyone else who'd had contact with Andrew Vlasto in the last few years. The picture that emerged was of an addled old gentleman living out his days in an Alzheimer's haze, seldom leaving home, and almost never venturing more than a block or two away. A wedding certificate confirmed a legal marriage to Sylvia Sabrina Mitchell, twenty-eight, in a storefront chapel on busy 125th Street less than three months before his death. On the document, the occupation of the retired lawyer, banker, writer and editor was listed as "shoe repair." Although he was born in a suburb of Athens, his birthplace appeared as Syrso, an island off Greece. The bride's birthplace was shown as Hawaii, her parents Steve and Elaine Mitchel, and her occupation designer.

The owner of the chapel confirmed that he'd performed the short service. "It did look a little suspicious to me," the preacher, known in Harlem as "the Prince," told *20/20*'s Greenberg. "I mean, him being so old." He said that Sylvia had made all arrangements and paid the wedding fee of $25.

LOOKING FOR THE source of the illegal prescriptions, Jim Vlasto and the TV journalists checked Manhattan hospitals and pharmacies. At a drugstore on Twenty-third Street, the search team found a cooperative druggist who'd dispensed a total of thirty-nine phenobarbital tablets and sixty codeine tablets to Andrew George Vlasto during the week ending October 12. The prescriptions were signed by a semiretired physician who practiced in a Brooklyn ghetto and admitted that he'd never met Mr. Vlasto before the old man paid a call with his young wife Sylvia. The doctor said that he'd thought the marital situation a bit unusual but prescribed the drugs anyway.

Jim Vlasto thought, Why the hell would my uncle go all the way to Bedford-Stuyvesant to get prescriptions for goofballs? Andrew hadn't traveled that far from home in years. He had no personal physician; like many elderly people, he checked himself into a local emergency room whenever he felt ill. Jim suspected that the doctor was one of dozens in New York who dispensed narcotics to anyone willing to pay his price.

AS FOR DIGITALIS and its derivatives, the investigative team could find no evidence that the heart medicine had been given to the old man at Bellevue or elsewhere. Jim Vlasto tracked down the male nurse who'd changed bedpans for his uncle for a few days, and the friendly aide said he'd been working under handwritten orders. He showed Vlasto a note in a scraggly handwriting: "Wife will give instructions to the aide as to what to do. Wife will give medications." The list of instructions had been signed by a man named Tom Brown on October 12, a day when the drugstore had filled prescriptions for thirty phenobarbital and thirty codeine tablets. Two days later, Andrew George Vlasto had been taken to Bellevue in a coma.

The searchers quickly switched their attention to the mysterious Tom Brown. Who was he, and why was he signing home-care orders for Andrew Vlasto? None of the friends or neighbors recognized the name. With help from the Rat Dog Dick Detective Agency and the Gypsy News Network, it took Jim Vlasto and the 20/20 team three months to piece together a grubby bicoastal puzzle.

TOM BROWN TURNED out to be Tom Tene, alias Ephrem Bimbo and other names. He was a pedigreed Tene Bimbo, grandson of the ruthless King George. With his Gypsy wife of nine years, Sylvia Sabrina Mitchell, alias Mona Stevenson, Sylvia Sabrina Stevens and other names, the Tenes had relocated to the east after Tom's conviction for a confidence scheme in California. The couple had moved into a small flat across the Hudson from New York, where neighbors complained that the family barbecued on their enclosed porch, parked illegally, and failed to control their two children, who didn't attend school and had a nasty habit of throwing rocks. The father, Tom Tene, walked with a heavy limp; he'd been shot in the leg but was afraid to go to the hospital to have the slug removed. He informed neighbors that he'd been hit by a stray bullet while watching a fireworks display; others said the wound was the result of a Gypsy feud.

From New Jersey the struggling Tenes had moved to a small apartment above a store a few blocks from Andrew George Vlasto's flat in Chelsea, representing themselves as Tom and Tina Goldman. In a sworn deposition after James Vlasto filed suit to protect his dead uncle's assets, the twenty-eight-year-old Sylvia described her husband and the father of her two children as "just a friend that I would always call and speak to and see." She claimed that she'd met old Andrew at a McDonald's restaurant on Twenty-third Street. After a second meeting, she said, he took her home and "my shoes were kind of tight. And he asked if I would like him to put it on a stretcher. And he put it on a stretcher. And as he was doing that, he indicated to me that he is not only a shoe repairman, but he also invented a shoe." None of Vlasto's survivors recognized their relative from the description.

The woman testified that a romance developed after she'd been hired as Vlasto's housekeeper, and in the spring of 1993 they'd had sexual intercourse in the Vlasto apartment. When Andrew proposed in August, Sylvia said, she thought he was joking. They were married a week later in Harlem. She claimed that he called her Rita after their favorite drink, margaritas. She testified that the ATM withdrawals had been made at her elderly husband's request. By bus, she said, they'd traveled to the Trump Taj Mahal Casino in Atlantic City and gambled away $20,000 of the $70,000 that was wired from his account in New York. Then he'd overdosed on self-administered opiates and pain drugs and spent twenty-four hours in a Philadelphia emergency room. Back home in Manhattan, he relapsed, was rushed to Bellevue, and died.

76

Who Is Sylvia?

THE GYPSY NEWS Network hummed with the latest on the intercontinental poisonings and inside information about the Tene Bimbos, always a popular subject. Sylvia, a Tene Bimbo by marriage, was described by a relative as looking "a little Pakistani. About five-five, attractive, slender, long black hair but not very good teeth. She's not a fortune-teller or a Tarot reader like most Machwanka. Sylvia plays old men, takes 'em shopping, uses their credit cards, stuff like that. She works sugar daddies because her Gypsy husband Tom Tene has cancer and he's too sick to work."

Among Fay's informants, Sylvia was quoted as strongly denying that she'd ever given Andrew Vlasto drugs. "He had several strokes," the woman had told friends. "He gets so hyper and nervous and he just pops his pills and mixes 'em up. When he was in the hospital, I bought nurses to stay with him around the clock, because I had to go back home with Tommy and our children. Andrew's nephew James Vlasto came to the hospital, but I wouldn't let him in because he was after our money. I had to go away for three or four days, and when I came back, my husband was dead. Sure I tied up his properties. We're legally married. I'm entitled."

A Gypsy friend had asked Sylvia if she'd been intimate with the old *gajo* and she responded with an epithet from her Machwaya tribe that sounded like *oo om gada*, meant "definitely not," and translated literally as "fuck my mother." She admitted that they'd tried sex, "but nothing happened." She explained her motivation for the strange marriage: "I'm tired of staying on welfare. I'm tired of being thrown on the streets. I'm tired of my children not having shoes. Welfare expects four people to live on a small income and pay rent and buy food. I wanted security."

A relative recalled another conversation: "I asked her if she gave the old guy poison. She swore that she didn't. She said, Hey, old people die! Don't blame it on me. She said, If I'm lying, may my son lay next to my mother's grave. When a Gypsy swears that oath, they *never* lie. You gotta believe her."

Long after Andrew Vlasto's death, Sylvia continued to back her story with passion and histrionics. "My late husband Andrew was a great guy," she told a reporter, wringing her hands. "I'm still not over his death. If I die, I die innocent." For a tabloid TV news program, she posed at the old man's graveside and said she would always love him.

HER GYPSY HUSBAND'S version of events, as relayed to Fay via GNN, was that he'd had no idea what was going on because Sylvia had taken a six-month leave from their marriage. Tom Tene told a reporter,

"I didn't know *what* she was doing with the old man. All that money? She gave it to her mother. I didn't get a dime."

Asked if he was willing to assist the authorities, the erstwhile Ephrem Bimbo provided an elliptical answer: "Me and Sylvia, we didn't kill nobody. We didn't poison nobody. I got a bullet in my leg and I ain't gonna talk to no detectives or media because I got kids and I ain't gonna get murdered for something that's so stupid." Asked who might want to murder him, he claimed that James Vlasto had hired Mafia hitmen who had somehow managed to shoot him in the leg while he was driving down Fifth Avenue in New York.

GYPSY GOSSIPISTES CONFIDED that Sylvia was the boss of her family because Tom was "pussywhipped." He was said to be dying of cancer, ulcers, a bad liver and his festering bullet wound, and his weight had dropped from 140 to 110. He'd always led a troubled life. He'd been spoiled by his doting father, Ephrem Tene Bimbo, AKA Big Al, sadistic villain of *King of the Gypsies*.

"Big Al gave Tom everything," a family member recounted, "and Tom's paying for it now. He can't go to work. He's stupid but thinks he's bright—a bad combination. He doesn't understand the simplest things—history, geography. He used to live off accident cases, fake injuries, other scams, till he got busted for fraud in California. He tried living in the non-Gypsy society, but he can barely read or write, and the *gaje* always found him out. He's had three wives—a Mexican, an Italian and a Gypsy. He ended up with Mona—that's Sylvia, the Machwanka one. Poor Tommy, he's not even forty yet, but you talk to him he sounds old, tired. He don't always make sense. There's something wrong with his head."

An investigator who reached Tom Tene by phone was treated to a rambling soliloquy that seemed to confirm the diagnosis: "I don't know what all the murder talk is about. There's only five dead bodies in San Francisco, right? Well, there was a lot more in the old days. Millionaires! The same sorta thing. My sister says our family learned how to do it in the sixties. I dunno. Listen, we're not killers. There was a lot of love in our family. My grandfather, the king, he might've murdered a few people, but they deserved it. A guy kept telling him that other Gypsies were saying bad things about him, so my grandfather said, Well, since you're the one that always hears about trouble, I'm gonna cut off your ear. And he did. Whenever he saw the guy after that, he'd say, Heard anything new?

"Another guy crossed him, and my father and my grandfather pulled out his tongue with pliers, put him in a sack and threw him off the Brooklyn Bridge. My grandfather was a man of principle. Did you know he was a captain in the Russian army? He was only fifteen or sixteen and he stole a boat to come to the States. He landed in Chicago and worked with Al Capone.

"In the depression he supported the family by stealing from banks. He'd ask to change a hundred-dollar bill. They'd give him twenties and he'd put on a thick accent and say, I no lika dis kinda money. Gimme different. While they're exchanging the money a couple times, he'd hide a twenty or a fifty. He would hit three or four banks a day and not go back for a year. He never got caught.

"A Chicago Gypsy named Charlie Mitchell tried to frame him. So my grandfather put out the word that the Tene Bimbos were *never* to marry a Mitchell, but I married one anyway. Grandfather was a brilliant *brilliant* man. When he died they rode him through the streets of Boston in a glass carriage. Did you know he's in the library? As a king? There's been lots of Gypsy kings, but he was *king* of kings. He had terrible headaches from a beating by the cops. He was addicted to Bromo-Seltzer. . . ."

ONE OF FAY'S informants claimed that the idea of slipping the nearly undetectable digitalis and other drugs to Andrew Vlasto had originated with California relatives of Tom Tene.

"Tom and Sylvia don't have enough smarts to come up with that kind of scam on their own," Fay's contact said. Another source reported that the toxic pills had been mailed to New York from the West Coast. Fay regarded the information as the usual Gypsy gossip and spin, unprovable even if true, and worthless in a court of law.

77

Aloha Oe

THE RAT DOG Dick Detective Agency was inundated with calls on Friday, January 6, 1995, the day the *San Francisco Examiner* brought news of the Vlasto case to a local audience. In a front-page article headlined "N.Y. Death May Be Tied to S.F. Gypsy Case: Widow's Link to Clan Investigated," the newspaper quoted a Manhattan District Attorney's office investigator: "We are in touch with San Francisco law enforcement authorities and are exchanging information." The article included a pointed reminder that "there have been no arrests in any of the deaths."

THAT NIGHT THE TV news program *20/20* aired a segment entitled "Dangerous Friends: Con Artists Preying on the Elderly." Barbara Walters appeared on-screen explaining that "*20/20* has uncovered what seems to be a heartless scheme." James Vlasto, Fay and others were interviewed on camera. In her voice-over, correspondent Catherine Crier reported, "Sylvia and Tom Tene have disappeared, their last known address this mail drop in New Jersey. But across the country in San Francisco, we found some of their cousins, members of the same Gypsy family who, investigators say, have made a virtual business out of collecting from one old friend after another."

A glamorous dark-haired woman materialized on-screen, and Crier said, "This is Angela, also known as Theresa Tene. She lives with her boyfriend, George Lama. The Mercedes you see? It's registered to George and a ninety-four-year-old friend who died. And the house? It used to belong to eighty-seven-year-old Nicholas Bufford. He signed the deed, making Angela co-owner of the property. She was listed as his granddaughter. Then they got married."

Fay Faron appeared next. "The next month they went back to the County Recorder's Office," she said, "and recorded another document that said, Oh, I'm sorry. I made a mistake. This isn't my granddaughter, it's my wife. And the next month . . . he was dead."

Fay went on to quote an unnamed San Francisco detective: "*You* know they're being poisoned and *we* know they're being poisoned, but sometimes these things just fall through the cracks."

Jim Vlasto provided a similar evaluation of the New York investigation: "Privately, they said that they feel yes, he was poisoned. Yes, he obviously was a victim of fraud. But it's hard to prove. Andrew Vlasto didn't have to die." He added mournfully, "Andrew Vlasto didn't have to die."

WATCHING THE PROGRAM over a late-night snack, Fay hoped that the one-two punch of the *Examiner* article and the TV documentary would shake the Foxglove investigators back into action. Producer Richard Greenberg phoned to tell her that ABC was already hearing from other victims and relatives. One of the first calls was from an aging San Diegan who paid $500,000 to revive his libido through Gypsy prayers and incantations. Greenberg quoted another caller: "I think my uncle's being taken advantage of right now. He's handed them two hundred thousand so far. This Gypsy woman uses his money to go to Hawaii—and sends him postcards."

Fay congratulated the producer on not shying away from using the key word "Gypsy" in the TV exposé. Whether it seemed racialistic or not, it was vital information for potential victims. In media coverage, the G-word was almost invariably omitted or underplayed. Fay had no more animosity against the Roma in general than she had against Methodists or Lithuanians or lefthanders, but she couldn't disagree with a published statement by Lieutenant Dennis Marlock, the Milwaukee PD's veteran *jawndare Romano*: "It is improper to judge a person's guilt or innocence based on race alone, [but] it is not improper to employ methods of classification in our attempts to identify, isolate and deal with criminal groups."

Fay recalled plenty of articles on "black crime," "Mafia crime," "juvenile crime." Why not "Romani crime" or "Gypsy crime"? For years, the media had sidestepped the issue by referring to criminal Roma as "eastern Europeans," "Serbian immigrants," "Rumanians" or "local fortune-tellers," or by simply omitting racial attribution. Now and then Fay wrote about Gypsy miscreants in "Ask Rat Dog," and some of her subscriber newspapers chose those days to omit her column. *The New York Times* seemed the most timid of all. In a lengthy study of the Vlasto case by Selwyn Raab, the *Times* omitted "Tene Bimbo" and "Gypsy" entirely, describing the suspects only as "members of an extended family." But in the same space, the world's greatest newspaper went into detail about Andrew Vlasto's Hellenic origins. In a follow-up, the *Times* described Tom Tene and his wife Sylvia as members of a Gypsy clan but deleted the ethnic designation after the first edition. In a review, *Times* TV critic Walter Goodman seemed to reflect his newspaper's sensitivity:

> It has not been a good week for Gypsies. They were portrayed as perpetrators of fortune-telling scams on both "N.Y.P.D. Blue" and "Dateline NBC." The "20/20" and "Dateline" descriptions are attributed to the police, but can you imagine anyone on the multiculturally correct networks referring to, say, a felonious Italian or Jewish or Hispanic family in that way? Are Gypsies the last unprotected ethnic species in the land?

When Fay read the review, she thought of a passage in *License to Steal*, a book coauthored by her friend Lieutenant Dennis Marlock and anthropology professor John Dowling of Marquette University: "No investigator can do field work among the Gypsies for long without knowing that they cheat, steal, and swindle. Police records document emphatically that Gypsy crime is a multibillion-dollar enterprise."

The authors had described a 1986 survey in which members of 150 police departments were asked if they knew of any Gypsies who owned legitimate businesses or held legitimate jobs. Eighty percent answered no. The other twenty percent cited fortune-telling as "legitimate," even though Gypsy palm readers had been involved in mischief for ages. In an eight-year period, Gypsy tea-leaf and palm readers were estimated to have scammed Illinois residents out of $5.1 million, a figure which didn't include the take from victims who didn't report.

Fay couldn't disagree with *The New York Times* that the Gypsy population as a whole might represent "the last unprotected ethnic species in the land." But it seemed to her that a far more endangered group, ethnic or otherwise, was the elderly.

* * *

SHE WAS TREATED to the Gypsy rebuttal on a call from GNN. She had the feeling that the basso on the other end of her phone line had been delegated by a Rom Baro to straighten out her warped thinking, and she welcomed the opportunity. She was tired of thinking ill of Gypsies.

"The *gaje* make too much out of this digitalis thing," he told her. "It's more of the same old shit—cops pushing us around. Listen, you can't victimize us anymore. This is America, not Germany. Your cops, they go into our *ofisas*, beat up our women and chase us outa town. We tell fortunes. So what? You *gaje* run sex phone lines on TV. Suckers pay three or four bucks a minute. You got these—whatta ya call 'em?— televangelists, pretending to heal people, stealing big bucks. How is that different from fortune-telling? Those rip-offs are run by Americans, not us. You say Gypsy women marry old men for their money? So did plenty of other *gaje*. It's not a crime. You Americans rob us with small print and pencils. Some of us Gypsies, not all—get that right: *not all!*—we steal with our hands, we steal with our smarts. You *gaje* force us to con and connive. But at least we're honest about it."

Fay tried to sort out the morality of the situation, but it wouldn't sort. She went to bed with a headache.

78

The Age of the Hitman

FOR WEEKS AFTER Jim Vlasto made the connection between Tene Bimbo operations in San Francisco and New York, Fay Faron's clipping service showered her with articles from the world press. The stereotypical perception of the Rom—violins and castanets, crystal balls and caravans—had always made good copy, and the addition of a Borgia-like clan with a colorful name proved tantalizing. An Associated Press report began, "Six elderly men, five of them from San Francisco, were apparently killed with the heart medication digitalis after being wooed for their money by younger women belonging to a San Francisco–based Gypsy family, authorities say." The AP story was picked up by dozens of newspapers, including the *Los Angeles Times* and the *Chicago Tribune*, under headlines like GYPSY ROMANCE SCHEME BELIEVED LINKED TO DEATHS OF 6 ELDERLY MEN. The *South China Morning Post* blared, GYPSIES, TRAMPS AND THIEVES FIND OLD ONES THE BEST, and made a few observations about the official investigation:

> In San Francisco, where around 4,000 Gypsies have settled, the tightness of their communities has traditionally resembled Chinatowns, notably in members' reluctance to talk to the authorities on criminal matters. The police have also tended to leave them to get on with it. But with seven elderly men dead, and not one arrest made in connection with the cases, somebody, somewhere is chalking up a record that makes the most violent of Chinatown hits look like a trip to the seaside.

A legal publication, the *Recorder*, informed members of the bar that six victims had been killed with digitalis, "which can be fatal in high doses." The London *Observer* ran a five-column article titled BIMBO TRIBE LURES MEN INTO FOXGLOVE TRAP, featuring large photos of a raven-haired Angela Bufford and a deskbound Fay Faron. A box on the opening page noted that "Angela was also having sex with the old men, but only to make their hearts pound a little faster." The story ended with a terse observation about Rat Dog Dick:

> Faron is disgusted at the inaction that means she still sees members of the Tene family on the streets. She cannot bear the fact that all these old men have been taken advantage of and the police do nothing. "We put that case together so well that we did everything but staple the suspect to the cover of the report and nothing has happened," she said. She has lodged an official complaint with the police. "I can't believe we live in a city where serial murder is just ignored," she said.

The London *Daily Mirror* splashed the *familia* name in its headline: ROBBED AND POISONED BY THE KILLER BIMBOS; THREE GYPSIES NAMED BIMBO MAY BE RESPONSIBLE FOR DEATHS OF SIX RICH MEN IN NEW YORK

AND CALIFORNIA. The text mentioned "an amazing marriage-and-murder plot hatched by three scheming women" and added that they were "blessed with brains which they used to deadly effect."

Fay found the article overly optimistic in its conclusion that "police are set to arrest the Bimbos and level murder charges in New York and California." In fact, there were still no signs of impending arrest or prosecution on either coast. She'd heard that Eastern authorities had allowed their two main suspects to fade into the ephemeral world of safe houses that extended from coast to coast and provided such amenities as forged identity cards and birth certificates and bail money. The San Francisco suspects seemed to feel no fear of the law. The pistol-packing *gajo* George Lama and his Gypsy paramour tooled about town in his white Mercedes and her blue-white BMW, making threatening gestures at John Nazarian and other suspected enemies. George sent his brother Jerry a terse message: "Remember, this is the age of the hitman." Everyone involved in the case seemed in a state of high alert.

Except the police.

79

Endgame

AS THE SUMMER of 1995 approached, the SFPD remained unmoved by its growing international image as cartoon cops. Fay's old adversary Nazarian told a friend, "This case has become a tragedy of errors. Instead of going after the killers, everybody's biting each other. It's one great big cluster fuck, the mad mad mad mad world over again. The victims are forgotten. The Gypsies? Hey, they're gonna walk! This is a big coup for the Tene Bimbos. It's made them celebrities with their own people. Believe me, they know about this operation in every *ofisa* from here to Marblehead Mass."

AS THOUGH TO confirm Nazarian's grim appraisal, his pal Greg Ovanessian and the *pistolero* Dan Yawczak were charged intradepartmentally with various feasances, including mis, mal and non. Fay learned that detectives rifled the beleaguered inspectors' desks at midnight, leading her to suspect that the department planned to work much harder on prosecuting it own officers than it had ever worked on Foxglove.

The only other police activity consisted of a belated raid in April on the white stucco house on Fourteenth Avenue. A posse led by the hard-driving Sergeant Phil Tummarello broke down a door and served a search warrant on George and Angela, but the SFPD declined to release results except to confirm the presence of human-shaped targets sketched on the garage walls. Neighbors reported that a Corvette, Mercedes, Mercury sedan and Mercury station wagon were impounded but soon returned. Fay couldn't help thinking what a dynamite idea the impromptu search would have been—two years earlier.

THE NEW RAMROD Tummarello appeared to be firming up his own turf as the SFPD's *jawndare Romano*, enjoying an early perk by traveling to Hawaii to deliver a lecture on Rom crime in place of his predecessor. "How'd he get to be a Gypsy expert so fast?" asked one of Fay's friends. "Is there a Cliff's Notes?"

The busy sergeant also took issue with ABC-TV news editors for the *20/20* piece suggesting that San Francisco Gypsies were getting away with murder. Around the Hall of Justice, he conducted an energetic publicity campaign against the Rat Dog Dick Detective Agency. When Fay was accepted into membership of the National Association of Bunco Investigators, he phoned the Baltimore headquarters to complain that she'd caused "real problems" for the San Francisco authorities. When Fay got the word, she commented, "I certainly hope so." NABI ignored the official beef and booked her as a guest speaker on Gypsy crime.

AT THANKSGIVING TIME 1995, Fay learned of the death of Richard Nelson. To the end, the ninety-four-year-old man had remained in contact with his Gypsy girlfriend. Two weeks before his death, he'd proudly shown his nephew Donald a box of soft candies. "Angie sent 'em," he said.

The younger Nelson had checked the wrapping and was relieved to find that it was mailed directly from the store.

"Angela was persistent," he told Fay after his uncle's funeral. "I think she'd given up on his money, but she kept him softened up in case she was brought to trial. We weren't worried about them getting together. She couldn't get past the reception desk. We'd seen to that."

NELSON REPORTED THAT several days after the death, his wife Gerry answered her phone. A female voice asked, "Is Rich there?"

Gerry said, "Who's calling, please?"

"This is Angela. Who's *this?*"

My God, Gerry thought, will we *ever* be rid of this greedy woman? She tried not to show her anger. "Angela," she said evenly, "this is Mr. Nelson's niece. Please don't call here again." She hung up and reported the conversation to her husband.

"Let's hope this is the end of it," Don Nelson said. "But . . . who knows what papers she got him to sign?"

"I guess we'll find out," Gerry said.

80

Go West, Young Rom

LOOKING BACK LATER, Fay Faron couldn't pinpoint the instant when she reached the conclusion that she'd resisted for so long: Foxglove was as dead as the four old men who'd been buried twice, and no one would be brought to justice.

By early 1996, almost four years after the digitalis poisonings first came to light, elder scamming flourished in San Francisco, despite the publicity. And a new technique began to surface: marrying AIDS patients, nursing them through their final days, and collecting on their life insurance. Fay headed an informal group of kindred spirits who shared her sense of outrage, including a young investigator named Ann Flaherty who had been chief of security at Nordstrom and had once placed Angela Bufford under surveillance on suspicion of passing merchandise to her boyfriend George. Another member of the ad hoc group, Ray Alsdorf, a DA's investigator in cross-bay Alameda County, pursued some twenty Gypsy-related matters, including several sweetheart scams on the elderly. In Santa Clara County, Assistant DA Judith Sklar and investigator Stephanie Avila began prosecuting a string of cases, including an elder-abuse charge that resulted in a rare jail sentence. J. J. Green, an investigator for the California Department of Insurance, kept valuable logs on crimes like slip-and-fall, faked injury accidents and other scams. IRS agents showed renewed interest in bringing tax evasion cases.

Fay was happy to see the new awareness but wondered why it seemed to stop at the San Francisco city limits. Most local bureaucrats remained blithely unconcerned. She handed the Fraud Unit a complete file on a ninety-two-year-old blind man from the Richmond District who wanted to prosecute a Rom woman for draining his retirement fund. Word came back that the inspectors had rejected his complaint because "we're not touching anything involving Fay Faron."

AFTER OTHER COMPLAINTS swirled down the same black hole, Fay and her angry new investigator Ann Flaherty decided to stop soliciting police help and to handle the elder-abuse complaints themselves, some for a small fee, most pro bono. There was no shortage. In the wake of the national publicity about unprosecuted poisoning cases, several *familias* had imploded on the city, adding to the eighty or so storefront *ofisas* that thrived in ethnic neighborhoods. Fierce new competition stressed the Gypsy underworld and sent the local Tene Bimbos into spasms of rage and frustration. A male informant told Fay that Pat Bimbo, AKA Potsy, was being set up on an extortion charge by another family member. Angela Bufford continued to defy her ex-pugilist father, Chuchi, also known as Richard Yonvanovich, Stanley Tene Bimbo and other noms de Rom, by refusing to break with her longtime *gajo* boyfriend. Fay heard reports that George Lama, no stranger to the game of bluff and bluster, had threatened to kill Chuchi for interfering with his life. Then a local Rom Baro, Larry Stephens, lost a bloody fistfight to Chuchi and a few weeks later was nearly killed when gunfire from a passing car ignited his gasoline tank. He informed *familia* members that he wasn't sure if the shooter had been a rival Gypsy or George Lama.

One of Fay's GNN correspondents told her in a shaky voice, "When that gas tank went, Larry and Jackie almost went bye-bye for good. They had to run through a cemetery to get away. They're scared shitless now. Larry walks down the street, he keeps looking around. I told him, God was wit' you and Jackie this time, man. He said, Yeah, God is wit' me, but for how long?"

Fay asked, "Jackie who?" The name sounded familiar.

"Jackie Peters. Larry's wife. She's a big-time fortune-teller." Fay was interested to hear that the Peters woman was back in business after bilking an Asian woman out of $230,000 and escaping with a light sentence. Baghdad by the Bay had turned into a free-fire zone for Gypsy sharks and con artists.

UNINTIMIDATED BY THE listless San Francisco police, local fortune-tellers did more business than ever with the continuing wave of Asian immigrants. Aggressive seers took ads in Chinese-language newspapers, used sandwich boards written in Cantonese, and even adopted Oriental names. Elderly newcomers seemed especially vulnerable to the suggestion that their money was cursed and required incinerating to a light ash, which was then flushed down the toilet while the real bills wound up in Madame Fatima's underpants. One Roma family used this ancient *bujo* technique to take a newly arrived Chinese woman for $100,000, a few thousand at a time. Most such crimes, as Fay knew too well, went unreported.

SOON THE ACTION spread south and began to include elder scams even more lucrative than the ones in San Francisco. A few miles down the peninsula, a Gypsy woman conned $250,000 from a frail man in his eighties. In San Jose, a lovesick ninety-year-old man gave $600,000 to his Rom girlfriend and doggedly fought his family's attempts to keep him from handing her more. A reader of "Ask Rat Dog" wrote to report that her senile father in San Leandro had paid a Gypsy workman $21,000 for a roof that blew off in a month. A Los Angeles police officer told Fay that the southern California area was "swamped" with elder scams. One Rom woman was convicted of swindling a dying man out of $180,000 but served only five months in jail. An old man in San Diego paid fortune-tellers $675,000 over eleven years, and another aged San Diegan reported that he was kidnapped and held for seventy days, then bilked out of $180,000 by his thirty-four-year-old Gypsy "bride."

* * *

FAY BEGAN TO wonder if there was something about her adopted home state that encouraged such crimes. *Go west, young crook, and take advantage of our abundance of rich old men.* But her new colleagues in the National Association of Bunco Investigators assured her that the problem was nationwide. In the United States alone, a million complaints of elder financial abuse were filed every year, many against the Rom. Gypsy criminals were so active in Houston that a local police official described their activities as "economic guerrilla warfare." In some Florida beach areas, the overworked police reverted to a "no-name" routine for Rom hustlers who preyed on elderly snowbirds. Instead of trying to keep track of the offenders and their many aliases, the beach cops ran their fingerprints and turned them loose if their identities couldn't be verified on the spot. Similar shortcuts were taken elsewhere, to the greater ease of the Gypsy Mafia. On the rare occasions when the scammers were caught, the old-style restitution-and-release policy continued in use. Lawmen figured it beat wasting a day in court.

FAY WAS ASTONISHED at the number of police reports involving the widespread descendants of King George Tene Bimbo. A twenty-seven-year-old great-grandson, who also used the name Danny Tene, died under mysterious circumstances in Illinois. Tom Tene and his wife Sylvia took to the road with the proceeds from the Vlasto affair. A Tene Bimbo woman was arrested in New Jersey for some fifty elder scams, including one for $10,000. A young Tene Bimbo was stabbed to death in New York. A *familia* member known as George Guy was arrested in Los Angeles and charged with masterminding a long-running elder scam. A San Francisco Tene Bimbo duped an aged heart patient out of $120,000 (and the victim was advised by the SFPD that the case was "a civil matter"). A fifteen-year-old family member from Boston was arrested for taking $160,000 from an old man. A burly young man who called himself Larry Stevens was charged with the strong-arm murder of a sixty-five-year-old woman in New York and suspected of other killings and a string of elder robberies. His mother, Doris Bimbo of Staten Island, told *The New York Times,* "Gypsies don't get steady jobs, but they are good people, they don't kill people. He's a nice boy, a good boy. He didn't do those things."

* * *

IN OTHER PARTS of the world, the violence went both ways, and prejudice against the Rom seemed on the rise along with Gypsy crime. With the approach of the millennium, *familias* that once had been tolerated in Europe found themselves driven from town to town. Fay recorded a segment on the TV program *Investigative Reports*:

> The small nomadic Gypsy population in Hungary is a major problem for the prison system. While the Gypsies comprise fifteen percent of the general population of the country, they make up about seventy percent of the prison population. The Gypsies are a stateless wandering people that live by their own laws. According to a Gypsy legend, God gave all the people of the world land and possessions except the Gypsies. As a result, Gypsy culture does not look down on stealing or thievery from other races and may even encourage it.

A socially aware prison guard attempted an explanation:

> The majority of the inmates are not here because they are Gypsies but because they commited a crime. They are criminals because of the prejudices and lack of skills they have to get proper jobs. So the only chance they have is crime. This has been a tendency in their culture for a long time.

Fay had drawn the same conclusion early in her research and wished she knew what she or the other *gaje* could do about it. A few Rom leaders made heroic efforts to reverse the dark trend, but plainly the Gypsy population needed help, economically and otherwise, and they didn't seem to be getting it. Fay wasn't surprised when now and then a Rom or two struck back in rage and desperation. A friend sent her a UNESCO report on two Gypsy men who'd massacred an Italian family. One of the killers surrendered, but the other asked for time to enjoy a cup of coffee and a cigarette in his courtyard. After one last puff, he shot himself in the heart.

81

A Faint Hope

UNTIL LATE IN the summer of 1996, Fay and Jerry Lama and the families of the San Francisco victims clung to the faintest hope that Angela Bufford or Mary Steiner or Danny Tene or *someone* might be brought to justice. Hot rumors bubbled up—*The grand jury returned secret indictments. . . . Mary Steiner's been charged with elder abuse. . . . The police have a new witness. . . .*

One by one the reports proved false. Fay suspected that some of the tidbits might be originating in a state-owned waterfront building where Sergeant Phil Tummarello and an aide had been detached to work exclusively on Foxglove, presumably to spare them the distractions at the Hall of Justice. The two inspectors assiduously avoided the press, severed working relationships with key investigative personnel, including the savvy Timothy Armistead of the City Attorney's Office, and issued no public reports.

"Investigations like this take on a life of their own," Tummarello explained in a rare public statement. "I'm sure all the parties involved would like to see the investigation concluded, but the complicated nature of the allegations dictates that a very thorough investigation is going to take a substantial amount of time."

Fay was annoyed by the pedantic phrasing. *A substantial amount of time?* Were four years substantial enough? Were a *dozen* solid witnesses enough? The two detectives didn't seem to be doing much investigating. Tummarello finally got around to interviewing her on the phone, explaining apologetically that he'd "saved the best for last," and spent a total of five minutes trying to squeeze out incriminating evidence against his interoffice rival Ovanessian. The rest, as far as Fay could tell, was silence.

*   *   *

SHE KEPT IN touch with most of the dramatis personae, and they were equally mystified by the inactivity. Jerry Lama checked with the authorities weekly, keeping tabs on his explosive brother, but no other member of the Lama family had been contacted by the Fraud Unit or the District Attorney's Office in three years. It seemed an odd way to prepare a murder case. The original Foxglove informants, Jerry's sisters Hami and Nicole, were out of touch, as were Nabib Atalla and Roland Dabai, key witnesses to the adulteration of the deli food. The nervous young Roland had gone on the "shoe-leather express," in John Nazarian's phrase, before returning to a cabbie's life in the Bay Area in the belief that the police were no longer interested in him or his testimony. Fay figured he was probably right.

IN SEPTEMBER SHE received a tip that George Lama and Angela Bufford were living in rustic Woodland, a short drive from San Francisco and the site of the original Lama family restaurant. The couple had been seen drinking chablis at the exclusive Olympic Country Club, and George was sighted driving an expensive sedan in Daly City, just south of San Francisco. He still seemed tightly bonded to his Gypsy girlfriend. Jerry Lama learned from other members of the family that George had vowed to go to prison for Angela if the cases were ever prosecuted.

"Some dumb fucks would call that love," Jerry told Fay by long-distance phone from his secret domicile in the East. He was still avoiding his brother, using phone cards so he couldn't be traced. "Me, I call it crazy. What's George gonna do in prison? Play Nintendo? Date the guards?"

"I wonder if he'll ever serve a day," Fay said gloomily. "I doubt it. Not *any* of them."

"Did I tell you what George said when my mother kicked him and Angela out of the house on Fourteenth?"

"No."

"He told her he had two bullets—one for her and one for my sister Nicole."

Fay laughed. "He's threatened to kill everybody but the Pope," she said. "How'd he ever miss Beans?"

"Don't joke, Rat Dog, I know my brother. Watch your ass."

Fay was saddened to hear that Jerry and some of his relatives were firmly convinced that a Gypsy curse was destroying the Lama family.

"My sister Nicole developed a mysterious problem with her hands and lost her job. My sister Hami's going through the divorce from hell. My sister Hilda's life is a major mess. My son has Lyme disease and he's losing his hearing and eyesight. I'm suing my wife for divorce. My life's a fucking nightmare and I don't know where to turn. George wants a piece of me and so does everybody else. I go to a fucking supermarket and get into a fight. I'm not a quitter, but I'm fucking losing it. You tell me, Fay—this is *not* a Gypsy curse?"

"You're just going through some bad times," she said. "Things'll turn around." She wished she was as certain as she sounded.

82

Goodnight, Sweet Frog Prince

ON A MORNING in November she was in the middle of her rope skips when she realized that she'd heard no firsthand news about Mary Tene Steiner for months. She made discreet inquiry among her GNN informants and was told that the woman had returned to Konstantin Liotweizen's old apartment building on Funston and seemed to feel as immune to prosecution as the other members of her family. A year earlier, the matriarch of San Francisco's elder scammers had flown to New York to attend a family funeral and *pomono* ("black feast"), then sheltered herself from the Foxglove heat in a Rom safehouse in Queens. Her sons Kelly and Teddy attended to her holdings in San Francisco until she returned to repaint and refurbish her apartment building and resume her life as a landlord.

WITH STEINER'S LOCATION pinned down, Fay installed Beans in the backseat and steered the Frog Prince to the corner house at 1045 Balboa to see if the Gypsy woman's oldest son Danny still occupied the green-roofed showplace he'd wrested from Hope Victoria Beesley. The windows were covered with blankets and sheets and reminded her of a line she'd read in her studies: "Some Gypsies don't feel comfortable indoors. They try to turn every house into a tent." She wished she could peek inside. Somehow she doubted that Mrs. Beesley's distinguished old residence would appear again in *Better Homes and Gardens.*

ON THE WAY back to the office the faithful old Frog Prince began to lurch and buck. Fay popped the hood and her head was enveloped in smoke. Two small fires appeared to be burning. She wondered if it was safe to drive with a burning motor. Probably not, she decided.

A tow-truck driver doused the flames and dragged the dying old car to Fay's favorite repair shop on Valencia Street, where the owner flung down his wrench and yelled, "No, NO! I will *not* work on this car again. Not for *any* amount! I'll give you thirty dollars for it."

Fay remembered that Dimitri "Jim" Egoroff rebuilt and sold old cars, among other exotic skills, and called him to the scene by cell phone. He offered ten dollars more. "Sold!" she yelped.

Over no-froth cappuccino and dietetic carrot cake, she asked her favorite Russo-Australian polymath how he was faring in Mary Steiner's apartment house with its memories of the landlord banging the pipes, the clicking of mah-jongg tiles, and the ghosts dancing on the roof.

"Fine and dandy," he said in his Aussie accent. "I sued Steiner for harassment and won a few dollars. Well, sixty thousand, actually. Then she tried to toss me out on my bum, so we went to court and I beat her again."

Fay smiled in admiration. "Gee," she said, "it must feel good to have the Tene Bimbos out of your hair."

His thick black eyebrows connected in a frown. "Out of my hair? Did I say that? Not bloody likely! They listen in on my phone. My door's been jimmied so many times it looks like a bloody artillery shell hit it. I get home from trips and find my mum's art works moved. Somebody opened my sealed water tank. Now I don't dare drink a drop. I still have nightmares about the night we ate the cottage cheese and *vishni.*"

"How is Mrs. Bar—Mrs. Baruk—"

"*Baruksopulo.* We lost my mum last year, Fay. She was never the same after the poisoning."

"Oh, Jim, I'm so sorry," she said. She was embarrassed about forgetting his mother's last name. Wasn't her first name . . . *Tamara?* Yes.

A fine artist. Apparently she'd been as eccentric and interesting as her son. And as multi-talented.

She broke the uncomfortable silence. "Do you see Mary Steiner around the building?"

The inventor seemed to welcome the change of subject. "Not quite as much as her sons. As soon as you see 'em in a car, they circle the block till you go away. They're like their mother; they don't even want you to know where they park. If you see 'em on foot, they disappear up an alley toward their brother Danny's house. They're like smoke. They absolutely do *not* want to be followed." He paused and frowned again. "Too bad the case wasn't solved. There wouldn't be as many bloody Tenes to cope with."

"Oh, the case was solved, all right," Fay said quickly. "It just wasn't prosecuted." To the proprietor of the Rat Dog Dick Detective Agency, the distinction was important.

83

Smarter Than the Cops

ON THE MONDAY morning before Thanksgiving, 1996, Fay cranked up Evie the Everex to help take her mind off the death of the Frog Prince and other recent unpleasantnesses. She'd almost finished the first draft of *Lily Kills Her Client*, but she was blocked on the ending. She took another stab, gave herself another rejection slip, and decided to do some shopping.

THAT AFTERNOON HER phone beeped just as she and Beans returned home with a pre-owned anthracite-black Ford Explorer that she'd christened Darth. The caller was Dan Reed, asking what was up.

"Nothing," she said. "I bought a car. I'm working on my book. Busy seatwork."

"Are you keeping track—"

"—of the unusual suspects? They're in town, every last one. Mary, Danny, Angela, George. They're running around like they own the Sunset."

The footloose journalist who'd broken the Foxglove story now worked for the *San Jose Mercury News*, where he was uncovering fresh cases of Gypsy crime against elders. "Fay," he said, "how come these crooks don't get prosecuted?"

"I wish I knew."

"It's like the cops can't win, so they don't even try. Are the Gypsies smarter than the cops?"

She didn't respond. They both knew the answer.

84

The RICO Solution

WITH THE ARRIVAL of 1997, Fay got word that the Vlasto case was in its death throes, and James Vlasto ventured the opinion that charges would never be brought against the Gypsy couple who, he was convinced, had cleaned out his uncle's accounts and helped the old patrician to his death. By now the files of the Rat Dog Dick Detective Agency bulged with similar cases, many of them involving the Tene Bimbo clan. Fay's campaign against elder scammers was encouraged over long-distance phone lines by a few experts like Lieutenant Dennis Marlock, but such dedicated lawmen were in a minority. In his book *License to Steal*, the Milwaukee *jawndare Romano* suggested a solution that made sense to Fay and others who struggled with the unique problems of combatting the Gypsy Mafia: vigorous prosecution under the RICO (Racketeer Influenced and Corrupt Organizations) Act. No one was surprised, including Marlock himself, when he was accused of racism for suggesting such a practical approach. Few policemen and prosecutors were willing to risk the animosity of the Gypsy underworld and its apologists, and the pattern of crime seemed destined to continue to the eternal detriment of *gaje* and Roma alike.

* * *

CERTAINLY NOTHING USEFUL seemed to be happening in San Francisco. On January 22, 1997, Fay opened her *Examiner* and found the problems of the poisoning cases reviewed on page one. Staff writer Jim Herren Zamora's lengthy article was headlined "S.F. Cops Rush to Beat Clock in Fraud Probe" and noted that the statute of limitations would run out on most Foxglove matters within a month. Zamora quoted Deputy Police Chief John Willett: "I anticipate that there will be a decision whether or not we proceed with the case in February. It's not going to be quietly given up. . . . We've done too much to just hope that it goes out into the sunset."

Fred Lau, now elevated to chief of police with the retirement of Anthony Ribera, made one of his typically tepid comments: "Because of this case, we've learned a lot about crimes against the elderly. It's a very complicated case."

Right on, Chief, Fay said to herself as she slammed the newspaper on her desk, and it's a heck of a lot more complicated if you don't investigate and don't prosecute and don't care. For months she'd suspected that the authorities had never intended to bring charges. Why else had they assigned an overburdened investigator like Dan Yawczak? Why else had they reassigned Gypsy expert Greg Ovanessian a few days after digitalis was found in Richard Nelson's blood? Why else had they allowed the fraud inspectors to compromise the investigation with errors so glaring that they'd resulted in departmental charges? Didn't Ovanessian and Yawczak have supervisors? Wasn't their work monitored? Or didn't anybody care unless prodded by a skip tracer who then was resented for interfering?

Maybe it's as simple as that, she said to herself. Nobody cares. The Tene Bimbos and the SFPD seemed in full agreement on one point: the final few years of life didn't count for much.

OR WAS THERE a kinder and gentler way of looking at the case? Seated in front of Evie the Everex, she remembered a conversation with a sagacious investigator a few weeks back. "The cops really *want* to nail the perps," the old friend told Fay. "But this damned Foxglove is too much for them. It's the worst possible assignment for typical police detectives—a *thinking* case. They know who the badasses are. They know their MO and where they live and where they came from, and they know they have a long history of murder for profit. So that means the detectives have to deal with a pattern that goes back years. They have to subpoena bank records and re-create family histories and take names and kick ass. They have to do what you and Dan Reed and Jerry Lama have been doing: dig through public records, nail down phone listings, addresses, marriage licenses, family trees. They have to collect all the goddamn paper they can get their hands on, and when it's all collected—they have to connect the dots."

"We connected the dots for them," Fay had said abruptly.

"Exactly! And that's another problem. *You* guys did the brainwork and the paperwork, and the cops didn't. Paperwork is the dirtiest word to detectives, even the best ones. They hate to write a goddamn grocery list. They like action, headlines, quick arrests—*bang zap* and on to the next case. Foxglove was *never* gonna be like that. So they feel intimidated, they get down on themselves, and they give up. Look at it this way, Rat Dog: If I'm a detective with twenty cases on my desk and one of 'em is gonna disappear all by itself, the old guy's a recluse and has no relatives and he won't even be able to testify because he'll be dead by the time I can gather the evidence, and on top of that I've got to deal with a bunch of smart crooks with a dozen different names and addresses . . ."

The conversation tailed off in Fay's mind. She was running on sensory overload, carrot cake and caffeine. She hefted the printout of *Lily Kills Her Client* and reread the ending that had eluded her for months. After the imprecision of Foxglove, it seemed so simple and clear.

> "Is he dead?" the cop asked.
> The coroner looked at his watch and said, "Nine twenty-seven."

Fay felt reassured by her own creation. *Some* things came to an end, even if they were only fiction. It was two hours past her bedtime. She looked down at Beans. His Rastafarian curls covered her instep, as usual. Better than anyone, her dear old dog knew what she'd been through. He was always there to keep her from harm.

He was snoring.

*   *   *

THE NEXT DAY the future best-selling author toasted the completion of her novel over brunch at the Grove, a trendy coffeehouse on Chestnut Street. The celebration didn't last long. Fay described the event to her colleague Ann Flaherty over the phone:

"Beans and I were sitting at an outside table and I was telling a neighborhood guy about the case. Just as I finish this outlandish story, who shows up but—yeah, *right!* She's in black stretch pants and black laceup boots with . . . those thin little heels that shape your legs? She's got on a fitted Brooks shirt and she's, she's—*strutting!* Backside twitching, hair swinging? Every guy in the place is clocking her action. She's hot and she knows it. The rest of us dweebs, we're mostly in shorts and sweats. You know, the gym crowd? The health nuts? The ones who don't poison people for their money?

"I told this neighborhood guy, I said, You're not gonna believe me, Lee, but that's the Gypsy I've been telling you about. He looked at me kind of funny. He says, Excuse me, Fay. I gotta run.

"After a while I walked inside and there she was, perched in my favorite seat in the corner with her legs crossed. The waiter brought her a carafe of wine. So sophisticated, so . . . Toulouse-Lautrec at the Moulin Rouge. I started to sit, but I thought, Oh gosh, I don't even want to be *near* that woman. I was *so* mad. People like her and her mother ought to be in prison, not strolling around restaurants, not breathing the same air as the rest of us. I just felt like jumping up and down and yelling, Mur-der-er! But then *I'd* be the crazy one. So Beans and I went home."

85

Deliverance

FAY SPENT THE first half of 1997 in seething silence as a colorful new district attorney showed no more interest in the elder scams than his predecessor. She was surprised at his apparent indifference. Terence "Kayo" Hallinan, a street fighter in his teens, freedom marcher in his twenties, convivial partylover and staunch admirer of womankind, was the son of the fiery Progressive Party presidential candidate Vincent Hallinan. Like his father, Hallinan the younger had always seemed less interested in prosecuting criminals than in a doctrinaire liberal agenda that included support for civil rights, transgender rights, legalized prostitution, loosening of marijuana laws and other social issues. Policemen who opposed his candidacy applied their cruelest epithet: "social worker." As a criminal defense attorney, Hallinan had represented Patty Hearst and mass murderer Juan Corona. As a prosecutor, he'd never tried a case. Fay admired the new DA for many of his public stands, but she decided that help for the Bay Area's beleaguered old people would have to come from a more aggressive quarter. But . . . where?

BIDING HER TIME, she formed a nonprofit organization called Elder-Angels, described in an opening press release as "a grassroots organization composed of laypersons, private conservators, civil attorneys, and police, state and private investigators who have long been donating their time and resources to provide support to the victims of elder abuse. ElderAngels proposes to continue and expand this effort by befriending the elderly, liasing with law enforcement to effect prosecution and restitution, alerting the public to current frauds and scams, and educating legislators and private enterprise about designing an environment where predators cannot freely operate."

As Fay and Ann Flaherty set to work gaining support for their latest pro bono venture, word began to circulate that the DA was convening a grand jury to look into the Gypsy cases. At first Fay thought the report was a joke. Why would Terence Hallinan risk identifying himself and his office with a case that had been so thoroughly muddled by his predecessors? Outside the postered walls of the Rat Dog Dick Detective Agency, who gave a damn about the poisoned old men?

When the rumor grew, Fay phoned an inside source in the mayor's office, who explained: "Hallinan was looking through old cases and came across this one. He asked everybody if it should be revived. The top police guys said, No way—you reopen this case, we're all down the tubes. Some of the DA's own people agreed, but for different reasons. They figured the city had spent too much time and money on the case and it was a sure loser anyway. They counted noses and it came out something like ten-to-one to give the Gypsies a pass. Case closed."

Fay sighed. "You mean, case closed *again*," she said. "For about the fifth time. So . . . why the grand jury?"

"For some reason known only to God, Hallinan took the Liotweizen file home one night. Bedtime reading, I guess. A few days later he took home some of the Angela stuff. Then he looked through a whole box of reports and came into the office yelling, 'Goddamn it, these Gypsies are *killing* people!' He put his senior man, Al Murray, on the case, told him to take as long as he wanted, and relieved him of his other duties. I guess it's a go, Fay."

"I hope so," she said.

THE GRAND JURY convened in July, 1997. Four months later, the members were still at work with no apparent result. Descriptions of the secret testimony arrived at Fay's office via anonymous phone calls, the Gypsy News Network, and members of the Friends of the Rat Dog Dick Detective Agency. It was said that Dimitri Egoroff and Graziana Gandolfi had reduced the jurors to tears with vivid descriptions of the last days of Konstantin Liotweizen. Nicole Lama, still angry about her treatment by the Fraud Unit, had refused to testify voluntarily, was dragooned from her office, and proved a reluctant witness, saying, "I'm trying to put this behind me." Jocelyn Nash gave a bravura recitation of Angela's run at her elderly mother in St. Francis Woods. Medical Examiner Boyd Stephens testified about the finding of digitalis, theophylline and other potential toxins in some of the exhumed bodies. Margaret Buchanan described the odd friendship between Harry Glover Hughes and his young admirers and their various sorties to Mexico and Alaska. Don Nelson talked about the lawn party and his Uncle Dick's arrival in a BMW driven by a comely young girlfriend six decades his junior. Social worker Glen Billy told of finding Richard Nelson so weakened and ill that he barely had the strength to write another check to his tormentors. Bank officials testified about their fired teller Angela Bufford and her dealings with George Lama. Druggists repeated their stories about providing Lama with Digoxin and other drugs for his father in the Holy Land. Inspectors Greg Ovanessian and Dan Yawczak were questioned, along with Sergeant Phil Tummarello and a half dozen other policemen. In all, 112 witnesses testified.

* * *

ON NOVEMBER 6, 1997, almost exactly five years from the date of the first anonymous call to the Fraud Unit, the grand jury returned a sealed ninety-six-count indictment, charging Mary Tene Steiner with two counts of conspiracy to commit murder, plus lesser charges; George Lama and Angela Bufford with six counts each of conspiracy to commit murder, plus lesser charges; Lama's nephew Roland Dabai with two counts of conspiracy to commit murder; Danny Tene with nine counts of stealing from a dependent adult and one of grand theft, and Teddy and Kelly Tene with stealing from a dependent adult. A local TV reporter described the case as "a family affair."

FAY ATTENDED THE first court hearing and learned a few fresh details about the suspects who had bedeviled and frustrated her for so long. According to the indictments, Angela "smiled and giggled" as George sprinkled the magic salt into takeout food for Harry Glover Hughes. George, Angela, Danny, Teddy and Kelly Tene, not just Mary Tene Steiner, had taken part in the fleecing of Konstantin Liotweizen in the late 1980s. George had muttered, "He's a tough old bastard" as he and Angela attempted to euthanize Stephen Storvick. Angela represented herself as a Storvick relative in the process of worming her way onto the retired stevedore's bank account, just as she'd once described herself as another old man's granddaughter. And after Harry Glover Hughes died, George brought the caper to a tidy end by rushing to the bank and zeroing out the old man's account.

The defendants entered innocent pleas. The judge set million-dollar bonds for the Tene brothers and held the others without bail. Like many of the courtroom observers, Fay's eyes were locked on the carefully groomed Angela. Nicholas Bufford's widow and the other defendants wore orange unisex jumpsuits provided by the City and County of San Francisco, but unlike her colleagues, Angela didn't seem fazed by the proceedings. As she took her place next to her *gajo* boyfriend, she brushed back the dark brown hair that fell to her shoulders and smiled graciously at the judge and her fellow defendants.

Fay thought, Isn't she the cool one? Just like that morning when I brought her the questionnaire. What's that six-dollar word? *Insouciant*, that's it. Why, she's as insouciant as the day I saw her at the Grove!

And she looks so good in orange.